Praise for *The City in Texas*

"This book is a treasure trove of information, representing a lifetime of research, and it will be indispensable... for years to come."
—David R. Johnson, Professor Emeritus of History, University of Texas at San Antonio

"This is the only comprehensive synthesis of the urban history of Texas that I'm aware of. Commanding the deep experiences of a lifetime of study of Texas and its cities, McComb combines an interesting narrative with a compelling analysis of the Lone Star State's urban places. His book will help a broad array of readers to understand that urban history, often dealt with as an afterthought when it comes to Texas, is fundamental to an understanding of the state's development."
—Robert Wooster, Regents Professor of History, Texas A&M University-Corpus Christi

"Individuals interested in knowing more about the various pathways to modern Texas cities will find much worthy of exploration in McComb's new book."
—*Texas Books in Review*

"After finishing the book the reader will no longer be able to ignore the many contributions that the cities of Texas have made to the state.... A valuable addition to the scholarship of the urban Southwest and should be read by those interested in Texas and its transformation from a rural to an urban state."
—*Annals of Wyoming: The Wyoming History Journal*

"[An] intriguing synthesis."
—*Pacific Historical Review*

"The broad, efficient sweep of McComb's writing style is remarkable.... The book represents a major accomplishment in Texas historiography and is highly readable. If you read one work in 2017 that examines the entire state, McComb's study would make a fine choice."
—*Central Texas Studies*

"Military towns, railroad outposts, lumbering centers, river communities, and port cities all get coverage in *The City in Texas*... [A] solid introduction to Texas urban history."
—*The Journal of Southern His*

BRIDWELL TEXAS HISTORY SERIES

The City in Texas

A HISTORY

David G. McComb

UNIVERSITY OF TEXAS PRESS　AUSTIN

Copyright © 2015 by the University of Texas Press
All rights reserved
Printed in the United States of America
First edition, 2015
First paperback printing, 2023

Requests for permission to reproduce material
from this work should be sent to:
   Permissions
   University of Texas Press
   P.O. Box 7819
   Austin, TX 78713-7819
   http://utpress.utexas.edu/index.php/rp-form

♾ The paper used in this book meets the minimum requirements of ANSI/NISO Z39.48-1992 (R1997) (Permanence of Paper).

LIBRARY OF CONGRESS
CATALOGING-IN-PUBLICATION DATA

McComb, David G.
  The city in Texas : a history / by David G. McComb. — First edition.
    pages   cm
  Includes bibliographical references and index.
  ISBN 978-1-4773-2856-9 (paperback)
1. Cities and towns—Texas—History. 2. Cities and towns—Texas—Growth—History. 3. City and town life—Texas—History. 4. Frontier and pioneer life—Texas. 5. Texas—History. 6. Texas—Social conditions. 7. Texas—Economic conditions. I. Title.
  HT123.5.T4M34 2015
  307.7609764—dc23
                             2014026616

doi:10.7560/767461

To Mary Alice

CONTENTS

INTRODUCTION: Theories, Definitions, Historians 1

PART ONE: FIRST THINGS

1. The Lay of the Land 13
2. The Influence of the Native Americans 14
3. The Towns of the Spanish Empire in Texas 16
4. The Coming of the Americans 31
5. The Towns of the Texas Revolution 44

PART TWO: THE DIRT ROAD FRONTIER, 1836–1900

6. Major Events 50
7. The Dirt Road 56
8. Migration: Gone to Texas 61
9. The Evolution of San Antonio 64
10. The German Towns of Texas 73
11. The Coastal Ports 76
12. The River Ports 86
13. The Political Towns 96
14. The Military Towns 107
15. The Railroad Towns 113
16. The Lumber Towns 140
17. The End of the Dirt Road Frontier 144

PART THREE: THE AMENITIES OF CITY LIFE, 1900–1950

18. The Rural to Urban Shift 148
19. The Great Galveston Storm 152

20.	Spindletop and Beaumont	157
21.	The Oil Towns	160
22.	The Elite Rule of the Cities	172
23.	The World War I Era	187
24.	The Enticements of the City	192
25.	The Great Depression	219
26.	World War II	226
27.	The Immediate Postwar Years	231

PART FOUR: GREAT TEXAS CITIES, 1950–2012

28.	Population and Urban Expansion	234
29.	Suburbs and Subdivisions	240
30.	Segregation and Integration	244
31.	The Hispanic Identity	253
32.	John F. Kennedy and Dallas	257
33.	The Voting Rights Act and the Cities	259
34.	Land Transportation	264
35.	Airlines and Airports	272
36.	Urban Excellence in Texas	277
37.	Houston, a Renaissance City	292
38.	The Infrastructure for Excellence	305
39.	The City and the State: A Conundrum	306

NOTES	309
SUGGESTIONS FOR FURTHER READING	334
INDEX	336

THE CITY IN TEXAS

INTRODUCTION

THEORIES, DEFINITIONS, HISTORIANS

It is currently estimated that 88 percent of the people of Texas live in urban areas and occupy about 6 percent of the land. In comparison, 82 percent of those living in the United States are urban and take up about 5 percent of the land. At the global level, 51 percent are urban (world land occupation is hard to estimate due to varying definitions of city limits). Although the actual number of rural folk in Texas has remained roughly the same since the 1930s, at 3 million, the percentages have changed in relation to total state population. The percentages reveal the decennial growth of the cities, with notable increases starting in the 1880s. Growth slowed during the years of the Great Depression of the 1930s, but Texas passed the median line of rural to urban in the following decade and then remained on course afterward to become an almost completely urban state in the first decade of the twenty-first century.

The shift of population from country to city is now complete and the rural-urban split is basically meaningless. At present, less than 2 percent of Texas inhabitants actually work as farmers or ranchers, and everyone is urbanized. This is not to say that farming and ranching are unimportant. There has always been a necessary symbiosis between country and city. Everyone needs the products of the countryside; dairy and vegetable farms, for instance, ring the cities. Most Texans, even rural folk, however, look to their urban centers for clothes, processed food, equipment,

TABLE I.1. Percent of Urban vs. Rural Population, Texas

YEAR	URBAN	RURAL
1850	4	96
1860	4	96
1870	7	93
1880	9	91
1890	16	84
1900	17	83
1910	24	76
1920	32	68
1930	41	59
1940	45	55
1950	63	37
1960	75	25
1970	80	20
1980	80	20
1990	80	20
2000	82	18
2010	88	12

Source: Compiled from U.S. Census and *Texas Almanac and State Industrial Guide, 1968–1969* (Dallas: A. H. Belo Corp., 1967), p. 168.

employment, medical care, politics, business, entertainment, and information. People are split only by distance.

In this rural to urban population shift, Texas trailed behind the United States until the 1940s and then surpassed the nation in the later part of the century. This is significant to the history of the state, because in the past half-century thoughtful Texans have begun to reject the inhibiting Texas mystique of narcissistic exceptionality, the myth of frontier independence, white male paternalism, and reckless wealth in order to associate with a greater world.[1] Human beings, albeit with setbacks, have followed a linear urban imperative that began with the founding of Jericho, the first city, some twelve thousand years ago. So also in Texas.

As has been long recognized, the greatness of human achievement has been incubated in an urban womb, and since 1950 people in Texas cities increasingly have contributed ideas, art, music, writing, and technology for the advance of American civilization. Examples are scattered throughout the text—for instance, Jack Kilby and the integrated circuit, Michael DeBakey and Dacron stints, Philip Johnson and Houston architecture, and Buddy Holly and rock music. Texans have become more creative.

A rough gauge of creativity is the number of patents registered with the United States Patent Office. A patent recognizes an original idea about how something works, what it does, and how it does it. Between 1963 and 1997, Texas, with a total of 78,000 patents, trailed seven other states. By 2010, in thirteen years, the total number of patents had doubled, to 161,000, and Texas remained behind only California and New York. In 2009 Texas passed New York in one-year registrations.[2] By itself, Austin's yearly production of patents leaped from seventy-five in 1975 to more than two thousand in 2001.[3] Texas had changed.

This is why the historical passage of Texas into an urban state is important; the transformation is a significant part of the state, national, and global human experience. To understand Texas it is necessary to know what it once was, to know what it has become, and to know how that came to happen.[4]

In Texas history the towns and cities have been an integral part of the settlement pattern. Town dwellers moved to Texas along with those who occupied the countryside. The settlers banded together to oppose the Indian groups, who were largely fought, killed, Christianized, betrayed, shunted aside, assimilated, and forced into Oklahoma. Pause should be given, however, to recognize that three current reservations now exist in Texas—the Alabama-Coushatta of East Texas, the Kickapoos of Eagle Pass, and the Tigua at El Paso—and that 315,000 Texans claimed Indian relationship in the 2010 census. The historic Indians provided foreknowledge of the land and exerted a pressure for consideration in city location and construction.

The Spanish imperialism that led the European occupation of the Southwest depended upon cities. Hispanics generally preferred to live in their towns and commute to the countryside to tend cattle and corn. Anglos, in contrast, lived on their outlying farms, ranches, and plantations. Rural Texas held the bulk of the population through the nineteenth century and provided an economic base. Overlooked by history, however, have been the towns and cities that supported the settlers with supplies, markets, technology, recreation, ideas, information, and political direction.

To survive, an early Texas town needed three ingredients: access, purpose, and water. Access, especially in the nineteenth century, required a gradually improving system of roads that spread from town to town and from farm to town. The towns led the way in this vital transportation evolution with pavement, railroads, and airports.

In a broad sense access also meant communication—the transportation of information through a network. According to information theory a closed system, one without a flow of outside energy (information), will wither and die. Thus, newspapers, libraries, telegraphs, telephones, radio, and television are channels of access. They are sources of information that can inspire change. It is important, in addition, that people be educated enough to understand and act upon the information they receive. Access is a two-way street.

Towns and cities also required purpose—a reason for being. This included commerce, churches, schools, hospitals, political institutions, military bases, and entertainment. At times a town lost purpose, as in the closing of coal mines at Thurber, the loss of quicksilver at Terlingua, a change in social habits at Mineral Wells, and the erosion of the beach at Sergeant, Texas. Such loss of purpose precipitated a decline into a ghost town. The wisdom, or luck, of a successful town was to find multiple purposes, a diversity that would stimulate change and growth.

A special feature of purpose involved location. Most important were places where there was a change in the mode of transportation, such as a port, where items of commerce transferred from water to land carriers—from boats to wagons, or the reverse. Such breaks in transportation attracted warehouses, banks, and merchants. Of somewhat less importance, but useful, were places that had simple river crossings, springs, or mineral resources.

Although neglected as long as it existed in generous amounts, adequate fresh water has been an uncompromising necessity for all cities at all times. In world history a prime example is the incomparable Fatehpur Sikri, the Mogul capital of India, which died in the early seventeenth century because of lack of water. It is now a magnificent ghost city for tourists. In addition, in our current search for life on other planets it is instructive that our scientists look first for evidence of water.

The eastern villages of frontier Texas seemed to have plentiful amounts. Yet, water has always been first on the list of necessary resources and a requirement for animal and municipal health. It also was necessary for fighting fires and providing sanitation as the towns grew. As can be seen on the map provided below, fewer large towns exist in arid West Texas compared to the rest of the state. This can be readily explained by a lack of water. Nature provided a statewide reminder of this fundamental need during the drought of 2011. Live Oak trees died in Houston, of all places; and at Robert Lee, a small town near the epicenter of the drought, the reservoir simply evaporated.

To reach beyond mere survival to greatness, a modern Texas city required openness so that ideas, leaders, and technology had a chance to bubble up. No one knows from whence the next formative idea or invention or piece of art will come. So, the tolerance and the diversity of the broad-based democratic rule of the United States was helpful. Public

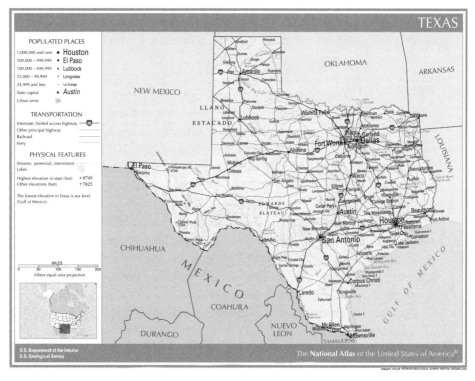

Major Texas roads and cities. Source: "Populated Places," U.S. Department of the Interior, U.S. Geological Survey, The National Atlas of the United States of America, *Reston Virginia, 2004.*

INTRODUCTION   5

education was needed not only to prepare students to work with the technical complexities of life, but also to support tolerance of people and government with understanding. It all merged together into a system that promoted high civilization. Thus, the working of a city council, the funding of education, the maintenance of libraries, and the fairness of the courts were all significant and interdependent.

Change, which is the essence of history, takes place as an interaction between people, the environment, the available technology, and the prevailing culture. Greatness can be found in change, but also destruction and death. Changes in urban life can produce both Beethoven and Napoleon. Dallas can produce grand opera and Galveston can suffer Hurricane Ike. No formula or reliable quantitative model for the interaction exists, but results often can be discerned and measured—such as the rural to urban shift in population. Changes in access, purpose, water, and greatness are emphasized in this narrative of Texas cities. This book, in essence, is an attempt to present Texas history from an exuberant urban point of view. Today's Texas is to be found in the evolution of its urbanized society.

DEFINITIONS

In order to avoid confusion, some clarification about the meaning of urban-related words is necessary. "Urbanization" can be defined as the process of becoming urban, but such circularity does not help much. Therefore, it is often conflated with the growth of markets or industry or religion or military bases or social life, which leaves the word with confused meanings.

Urban sociologist Hope Tisdale, however, captured the essence of the word in 1942. It was simply "the process of population concentration," a movement of people to a central place. Urbanization stopped when concentration stopped. Her definition avoided the contentious listing of urban traits across times and cultures. For Tisdale the process of concentration was the only constant factor, though she admitted the importance of varied technology in the movement.[5] Her insight about concentration is used in this book; size is important.

In addition, there are words that denote settlements by their population amount. In ascending order these are village, town, city, metropolis, and megalopolis. A lack of sharp lines, a vagueness, exists, however. The word "city," for example, is commonly defined as a large town. How large? How small? This is left unexplained. These words also indicate a place led by a local government, sanctioned by the state, with a clustered population and restricted in space by corporate limits. State definitions can vary, yet we know by experience that a village is smaller in space and population than a city, and a city is smaller than a metropolis. Often in this book I use the word "city" in this loose generic, conversational manner.

In an effort to be more precise, the United States Bureau of the Census, our most reliable source of statistics, assigns additional definitions, identifying unincorporated places of 2,500 people or more; incorporated units of 2,500 or more (cities, boroughs, towns, and villages); a city of at least 50,000 people with 75 percent of the labor force in nonagricultural activity (metropolis); and central metropolis with extended economic subregions (metropolitan statistical area [MSA]). Rural areas are simply those places that are outside the urban definitions.

The Census Bureau changed its definition of metropolitan areas in 1949, 1958, 1971, 1975, 1980, 1990, and 2000, and warns about cross-comparisons. Before 1950 the census counted only incorporated places of 2,500 population or more as urban. At that date the bureau began to include unincorporated places as well—an acknowledgment of suburban growth. This meant an increase of about 3 percent in the urban column and a similar decrease in the rural line in the tables about the rural to urban shift in population. All of this adjustment demonstrates that demographics can be tricky, and some caution is needed.

THE LINEAGE OF URBAN HISTORY

Historians expressed interest in cities in the early part of the twentieth century. Lewis Mumford (1895–1990) of New York, who hated the sprawl of the modern city, devoted most of his writing to global urban matters and technology, starting in 1922. He is one of the relatively few historians to ponder the meanings of city growth and civilization. "The final mission of the city is to further man's conscious participation in the cosmic and historic process," he concluded in *The City in History: Its Transformations, and Its Prospects* (1961).[6]

Mumford was later joined by British geographer Peter Hall in 1998 with *Cities in Civilization*. Hall provided a historical probe into creative ages for clues to their success. All golden national ages were urban, he discovered, but cities were not necessarily calm or comfortable or equitable. Democracy was not the norm until the great American experiment of governmental rule, but important cities of the past were cosmopolitan, comparatively free of traditions, and heady with opportunity.[7]

Academic urban studies in the United States experienced a jolt when Richard C. Wade, in *The Urban Frontier: The Rise of Western Cities, 1790–1830* (1959), provided a counterbalance to Frederick Jackson Turner's revered "frontier thesis" about the settlement pattern of the American West. Turner had said in a speech to the American Historical Association in 1893 that successive waves of Indian traders, hunters, farmers, cattle ranchers, and miners established a frontier line between "savagery and civilization" and forged the character of the American people. That line, based upon density of population, had disappeared by 1890, according to Turner.

Wade challenged Turner's widely accepted "frontier thesis" with the thought that in reality urban places led the way into the wilderness, carrying the ideas of civilization with them. "The towns were the spearheads of the frontier," he proclaimed in the first sentence of his revolutionary book about cities in the Ohio Valley. Overlooked was that throughout history some peoples have preferred a city life, even on a frontier. In Texas this can be seen in the proclivities of the Spanish, Mexicans, Jews, Germans, Chinese, and the merchants from the eastern United States. These were people who preferred urban culture, ventured into the wilderness, and planted the seeds of civilization on town squares.

Wade (1921–2008), a professor at the University of Chicago and later at the City University of New York, became the first president of the Urban History Association, founded in Cincinnati in 1989. The forming of an association and publishing of a journal are common markers of academic maturity. Wade looked at cities with a broad view that examined political, economic, and social matters and encouraged urban research among his students and others.

He was followed by a generation of scholars such as Sam Bass Warner, Jr., Carl Condit, Nelson Blake, Gary B. Nash, Joel A. Tarr, Allen Pred, John W. Reps, Kenneth T. Jackson, Clay McShane, Carl Abbott, and Roy Lubove. Cities, however, are multifaceted, with a history for each facet, and it is not surprising that scholars have followed individual themes of growth, politics, suburbanization, regional influence, technology, planning, immigration, class stratification, ethnicity, gender, and culture.

Urban history has remained, consequently, a splintered historical field of study with no overarching thesis.[8]

Of some help, nonetheless, was the central place theory of German geographer Walter Christaller (1893-1969), who explained regional urban settlement patterns by looking at the locations of large cities in relation to others. Essentially, Christaller modeled a commonsense hierarchy of cities in which a few large central places serviced a group of intermediate-sized cities that in turn helped an even larger group of small towns. The model was based on population size, central location, distance, and transportation.[9] The realities of transportation, terrain, culture, and politics eventually diminished Christaller's ideas as an urban planning tool of the mid-twentieth century in Europe and the United States.[10]

Still, in the history of Texas a few large cities came to dominate. They served intermediate-sized cities that affiliated with them and the intermediate-sized places supplied a blanket of dependent small towns that speckled the countryside. This development is especially apparent in parts 2 and 3 of this book, with the proliferation of small towns related to the activity of railroads, cattle, ports, politics, lumber, and oil. They demonstrate the concentration principle of Hope Tisdale, while the large places fulfill the permanence predicted by central place theory.

For hard factual Texas information, an assemblage of historians, genealogists, dilettantes, and students put together brief, factual, authoritative, historical articles about some 7,200 Texas communities for *The Handbook of Texas* (1952, 1976), *The New Handbook of Texas* (1996), and *The Handbook of Texas Online* (ongoing). These handbooks are a unique accomplishment started by University of Texas historian Walter Prescott Webb (1888-1963). A remarkable reference tool, they provide encyclopedic information for people wanting to know about specific places.

Also, there have been written a variety of books and academic papers about women, race, business, architecture, politics, entertainment, transportation, and special events that have used the city as a setting. Texas writers such as Jesús F. de la Teja, Gilbert R. Cruz, C. L. Sonnichsen, W. H. Timmons, David G. McComb, Darwin Payne, Paul H. Carlson, Mary Jo O'Rear, Roger M. Olien, Diana Davids Olien, Thad Sitton, James H. Conrad, Char Miller, Martin V. Melosi, Joseph A. Pratt, and T. Lindsay Baker have made noteworthy contributions.

This book owes a great deal to all of these people who saw towns and urban history as interesting and important to Texas. To a large extent this study is a synthesis of their ideas and research, and they are saluted in the endnotes. A special acknowledgment, in addition, goes to the anonymous readers of this manuscript for their endurance, comments, suggestions, and corrections. Their work and attention made this a better book. Theresa May of the University of Texas Press, in particular, deserves special recognition and thanks at this time of her retirement from the Press for guiding the book to publication with the same steady hand she used with my other books over thirty years.

PART ONE

First Things

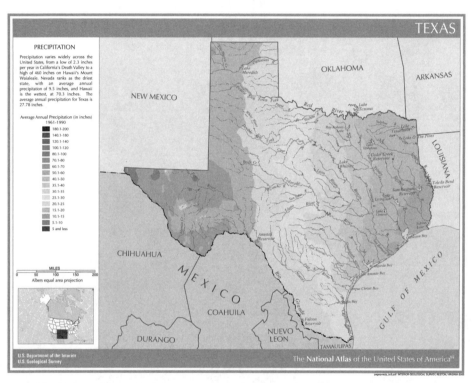

Rainfall regularly diminishes from east to west with the historical result of, first, American settlement in the east and, later, concentration in a vertical line of cities from Lake Texoma to the San Antonio River along the Balcones Escarpment. The rivers flow in a southeasterly direction, which meant that early Spanish explorers and travelers had to contend with multiple river crossings. Source: "Precipitation," U.S. Department of the Interior, U.S. Geological Survey, The National Atlas of the United States of America, Reston, Virginia, 2004.

1

THE LAY OF THE LAND

The physical features—rainfall, temperature, soil, configuration of the coast, forests, run of the rivers—that initially attracted hunters, farmers, and ranchers to the land have been fundamental also to the gathering of people into Texas cities. Across its face the state displays four of the eight major landforms of the United States—Rocky Mountains, Great Plains, Interior Lowlands, and Coastal Lowlands. From west to east—773 miles—average rainfall increases from desert in the far west to swampland near the Louisiana border. From north to south—801 miles—average temperatures range from chilly in the Panhandle to pleasant in the Rio Grande Valley. The sheer expanse has impressed people from the beginning to the present, and largeness has been always a part of the Texas mystique.[1]

The growing season is almost all year long in the Valley, and half that time in the Panhandle. The country is raked by yearly tornadoes in the midsection, ravaged by summer hurricanes on the Gulf Coast, and parched by periodic drought during odd-numbered decades. The decade beginning in 2011 has been among the worst. The desultory rivers, rarely in any hurry to scour deep channels, run from the northwest to the southeastern coast. Such environmental factors have all influenced the development of Texas cities.

2

THE INFLUENCE OF
THE NATIVE AMERICANS

About the same time that sedentary Neolithic people established Jericho, the first city in the world, Paleo-Indians entered Texas from the north. Over time these Indians deepened their technology and culture to evolve into some two hundred bands in ten cultural "tribes" that occupied Texas when the Spanish arrived to challenge their sovereignty. Unlike the high civilizations of Central and South America or the Pueblo Indians of New Mexico, the Texas Indians remained for the most part hunters and gatherers.

In the eastern pine forests the exceptional Caddo Indians lived in semipermanent villages of round, thatched huts; planted corn, squash, beans, and tobacco; hunted and fished; sported elaborate tattoos; made pots and flutes; and played a game like field hockey. The Spanish adopted their word for a friend, "Tejas." From this came the word "Texas," and the motto of the state, "friendship." The north-south Hasinai Trace connected the Caddos to the Mound Building culture of Arkansas and Illinois. They bartered widely with other Indians and even hosted annual trade fairs. Anthropologist William C. Foster considered them the most "cosmopolitan" of the tribes.[1]

A major east-west Indian trading route through Kentucky, Tennessee, and Mississippi crossed the Mississippi River at Natchez and went westward over the Red River near Natchitoches and thence through the Caddo nation of East Texas. The trace crossed the Angelina and Neches Rivers on the way to the vicinity of San Antonio, angled to the Pueblo villages of northern New Mexico, and dropped southward to the high civilizations in Mexico.[2]

It is likely that Cabeza de Vaca, who provided the first European description of the interior of Texas, intersected this trail just south of the Rio Grande during his escape to Mexico in 1535.[3] Explorer Alonso de León in 1689-1690 used 500 miles of this Indian trade trail to blaze the Camino Real, which developed into the first Spanish road across Texas.[4] The Caddos thus thrived at a crossroads of trade, but their interactions with outsiders meant that they suffered greatly from European diseases such as smallpox and cholera. Once counted as the largest group in Texas, with eight thousand members, by 1800, after successive epidemics, the Caddos amounted to only several hundred families.

The Indians, particularly the fierce Comanches of the Great Plains, are significant also for their resistance and the fear they created in settlers until the mid-1870s. The Comanches were hit-and-run raiders who ate the cattle, killed and scalped men, stole horses and mules, ransacked cabins, and kidnapped women and children. When chased by vengeful pioneers the Indians divided their loot and split into separate directions, which made them hard to track. They so harassed the farmers working the outlying fields at San Antonio that it was hard to produce a crop of corn. In 1840 four to five hundred Comanche warriors attacked Victoria and the small port town of Linnville at Lavaca Bay. This was their largest raid and they left the Linnville warehouses plundered and smoldering into ashes.

The cultural clash of violence and mistrust between natives and settlers thus cast a dark shadow over the early history of the region.

3

THE TOWNS OF THE SPANISH EMPIRE IN TEXAS

The outline of the Spanish expansion into Texas is well known. Starting with explorations of the coastline, the adventures of Cabeza de Vaca, and the entrada of Coronado in 1540, knowledge of the Texas landscape slowly emerged.[1] Coronado did not find the golden cities that he sought; only poor Indian pueblos and vast grasslands. Following this failure the king ordered the end of the brutal entradas and the killing of innocent Indians. Afterward, a gradual settlement of the upper Rio Grande Valley, supervised by a patriarchal bureaucracy, commenced with commands from the king in Madrid to the viceroy in Mexico City.

Reports from parallel civil (pueblo), military (presidio), and church (mission) institutions trickled upward through a chain of command while special inquiries investigated complaints and the performance of officials. The greatest difficulty in this system of empire was slowness, an unavoidable trait explained by the great distances and the tools of communication—couriers, roads, horses, ships. Nonetheless, this trinity of institutions, like a three-legged stool, represented Spanish civilization in the wilderness. It was an urban empire organized around cities with a gateway town into Texas—San Juan Bautista, a mission and presidio located in Mexico five miles south of a favorable crossing of the Rio Grande.

Royal decrees issued over five centuries to regulate the Spanish Empire, known as the Laws of the Indies, included rules to guide the building of towns. A codification ordered by Philip II in 1573 collected ideas of organization that included a rectangular, central plaza with the corners at the cardinal points of the compass; streets intersecting at right angles; an elevated site with nearby timber, water, fertile land, and native population; buildings of similar style to enhance beauty; a segregated area for slaughterhouses with drainage for filth; a separate plaza for the main church; and a commons area for recreation and cattle.

It was expected that vacant land would be used and that no harm would come to the Indians. The natives were to be converted to Christianity by persuasion, not at the point of a sword. Mission compounds, with their chapel and farmlands, were thought to evolve into pueblos. The walled presidios, which were designed by commanders on the spot for the protection of soldiers, missionaries, and village folk, stood apart as forts. Variation by site and circumstance inevitably occurred, but the Laws of the Indies can be considered the first Western attempt at city planning in the New World.[2] Remnants are still visible in modern cities of Spanish heritage, particularly Santa Fe and San Antonio, and less so in Nacogdoches, Gonzales, Laredo, and Goliad.

THE ROLE OF THE ROMAN CATHOLIC CHURCH

In history it is sometimes difficult to track the influence of religion, but this is not the case in the Spanish Empire. To save the soul of the heathen was almost as important a motive as acquiring gold and conquering land. Zealous missionaries, sometimes barefooted, paced alongside the avaricious conquistadors. After the Coronado failure, the missionaries commenced a slow, determined program of persuading Indians to embrace Christ. Franciscan friars—noted for their simplicity, gentleness, and subsistence on alms—founded the first Texas mission near present-day San Angelo in 1632 and thirty-seven more, including one in Louisiana, by 1794. The areas of concentration were in East Texas near Nacogdoches, the upper Rio Grande at El Paso, and in south central Texas along the San Antonio River.

Working in pairs the friars would build a chapel, plant crops, and start handicrafts such as metalworking to interest the natives. They handed out small presents and tried to teach the Indians about Christ and the Spanish way of life. They expected to change the Indians into fervent subjects of the king and thus eventually end the need for a mission. Although there were some conversions and inevitable intermarriage with Spaniards, most nomadic Indians had slight use for the strange men in light-blue frocks cinched at the waist with a cord, preaching an odd faith in an unfamiliar language.[3] Worse, the Indians used the overeager Franciscans as pawns in warfare, and the Spanish government manipulated the missionaries as a means to maintain a presence in a weak frontier.

After a century and a half of unrewarded efforts at persuasion, the Viceroy Revilla Gigedo II ordered secularization of the missions and distribution of the assets—grain, oxen, horses, cattle, farming tools, land, irrigation water—to church members. It meant that the crown no longer had to fund the missions; that conversions of Indians ceased; that neophytes became tax-paying citizens and a low-ranking minority of society; and that the presidio became the most important institution. Secularization, 1793–1824, was accomplished under the direction of local civil authorities with the approval of the withdrawing Franciscans.

By the end of a generation of Indian ownership the nearby mission land generally fell into the hands of townspeople and the distant pastures went to traditional ranchers. The buildings decayed to rubble useful only for outside construction projects until the Republic of Texas recognized church ownership in 1841.[4] The retreat of the friars marked a triumph of warfare over pacification, a victory for an intractable native culture, and the loss of an important Christian moral force on the frontier. One of the three supports of empire had been removed.

EL PASO DEL NORTE

Spanish exploration and settlement in the seventeenth century brought an empire of livestock ranches and small wheat farms into New Mexico to just south of the Rio Grande at El Paso del Norte (the Pass of the North) in northern Mexico. El Paso was an oasis area where the Rio Grande cut southeastward between the Franklin Mountains and the Sierra de Juárez. It was a passageway and stopping place for travelers to New Mexico. The Pueblo Revolt of 1680 in New Mexico pushed 2,500 bedraggled Spaniards and their Indian allies eastward into this remote western point of Texas to five connected settlements along the south bank of the river.

The El Paso area, already a way station for western traffic, thus became a refuge and a launching point for a retaking of New Mexico.[5]

At their El Paso missions industrious Franciscans planted irrigated corn and wheat and raised cattle. Their vineyards produced the best wine and brandy in the Spanish Empire—an accomplishment that reflects into the present time. In El Paso, moreover, can be detected the earliest urban pulsebeat of Texas. In 1682 Franciscans built the Corpus Christi de la Isleta Mission and Pueblo for the Tigua Indians. It endured and a shift of the Rio Grande in 1829 placed it in the United States. Now "Ysleta" claims to be not only one of the three Indian reservations in the state, but also its first township.

ALONSO DE LEÓN AND THE FRENCH THREAT

Spanish attention at the time, however, was redirected by French imperial ambitions on the Gulf Coast. Reports of spies about a La Salle expedition in 1685 to establish French control at the mouth of the Mississippi River, plus the appearance of a Jumano Indian in northern Mexico carrying a letter written in French, alerted them to rival ambitions. Ten expeditions by the anxious Spanish to locate and oust La Salle failed, but the Spanish distress was needless. The new governor of the province of Coahuila, Alonso de León, in 1689 finally found on his fourth attempt the remainder of the misdirected French expedition at Garcitas Creek near Matagorda Bay—the ruins of a small fort and three skeletons.

Meanwhile, de León blazed a road, the Camino Real, along the old Indian trading path that reached from the Rio Grande to Louisiana, listened to the request of the Caddo Indians for missions, and released unneeded cattle and horses into the wilderness. This feral livestock thrived on the prairie grasses and contributed to the breeding of Texas longhorn cattle and the mustang pony.[6]

The Franciscans founded several short-lived missions in East Texas in 1690 in response to Indian requests; pulled back to Mexico when the Indians proved difficult; and then marched out again under a Spanish-French détente in the second decade of the eighteenth century. Los Adaes in Louisiana became the capital of Spanish Texas in 1729. It remained a focal point of Spanish occupation until 1772, when the viceroy of Mexico recalled all Spanish settlers and missionaries to Bexar in an effort to strengthen frontier defenses.

THE SURVEY OF THE MARQUÉS DE RUBÍ

The Marqués de Rubí inspected and reported on the presidios and missions from California to East Texas in 1768. It was as disheartening as the similar inspection by Pedro de Rivera in 1727. What Rubi reported was corruption, incompetence, poverty, abusiveness, and uselessness. He offered as an example the destruction of the mission at San Saba by Indians within three miles of a fully armed presidio commanded by Colonel Diego Ortiz Parrilla.

Lipan Apaches, squeezed by Comanches in the north and the Spanish in the south, cleverly obtained a mission at San Saba to the northwest of San Antonio in 1757. The Apaches hoped to provoke their enemies to fight, and the naive friars fell into the trap. The churchmen insisted on distance between their mission and the presidio due to the corrupting influence of the soldiers. When two thousand Comanches arrived in the spring of 1758, painted red and black and mounted on horses with their bows and lances, the three missionaries refused military protection and rushed out to greet them with gifts of tobacco and beads. In return they received war whoops, death, and mutilation.

In reaction to the destruction of the mission at San Saba the Spanish government sent out a punitive army of six hundred soldiers, volunteers, and Indian allies under the command of Ortiz Parrilla. Marching northward the Spanish force attacked a Wichita village protected by a moat and stockade. Armed with French guns and apparently aided by French advisors, the Indians repulsed the attack and encircled the Spanish. Ortiz Parrilla fought loose at the cost of his supplies and cannon, and retreated to Bexar. It was the worst defeat for Spanish arms in Texas history and a signal victory that Indians, when equipped with similar weapons and tactics, could halt Spanish incursions.

Rubí recommended annihilation of the perfidious Apaches, the establishment of a defensive line along the Rio Grande, and a pullback from East Texas and Louisiana, where he found no Indians converted by the missionaries. Although supported by governmental authorities, this forced removal faltered when Antonio Gil Ibarvo, a landowner and Indian trader of Los Adaes in Louisiana, successfully petitioned for a group of settlers to return partway home. They stayed four years on the banks of the Trinity River, until floods and Indian raids forced them to move eastward, without authorization, to the abandoned mission site of

Nacogdoches in 1779. The Caddo Indians at the old mission were much more tolerant. Spanish enthusiasm for the pullback had ebbed by this time and Ibarvo became the official commander of the militia and the magistrate of the pueblo.

NACOGDOCHES

Nacogdoches, named for a local Caddo Indian band, evolved into a center for illicit trade with the French and Americans, a stopping point for drifters moving westward across the leaky border from Louisiana, and a touch point for revolutionaries. It looked eastward to New Orleans for its sustenance, not southwestward to far-off Mexico. Ibarvo constructed a substantial two-story stone house, later called the Old Stone Fort, for his commercial and governmental work. Made of native stone and lined with adobe, its walls were two-and-one-half feet thick. It was built facing a plaza along the Camino Real (also called the Old Spanish Road), which followed the Indian trading network. Streets crossed more or less at right angles around the central square, as might be expected of a Spanish town.

Ibarvo, the magistrate, gave out land grants without bothering to write them down, and issued a criminal code of fifty-four offenses with almost half calling for punishment by death. He prohibited gambling, dancing, and selling liquor to Indians. Unhappy settlers accused Ibarvo of smuggling and forced his removal to Bexar for judgment. After much delay, 1791–1796, he was acquitted for insufficient evidence. The officials in Bexar, however, banned his return to Nacogdoches.

In 1788 French frontiersman and Indian interpreter Pedro Vial reported that Nacogdoches had eighty to ninety wooden houses and 250 population, mainly Spanish and French.[7] At the turn of the century it was reported to have 660 persons and a church plaza, with businesses located around the plazas.[8] American adventurers in the vanguard of their westward movement had begun to slip into East Texas by this time. Four of them formed a trading company with William Barr and Peter Samuel Davenport located in the Stone Fort at Nacogdoches, and partners Luther Smith and Edward Murphy established at the French trading post in Natchitoches, Louisiana. European trade goods came more cheaply through New Orleans than through Saltillo, Mexico, a longer distance.

From 1798 to 1812 the House of Barr and Davenport was the leading mercantile company in East Texas, with a prosperous business that supplied the Indians, Spanish troops, and settlers. The Spanish quartermaster paid them cash for flour, beef, salt, and candles, while the Indians exchanged horses and pelts for tobacco, lead, gunpowder, axes, knives, blankets, scissors, mirrors, beads, and vermillion. The company's merchandise traveled from a Natchitoches warehouse by ox or mule train over the Camino Real, and in reverse the company sent horses, mules, and pelts to Louisiana. Facing the hazards of bandits and shifting governmental policies, the items had to traverse a treacherous and lawless "Neutral Ground," 60 miles designated to keep peace between the United States and Spain from 1806 to 1821.

Following the deaths of Smith and Murphy in 1808 and Barr in 1810, Davenport turned against Spain, then under the control of Napoleon. He supplied the ill-fated revolutionaries of Bernardo Gutiérrez de Lara and Augustus Magee, and after their defeat Davenport fled to Natchitoches Parish, where he resided on a luxurious sugarcane plantation until his death in 1824.[9] Although revolution against Spain was simmering, as a result of the aborted Gutiérrez uprising the forces of royalist Joaquín de Arredondo enacted a bloody purge that scattered the population of Nacogdoches and left the town practically deserted until Mexico gained independence from Spain in 1821.

SAN FERNANDO DE BEXAR (SAN ANTONIO)

The Marqués de Rubi's reconnaissance of 1768 came too early to witness the lively development of Nacogdoches, but he praised the success of Bexar as a base between Mexico and East Texas, and made it an exception to his Rio Grande defense. Early Spanish explorers Domingo Terán de los Ríos in 1691 and Fray Isidro de Espinosa in 1709 had spotted the pleasant spring that would later supply fresh water to Bexar. Espinosa wrote:

> We named it San Pedro Springs and at a short distance we came to a luxuriant growth of trees, high walnuts, poplars, elms, and mulberries watered by a copious spring which rises near a populous "rancheria" of (500) Indians... The river, which is formed by this spring, could supply not only a village but a city which could easily be founded here because of the good ground and many conveniences.[10]

San Pedro Springs, located now in a park in the center of San Antonio. Photograph by author.

An example of the Franciscan energy at this time is the stone aqueduct built in 1725 over Piedro Creek to carry irrigation water to the Espada Mission below Bexar. Photograph by author.

Captain José Domingo Ramón opened a route to the site in 1716 from San Juan Bautista during his expedition to Los Adaes in Louisiana with the flamboyant Louis Juchereau St. Denis to found the East Texas missions. Trade roads to Monclova and Saltillo linked San Juan Bautista to the interior of Mexico. In the same burst of energy that inspired the Franciscans to trudge back into East Texas they dotted the San Antonio River with five successful missions, 1718–1731.

The most historically significant was San Antonio de Valero, known as the Alamo, founded May 1, 1718. Four days later the San Antonio de Bexar Presidio and the Villa de Bexar followed at the same location. Due to hostile Indians and a hurricane the mission moved three times, but could boast of a permanent priests' residence made of stone in 1727. The three-acre compound eventually included offices, kitchens, guest rooms, dining rooms, a church, storerooms, workrooms, and an irrigation ditch. Because the mission often had to look to its own defense, and after the lesson of San Saba, the friars erected eight-foot walls around the compound armed with light artillery and a fortified gate. Outlying irrigated fields of corn, beans, cotton, and orchards attracted settlers and some three hundred Indian neophytes.

Because of its storied history the modern Alamo became the most revered tourist site in Texas. Photograph by author.

The San Antonio de Bexar Presidio, which shortly moved across the river from the mission, consisted at first of a single adobe building with a varying number of soldiers, twenty to fifty, living in brush huts. They constructed a rude stockade, and their main duty was to guard the missions. In 1793 the Spanish government secularized the Alamo mission, and the site with its walled defenses became the chief location for the military. It briefly became the site of the first Texas military hospital in the early nineteenth century.

The population for the town, or villa, came primarily from volunteer peasants of the Canary Islands after the king ordered the island to provide two hundred settlers for Texas. Following various mishaps fifteen families—fifty-six people—arrived at the presidio on March 9, 1731, formed the first civil government in Texas, San Fernando de Bexar, and merged after initial resentment into the military community. The new settlers had the right to form a local government, receive land grants, including residential town lots, and carry the low nobility title of "hidalgo." Immigration to Texas gave the peasants of the Canary Islands an unusual opportunity in life. On the Texas frontier they experienced less class discrimination, obtained land and support for the first year, and had a chance to lead society.

Elaborate instructions following the Laws of the Indies for the construction of a villa accompanied the Canary Islanders. The plan called for a rectangular plaza with corners at the cardinal points of the compass, streets meeting at right angles, farmlands, pastures, and commons, all totaling 12 square miles. Hardly anything in the instructions remained unchanged by conditions on the spot, but the distribution of town lots became the first recorded survey in Texas. After agreement at a town meeting and with funds from the king, the citizens completed a church on the plaza in 1758.

Following reconstruction it became San Fernando Cathedral in 1873. The unpaved Main Plaza was a peaceful place for commercial activity, religious ceremony, and entertainment. The church separated it from Military Plaza, which was a parade ground for the presidio and a place of executions. A third plaza developed at the Alamo Mission, which became a blood-stained battleground during the Texas Revolution.[11]

The viceroy designated San Fernando as a prestigious "cuidad," or city, to be governed by a "cabildo," or town council, with initial members selected by the captain of the presidio. The cabildo had the power to

The Main Plaza is but a remnant in front of the current San Fernando Cathedral. Photograph by author.

regulate local affairs, including taxation and fines, subject to the governor's approval. It designated, for instance, the prices at the first public butcher shop in Texas in 1805. The council also appointed a public attorney to defend those unable to pay legal fees. Citizens (married adult males) elected officials with a secret ballot and made decisions at open town meetings. San Fernando was a seed of democracy. When San Fernando was established, only four of its nine officers were literate.[12]

Although Spanish officials dictated orderly urban development and Spanish culture embraced urban life, San Fernando built outward in haphazard fashion on dirt streets, with farmers living in town and needing military protection to maintain flocks, fields, and irrigation systems. When Fray Juan Agustín Morfí visited San Fernando in 1777 he found that "the town consists of fifty-nine houses of stone and mud and seventy-nine of wood, but all poorly built, without any preconceived plan.... The streets are tortuous and are filled with mud the minute it rains."[13] Indian raids and the competition from nearby missions cramped growth. Nonetheless, San Fernando, or Bexar, as it was generally known, had a population of about 500 in 1750 and 1,500 in 1800. It was known as San Antonio after 1836.

Bexar became the capital of the province in 1772 during the pullback under the Rubi plan of defense. Pedro Vial reported in 1788 that Bexar had seven hundred Spaniards who carried on a moderate trade in clothing and food.[14] Pack trains of mules carried cow hides, wild animal pelts, beef jerky, and tallow to Saltillo and returned with blankets, flour, soap, pans, salt, raw-sugar candy, and sugarcane rum.[15] The governor of Texas from 1770 to 1778, Baron de Ripperda, housed his family in the tiny military jail while the barracks at the presidio served as a prison, workshop, and dormitory for single soldiers. They had to be evacuated for special moments, such as when the baroness gave birth, as she did on six occasions.[16]

Governor Domingo Cabello, who followed Ripperda for the next eight years, complained mightily about Bexar, where he said his living quarters were better suited for pigs. Also, barking dogs kept him awake at night, teenage boys roamed about in gangs, and their parents went to unruly parties called "fandangos." Even God was lax, he thought, and did not protect him when he fell off his horse and broke an arm. He was miserable.

In spite of his complaints Cabello carried out a census, started a permanent mail service through the missions and presidios in the province in 1779, made a shaky peace with the Comanches in 1785, and under orders sent cattle drives to Louisiana to support the American Revolution. His taxation of livestock and confiscation of unbranded cattle for the crown, however, engendered long enduring unsuccessful lawsuits from ranchers and spelled economic doom to the mission system. The Franciscans had sold their excess unbranded range animals in Coahuila in exchange for manufactured products. Now, this was no longer possible and it hastened the decline of the mission institution.[17]

LA BAHIA

The Marqués de Rubí in his survey praised not only Bexar but also La Bahia, a settlement he visited toward the last of his inspections. The Spanish had established a presidio at the site of La Salle's failed colony on Matagorda Bay in 1720, followed by a mission two years later. Bad weather and mosquitoes, however, drove them in two jumps to the San Antonio River by 1749, where a pueblo grew up around the presidio. It flourished as a connecting point between Bexar and the coast. Along with Nacogdoches and Bexar it was one of the three most important Spanish settlements in Texas. In 1829 the name changed to Goliad, an anagram to honor Father Miguel Hidalgo, who inspired the move toward independence from Spain.

LAREDO

After traveling 7,600 miles in twenty-three months on horseback from the Gulf of California to Louisiana for his survey of missions, presidios, and pueblos, Rubí, exhausted, left Texas by way of Laredo and San Juan Bautista. In 1755, during the Spanish settlement of Nuevo Santander in northeastern Mexico, Captain Tomás Sánchez took cattle, horses, sheep, goats, and a handful of settlers across the ford of the Rio Grande near San Juan Bautista and founded Laredo. The semi-arid range proved ideal for livestock, but impractical for farming. The Indians were passive and more ranchers arrived by way of a newly discovered ford just south of the pueblo. By 1757 the population had eleven families, and when Rubi came through ten years later he found twelve huts made of branches and leaves. A census in 1789, however, listed 700 inhabitants consisting of

Spaniards, mestizos, and mulattoes, plus 110 Carrizo Indians who sought protection from the Apaches.[18]

THE KING'S CENSUS

The monarch ordered an annual census of the empire and reluctant officials—Governor Domingo Cabello had to threaten the alcaldes in San Antonio with fines and prison for the extra work—carried out the command in 1777-1793. The data collection was irregular, focused on the major towns, and some of it was lost in the erosion of time, but Alicia V. Tjarks, a bibliographer and social demographer from the University of New Mexico, pieced together a statistical portrait of Spanish Texas at the time. The 1790 census, the most reliable, reported 3,169 total population, a figure that matches the estimated sparse density in Texas of two people per square league (nine square miles). Bexar had 1,878; La Bahia 767; and Nacogdoches 524. The 1795 Bexar census counted sixty-nine ranchers and sixty farmers—not everyone was urban.

The population remained stagnant through the census periods with a proportion of 55 percent male. A high rate of infant mortality meant that two-thirds were adults in spite of an average birth rate of 6.3 percent. The average lifespan was forty years and the number of widows and widowers was high.[19] Unlike the situation in English colonies, Spanish women could inherit and own land. Women could sue or be sued, write wills, and manage their own property. Three of the top ten cattle owners in the Bexar area, for instance, were women. Altogether, this census data meant that life was short, that women could expect to have six children, more or less, and that by necessity in a small population of men and women there would be a heterogeneity of races and ethnic groups.

Spain transferred its ideas about caste based on race to the new world. Light-colored skin was at a premium and at the top were white people, mainly Spanish, followed by Indian mixtures of mestizos (Spanish-Indian), mulattoes (Spanish-black), and on the bottom blacks, Indians, and slaves. Despite the scolding of the friars in the Texas borderlands, a certain licentiousness prevailed. The scandalous Felipe de Rábago, for example, who was the commander of a presidio to protect the San Xavier missions in the 1740s, lusted openly after Indian and Spanish women, married or not. His soldiers followed his example and the outraged local missionary, Father Miguel Pinilla, had to excommunicate the whole lot.

Illegitimate (not sanctioned by the church) births reached almost 20 percent on the frontier and the resultant mixing of peoples influenced the data of the census. All military personnel of the presidios were listed as "Spaniards" even though it was known that most were mestizos or mulattoes. Antonio Gil Ibarvo, the founder of Nacogdoches, was listed as a Spaniard in the records, but everyone knew him to be a mulatto, as his enemies reminded everyone.[20] Honor, status, and race were social tools upheld by the Spanish, and, as historian Jesús F. de la Teja brought out in a study of a 1781 Bexar marriage case, people "gamed" the system if they could and changed official race designations to their advantage.[21]

In summary, what Spain had accomplished after a century and a half on the remote Texas frontier was a courageous but mostly failed effort to convert the Indians for Christ; an expensive slow-growing fringe of empire held together by three towns—Bexar, Nacogdoches, and La Bahia—linked by insecure roads; Castilian law enforced by a governor; legal property protection for women; acceptance of the concept of private property; the idea that cities and towns should have rational planning with self-governance; livestock breeding and cattle ranching; a lasting imprint of Spanish place names and customs; and a shaky peace with the Comanche Indians.

The Spanish presence was impressive. When King Philip V died in 1746, a six-month period of mourning was decreed and announced with church bells, draped bugles and kettledrums, and the wearing of black clothing throughout the empire, including Texas. This was followed in Bexar as elsewhere some months later by three nights of festival lights in homes and barracks, the unfurling of the royal standard, pledges of allegiance, bullfights, and dramas to celebrate the ascendancy of a new king in 1747.[22] It was an extraordinary global statement. All total, considering technology, terrain, and culture, Spain had made a grand effort to impress its civilization on the world and the Texas wilderness. All was not well, however, and it did not last.

4

THE COMING OF THE AMERICANS

Zebulon M. Pike was a harbinger. United States Army Lieutenant Pike had been ordered to explore the land west of St. Louis and after reaching the northern Rio Grande in Colorado became lost in a snowstorm. Spanish soldiers captured the "Lost Pathfinder," as he became known in history, and escorted him to Santa Fe along with seven of his men. Suspicious—why were Pike and his men snooping in Spanish territory?—but not knowing what to do with them, the Spanish authorities respectfully marched them across Texas to an exit at the nearest U.S. post in Natchitoches.

His captors had instructed Pike to take no notes, but the enterprising lieutenant took frequent "toilet" breaks in the bushes; wrote observations about geography, military might, and culture; rolled them; and secreted them in the gun barrels of his soldiers.[1] Later retrieved and published, the descriptions of a fertile, well-watered, lightly populated Texas encouraged land-hungry migrants from the United States. Pike's observations are second in importance only to the Lewis and Clark reports a few years earlier for information about the American frontier.

Concerning Bexar in 1807 Pike observed: "It contains perhaps 2,000 souls most of whom reside in miserable mud-wall houses covered with thatched grass roofs." In a conversation with a resident priest, Pike asked about the absence of Indian neophytes. "He replied that it appeared to him that they could not exist under the shadow of the whites as the natives who formed these missions had been nurtured, taken all the care that was possible, and put on the same footing as the Spaniards; yet notwithstanding, they had dwindled away until the other two missions had become entirely depopulated." This was confirmation of the decline of the mission institution. It may also reflect a diminished Indian population due to warfare and disease. Pike nonetheless found San Antonio "agreeable" and "laid out on a very grand plan."[2]

He enjoyed the people of New Spain with their singing and dancing to guitar and violin music. The women sang in French, Italian, and Spanish, and danced to the soft and voluptuous music with the snapping of fingers. Billiards, cards, horse racing, and cockfighting were amusements. "For hospitality, generosity, and sobriety the people of New Spain exceed any nation perhaps on the globe," he wrote. "But in national energy, patriotism, enterprise of character, or independence of soul, they are perhaps the most deficient."[3] Although prejudiced in favor of his own country, Pike had touched upon a vulnerability that shortly would subsume the decaying Spanish civilization into a more energetic American culture.

THE MEXICAN REVOLUTIONS

The defeat of Spain by Napoleon in 1808 promoted opportunistic wars of independence within the far-flung Spanish Empire and prompted dreams of exploitation by adventurers wanting to fish in troubled water. In Mexico the creole Father Miguel Hidalgo rallied the Indians and mestizos in 1810 with "Long live our Lady of Guadalupe! Death to bad government! Death to the gachupines!"[4] With a rampaging, mob-like army he threatened Mexico City but was captured on a northward retreat by Governor Manuel Salcedo of Texas near Monclova, in Coahuila. The "Father of Mexican Independence" was defrocked, executed by firing squad, and decapitated. The Spanish authorities impaled his head on spikes in an iron cage at Guanajuato as a warning to future rebels.

In Texas, nevertheless, other opportunists arose, such as James Long and Francisco Xavier Mina, but the most important for urban impact was Bernardo Gutiérrez de Lara of the Gutiérrez-Magee expedition of 1812–1813. Gutiérrez, who was from Revilla, Tamaulipas, was a participant in the Hidalgo revolt who refused to quit and who traveled to the United States to gain tacit and limited support for Mexican independence.

With Augustus W. Magee, a former artillery officer at Fort Jessup, near Natchitoches, he recruited free-spirited volunteers from the Neutral Ground with a promise of $40 a month and a league of Texas land. The "Republican Army of the North" crossed the Sabine River with 130 men, gathered more recruits, and captured Nacogdoches unopposed. They took over Spanish supplies of flour, powder, ammunition, mules and horses, and specie; and merchant Peter Samuel Davenport agreed to supply the army.

They marched on to La Bahia, where the Spanish garrison joined the rebels—soldiers often switched sides when it was to their advantage. The Republican army took over the stone fort. Since the first task of an army is to feed and water itself, the men scoured the neighborhood for corn and cattle belonging to the "gachupines," who had fled at their advance, and stored a one-month supply at the fort. The soldiers brought the cattle in at night and let them out, under guard, during the daytime. Six days later a royalist army led by Governor Manuel Salcedo and Simon de Herrara arrived to lay siege to the fortress. The four-month long siege was a standoff, but the defenders eventually had to purchase more food and suffered a continual plague of lice.

Magee, who was unpopular with the men due to earlier prosecutions in the Neutral Ground, died at La Bahia, maybe poisoned, and was replaced by tavern owner Samuel Kempner. After a skirmish where the Republicans surprised and killed one hundred men in a ravine, Salcedo and Herrara quit the siege and retreated to Bexar. The rebels, who gained strength from additional volunteers and Spanish army deserters, prepared to pursue and expected each man to provide his own food and ammunition. They parched corn and made jerky and hoped to be fed at the missions along the San Antonio River. Herrara tried to stop the insurgents, but the Battle of Rosillo, outside the city, turned into a rout and the Republicans captured the Spanish supplies. This forced Governor Manuel Salcedo to surrender Bexar, which had been stripped of sustenence except for beef, mutton, and water.

Gutiérrez, in charge of the occupation of the town, allowed a biased court-martial to condemn the government officials. At night, under a guise of safekeeping with their hands tied behind their backs, Governor Salcedo, Colonel Herrara, and their aides were led by a squad of Mexican rebels to the nearby site of the Battle of Rosillo. They were told to dismount, and after yelling insults, the rebels stripped the prisoners of their clothes. The guards then pulled out knives and left the field littered with mutilated bodies. Back in Bexar the next day, in spite of Mexican explanations that this is what always happened to enemy officers and an offer to be first to buy the clothes of the murdered men, Kempner led some hundred disgusted American volunteers back to Louisiana.

Gutiérrez proclaimed the independence of Texas and assumed the lofty title of "President Protector of the State of Texas." His glory was brief, however; he was tied to the murder of the Spanish officials, found guilty by a willing court-martial, and resigned. He was replaced by José Álvarez de Toledo, who had the difficult task of imposing discipline and organization on a loose gathering of Mexican patriots, leftover Americans, deserters, and Indians. Citizens who had fled returned to Bexar, and the lax army softened under the charms of afternoon siestas and evening fandangos. Meanwhile, a royalist army of 1,100 men with sixteen cannons, led by the former governor of Nuevo Santander, Joaquín de Arrendondo, marched northward from Laredo to restore Spanish control.

A subordinate, Lieutenant Colonel Ignacio Elizondo, against orders unsuccessfully challenged the Republican army with a contingent, but captured a herd of horses and retreated to rejoin Arrendondo. Republican scouts thus discovered the combined army 50 miles from Bexar, and Toledo led the rebels out to meet them on the banks of the Medina River. After a four-hour battle the Spanish forced a retreat that deteriorated into a chaotic runaway. Elizondo and his cavalrymen were ordered to kill the running fugitives with sword and lance all the way to the gates of Bexar, which by this time sheltered only panic-stricken noncombatants.

Arrendondo sent Elizondo with five hundred soldiers on to Nacogdoches to exercise a policy of pacification through execution, imprisonment, and confiscation. Another unit was sent to La Bahia. Fugitive men were jailed or executed by the hundreds as they raced for their lives to the Neutral Ground, and suspected women were put to work converting bushels of corn into tortillas for the Spanish occupying force in Bexar. Their children were left to beg on the streets.

The stock-raising industry collapsed and the people grew no crops beyond a subsistence level. Arrendondo admitted in 1814 that his men lived entirely on meat, without enough corn for a tortilla.[5] Nacogdoches remained abandoned until Mexican independence in 1821; the bodies lay unburied at the Medina battle site for nine years; and the province was deathly quiet, with only San Antonio standing as a ghost of urban expression in Spanish Texas.[6]

The draconian peace lasted but a few years, however, before other outside adventurers began to probe the weakness of the empire and encourage the discontent that boiled up from within. José María Morelos continued the Hidalgo revolt until captured and executed, and the independence spirit sparked sporadically in the mountains and forests between the coasts. Weary of war and wary of the liberal policies of the new King Ferdinand, the creole class of Mexico backed Agustín de Iturbide, who declared Mexico independent in 1821 and himself Emperor Augustin I in Mexico City in 1822.

His excesses forced an abdication the following year, which in turn led to the writing of the 1824 Constitution. This document established Mexico as a federal republic with a bicameral legislature. The Catholic Church retained a religious monopoly, the president was given extraordinary emergency powers, and the clergy and military were confirmed in their time-honored exemption from prosecution in civil courts. Mexico thus set out on its troubled future path as an independent nation, and one of its major problems was Texas.

Texas was remote, vast, and unattractive to most Spanish settlers. The implacable Indians, who had been neither pacified nor converted to Catholicism, merely fought to a standstill in the plains north of San Antonio. The Adams-Onis Treaty in 1819 had eliminated the Neutral Ground and placed a recognizable boundary at the Sabine, Red, and Arkansas Rivers between the United States and the Spanish Empire. Restless Americans, however, had already crossed these rivers. Nacogdoches became repopulated and illegal American squatters with slaves were seeping in from Arkansas. Slavery and caste had been implicitly opposed by Mexican rebels during the independence movement, and in September 1829 the Mexican government explicitly abolished slavery.

THE EMPRESARIOS

The Spanish crown had wanted to populate Texas with loyal subjects, and in 1821, just before independence, the governor at Monterrey granted Moses Austin, an impecunious promoter from Missouri, a contract to settle three hundred Catholic families in Texas. Before anything happened,

Moses Austin died and Mexican independence occurred. The new government, however, confirmed the agreement with his son, Stephen F. Austin, who quickly commenced bringing in settlers.

According to the contract the settlers agreed to profess the Catholic faith and obey Mexican law. Land sold for as little as four cents per acre compared to $1.25 in the United States; initially slavery was permitted; and the East Texas population boomed as Mexico granted other colonizing contracts. In 1827 there were 12,000 Americans in Texas and 7,000 Mexicans; by 1835 there were 30,000 Americans and 7,800 Mexicans.[7]

Empresarios did not sell land or receive fees, but gained a bonus of 23,000 acres for each hundred families settled. By the end of his land promotion career, Austin had brought in about 966 families and acquired 197,000 acres. He founded San Felipe as his capital in 1824 on a bluff on the west bank of the Brazos River near the ferry crossing of the Atascosito Road to Nacogdoches. It possessed timber, fresh drinking water, and fertile soil. Although planned according to the old Spanish town concept, with plazas and streets crossing at right angles, settlers sprawled along the main roadway and placed their log cabins as they pleased.

Within four years the town had forty to fifty houses; a population of two hundred, largely American and European, where males outnumbered females ten to one; a hotel; two taverns; a blacksmith shop; and three general stores. Austin ran the colony from his residence, a dog-trot log house with chimneys on each end, until he was replaced by a three-man "ayuntamiento" in 1828 that acted like a county government. Requirements for election included the following: male, twenty-five years of age if unmarried, twenty-one years of age if married; three years of residency; some capital or a trade; and literacy. Although the regulations for the right to vote are not mentioned in the various documents, historian Eugene C. Barker assumed the franchise was the same as the requirements for election.[8]

The town became a hub of commercial activity with a postal system, gristmill, lumberyard, and an irregular four-page newspaper, *The Texas Gazette* (1829-1832), which was published mainly in English. Nearby cotton plantations made San Felipe a shipping point for the staple by wagon to the coast 60 miles to the south. Baptist preacher Thomas J. Pilgrim established the first school in town—mainly boys in attendance—and began an illegal Protestant Sunday school in 1829. The first Catholic priest arrived two years later.

Noah Smithwick, the resident blacksmith, recalled that the wealthier people preferred to live independently with their families outside of town on their farms and plantations. Symbolic was Captain James "Brit" Bailey, who lived stubbornly on a squatter's claim. He instructed his wife, "I have never stooped to any man, and when I am in my grave I don't want it said, 'There lies old "Brit" Bailey.' Bury me so that the world must say, 'There stands Bailey.' And bury me with my face to the setting sun. I have been all my life traveling westward and I want to face that way when I die." His widow followed his wishes when the time came. His coffin was lowered feet first into a deep, well-like grave facing the setting sun.[9]

Those who lived in town were for the most part unmarried, rowdy, disrespectful, and disreputable. "It was a regular thing to ask a stranger what he had done," recorded Smithwick, "and if he disclaimed having been guilty of any offense he was regarded with suspicion." Bachelors who lived together received a family land portion, and this added to the singleness of the population. Amusements were shooting contests, card playing, and drinking. The popular barroom ballad "Mrs. Williams' Lament," inspired by a local love affair gone awry, claimed:

> The United States, as we understand,
> Took sick and did vomit the dregs of the land,
> Her murderers, bankrupts and rogues you may see,
> All congregated in San Felipe.[10]

Empresarios, including Stephen F. Austin, were required by the Mexican government to establish a central town. Thus the policy spawned not only San Felipe, but also Victoria (De León colony), Gonzales (DeWitt colony), Refugio (Powers and Hewetson Colonies), and San Patricio (McMullen and McGloin Colonies), as well as adding to the reoccupation of Nacogdoches. The newcomers were only nominally Catholic, refused to learn Spanish, and had different political and cultural customs, particularly about slavery.

When Padre Michael Muldoon finally showed up in San Felipe, there was an initial incident that threatened the stability of the colony. Muldoon, an Irishman who enjoyed strong drink, entered Frank Adams' grocery store as the men of the town were preparing to start their usual evening drinking ritual. Adams politely invited Muldoon to join and the priest sniffed, "No, I never drink with any but gentlemen," upon which

Adams slugged him between the eyes. This was an affront to a spiritual representative considered sacred by the Mexican community. It was a sacrilege.

People held their breath. Muldoon, however, recognized the difficulty, apologized, and accepted a drink in reconciliation. The loquacious priest, who enjoyed wedding parties, christenings, and evenings in the saloon, went on to become a popular member of the colony. Settlers referred to themselves jocularly as "Muldoon Catholics."[11]

The so-called roads of Texas rarely amounted to much more than a path for horses to move in single file. Fray Gaspar José de Solis dutifully inspected the missions for eleven months in 1767–1768, mainly during the rainy winter season, on mule back, and accompanied by a squad of armed soldiers for protection. It was cold and wet, his mule slipped and fell, and when they traveled eastward they had to ford the swollen streams that naturally flowed southeastward. There were no bridges in the countryside except one they made by felling large trees across the Navasota River. Otherwise, they crossed on rafts.

The friar found the Indians "cruel, inhuman, and ferocious," "dirty, foul-smelling, and pestiferous," and "cowards and pusillanimous."[12] In July 1768, on the return home, he recorded, "I remained at the Mission of La Bahia resting and bathing because I needed it."[13] In October he returned the six mules, tack, and gun that had been loaned to him at the Hacienda de Cedros. Gaspar José de Solis was not a happy camper and was delighted to escape the Texas wilderness. He concluded his diary:

> On the 13th [October 13, 1768] we passed through Los Tecolotes, through Guerreros, and came back to the Holy College of Our Lady of Guadalupe. Thanks and praise be given to God, Our Lord, through all eternity in heaven and earth who has given me such great and peculiar benefits without my deserving them, only because of his goodness and infinite mercy; for all of which may He be praised, glorified, and blessed through all the centuries. Amen! Amen! Amen![14]

Appointed by the king, Bishop Martin de Porras thought that he too should visit the towns in his jurisdiction of New Spain and Texas, and embarked on a similar journey in 1805. He traveled with twenty-five men during the rainy season from February to June from the Rio Grande to Louisiana and back through Nacogdoches to San Antonio. The cleric was impressed by the openness of the land, the lack of settlement, and the difficulty of travel.

He crossed nine large rivers on a raft drawn by swimming men and lost much of his baggage. The current was so swift on the Colorado River that the raft drifted 200 paces downstream from the starting point on the opposite side. The bishop was disconcerted to find that the "roads" accommodated only people on horseback, and so he took ten woodcutters in his group to clear the trail. "Thus," he concluded with some satisfaction, "we left a good road open for the benefit of the public."[15]

Mexican independence did not change much in the manner of politics or customs or roads or cities in Texas. Tejanos, the native Hispanics of Texas, continued to rule the towns, elect officials, collect fees, and send out military patrols to enforce the laws in the municipalities. In view of the small and scattered population, the Mexican government in 1824 logically combined Coahuila and Texas into a single state. The Texas colonists, however, grumbled about the long distance to the capital at Saltillo, where all appellate courts were located, and about their representation; they were outvoted ten to one.[16]

Haden Edwards, who possessed a colonization grant in East Texas, took advantage of the long distance and tried to force old settlers to produce ownership documents for their land or buy land from him. When he was blocked by the Mexican authorities in 1826, he led a band to Nacogdoches, took over the Stone Fort, and declared the Republic of Fredonia. Mexican soldiers, aided by militia from Austin's colony, suppressed the revolt and chased the rebels across the Sabine River.

THE TOUR OF MIER Y TERÁN

Disturbed Mexican politicians sent out a commission under General Manuel de Mier y Terán to inspect the new boundary with the United States, catalogue the natural wealth of Texas, and assess the suggestion that colonization with Europeans might be better than with Americans. Terán had fought for Mexican independence, served in Congress, and was the head of the artillery school. He had an interest in engineering, math, and natural sciences and rode in a grand, silver-inlaid carriage with large wheels in back. His entourage, which included a team of specialists in botany, mineralogy, zoology, geography, and military affairs, traveled on horseback and in wagons.

They arrived in Laredo early in 1828 and went on to visit San Antonio, San Felipe, Gonzales, and Nacogdoches. Terán's diary and those of two of his subordinates, José María Sánchez y Tapia and Jean Louis Berlandier, provided a unique window on East Texas towns, roads, and settlement for the time just before the Texas Revolution.

A group of fifty to sixty people, including cavalry, pack mules, an instrument wagon, a supply wagon, Terán's carriage, and cavalry for protection left Laredo for Bexar in late February 1828. Laredo proved unimpressive, with a "lazy" two thousand residents living in "jacales." The walls of these huts were made by filling the gap between two lines of vertical mesquite poles stuck into the ground with branches and mud wattle. A dirt floor and thatch roof completed this northern Mexico equivalent of the log cabin in a land where trees were rare.[17]

Laredo had two plazas, scant crops, and no irrigation due to the high banks of the Rio Grande. The expedition was nonetheless able to purchase travel rations of corn cakes flavored with anis seed or cinnamon, and dry, salted beef. Foodstuffs came from Mexico and were resold at high prices. Shepherds taking flocks to sell at Bexar joined the Terán group for protection against Indian raids and supplied mutton to supplement their diet. The soldiers posted guards at night to protect the horses and mules, and after a human skull was discovered at an abandoned Indian camp, it seemed prudent to double the guard.[18]

They traveled six to eight leagues (18 to 24 miles) per day and had to look for fresh water to drink and pasturage at each campsite. A guide was necessary because the road had been obliterated by wild horse trails leading to water. Since it was the rainy season the wagons had to be unloaded for crossing rivers, where swarms of mosquitoes irritated both man and beast. The outlying fields at Bexar were untended because of Indian raids, and human bones were still visible as they crossed the battlefield of Medina, where Governor José Félix Trespalacios had buried all he could in 1822. They discovered that the garrison of about 120 men had been left unpaid and that the soldiers had to rely on hunting, farming, and charity. This situation affected the rest of the community, and the town had declined in vitality.[19]

In Bexar, Sánchez found the crooked streets neither attractive nor convenient. Commerce was dominated by foreigners, and the unpaid soldiers had gone without supplies for months. When paid, the soldiers had to pay double the price for goods. The people, a population of 1,400, were nonetheless carefree and enthusiastic dancers. "The worst punishment that can be inflicted upon them is work," Sánchez grumbled.[20]

Joseph Chambers Clopper, a young farmer and trader from Pennsylvania who visited Bexar a few months later, recorded in his diary much the same observations, although he felt the population was twice as large. The Main Plaza was lined with walls and dwelling places with a canal cut through for watering garden plots. It was against the law to wash clothes, litter, or dump trash in the irrigation ditches. Every family, he observed, had a cone-shaped oven in the yard and ate a hash made of roasted meat with peppers. They used ground Indian corn to make flat cakes heated on iron pans and eaten with butter or gravy. Seated on skins on the earthen floor, the family used the tortillas as spoons to dip into the hash. There were few chairs.

While Clopper was in town the citizens celebrated Mexican Independence Day, September 16, with a candlelit fandango in the square. There was a large table with free wine and liquor; a priest gave a speech; and people danced waltzes and reels, with the women choosing their partners. Clopper was enraptured by a lustrous, dark-eyed daughter of a wealthy Gachupine family whose "pouting cherry lips were irresistible." Even so, reflecting Anglo prejudice, Clopper thought Mexicans to be "too ignorant and indolent for enterprise."[21]

In April 1828 Terán left Bexar for Nacogdoches along a poorly marked road through woods and steep arroyos. At Gonzales they crossed the Guadalupe River on a raft made of two canoes that was propelled by two "tight-lipped North Americans." The village of six square log cabins chinked with mud housed seven Americans and one Mexican. Terán was not welcomed and was not invited into any of the cabins. Gonzales marked the eastern edge of Anglo frontier settlement in Texas.[22]

On the way to San Felipe they twice lost their way because of the rough road, and broke a wheel and the front assemblage of the instrument wagon. The wagon was repaired with the use of an oak tree. At San Felipe on the west bank of the Brazos River, Terán found two hundred people, mainly Americans; forty to fifty cabins irregularly arranged; and two stores selling whiskey, rum, sugar, coffee, cheap cloth, flour, lard, and rice.

Sánchez said that the Americans ate salted beef, cornmeal bread, coffee, homemade cheese, and strong liquor. They prepared winter fields for planting in the spring to produce cotton for sale in England; shipped their cotton through Brazoria, a small port town on the Brazos River; and worked on their roads to prepare them for wagon traffic moved by oxen, horses, or mules. Still, Sánchez judged the Americans a "lazy people of vicious character" and opined that Stephen F. Austin, the leader of the colony, had lulled the Spanish authorities with a false sense of security. "In my judgment," he wrote prophetically, "the spark that will start the conflagration that will deprive us of Texas will start from this colony."[23]

Rains and floods kept Terán in San Felipe for almost two weeks, and then he crossed the river on a ferry without having to dismantle the wagons. That was a blessing. They bought corn for the animals from Jared Groce, the richest man in the colony. Groce arrived from Alabama in 1822 with fifty wagons and ninety slaves to establish a plantation in Austin's colony. He raised one of the first cotton crops, built a cotton gin, and became noted for Texas patriotism as well as his generosity toward strangers. Sánchez, however, found him stingy and was insulted that he had named a dog "Bolivar" after the South American liberator.[24]

On the road to Nacogdoches the men had to unload the wagons to get across large mud holes and struggled to pull the carriage and horses through by hand. Heavy rain, marshes, thick woods, and clouds of mosquitoes surrounding their faces and getting into their eyes hindered the march. Fevers sickened the men, including Berlandier and Terán. The axle of the baggage wagon cracked, the shaft of the instrument wagon broke, they had only corn left to eat, and at this point they faced crossing the rapidly moving Trinity River. Terán decided to take Sánchez and eight men, cross the river by flatboat, and travel on to Nacogdoches on horseback; the wagons, carriage, and the rest of the men returned to Bexar.

The town was located on a hill, surrounded by pine, walnut, maple, and live oak trees, and blessed with two springs of cool, fresh water. It took Terán fifty-one days to reach this point from Bexar. He found a mixed population of seven hundred North Americans, French, Mexicans, Indians, and black slaves. They lacked schools, education, or culture, but engaged in a brisk Indian trade to purchase necessities such as whiskey, cloth, flour, salt, rice, sugar, beans, and corn through Louisiana and New Orleans. Terán summarized:

> The Mexican is dissipated and constantly in town. The French invest all their tasks with a certain courtesy and much bombast. The North

Americans are haughty; they shun society by inclination and because they disdain it. They devote themselves both to industrial enterprises and to the hardest labors—as well as to the grossest vices—with exceptional ardor. They do not think they have relaxed from their grueling tasks until drunkenness dulls their senses, and in that state they are fierce and scandalous.[25]

It was of little surprise, then, that in his final report Terán recommended greater settlement by Mexicans and Europeans, additional garrisons in the towns, and closer trade ties with Mexico. His ideas became a part of the alarming "Law of April 6, 1830," which prohibited slave trading and closed the border to Americans.

THE WARNING OF ALMONTE

Mexican authorities, anxious about the ambitions of the United States and worried that Texas might revolt, sent Colonel Juan N. Almonte from New Orleans into East Texas to secretly assess military capability in 1834. On the way to Nacogdoches along the Camino Real he passed through the new town of San Augustine on the banks of Ayish Bayou, a place of 350 people with a great deal of "traffic" to Louisiana. Established by a joint-stock company of Anglos in 1833, it traded in cotton and corn and was platted in typical American grid pattern. The origin of its Spanish name was a mystery, but it became one of the stopping points for migrants crossing the Louisiana border into Texas, a place for smuggling, and, briefly, a competitor to Nacogdoches.[26]

Almonte compiled a statistical account that confirmed the richness of the land and the passable nature of the roads in the dry months of May to November. He noticed also the increasing settlement of self-sufficient Americans east of San Felipe, the lack of schools and priests, and the predominance of the English language. The Spanish pattern of farmers and ranchers living in towns had given way to the American pattern of settlement on individual farms in the countryside. Almonte estimated two thousand rebel fighting men and recommended that more troops be assigned to Texas.[27] But it was much too late. Contempt bubbled in the relationship of Mexicans and Americans, and the Anglos outnumbered Hispanics about four to one. Texas was already North American in culture and occupation, and ready to explode.

5

THE TOWNS OF THE TEXAS REVOLUTION

Probably, the engrossing subject of Texas independence, with its heroes, battles, politics, and consequences, is the single most researched and written about event of Texas history. At the University of Texas library, which is the foremost academic library in the state, there are 1,462 entries for "Texas Revolution, history." In contrast, there are only thirty-four entries for "Texas cattle industry, history," another popular topic. The history of the revolution, consequently, has been told often and needs little repetition. The role of Texas towns and their connecting roads during the revolution, however, is treated mainly as backdrop for the dramatic events of war.

Conflict was inevitable considering the reports of Almonte and Terán, and it boiled over, as Sánchez had predicted during his visit to the Austin colony. Argument about an inconvenient new customs station at Anahuac on Trinity Bay in June 1832 resulted in an attack on the Mexican fort at Velasco, an entry point on the Brazos River for the Austin colonists. Texan patriots borrowed a cannon from Brazoria, also a Brazos port village, to use at Anahuac, but the fort blocked the easy transport of the cannon by water. Fighting erupted. The Mexicans surrendered after running out of ammunition, but seven Texans and five Mexicans died. Blood had spilled and disruptions continued.

Colonel José de las Piedras was able to calm the insurgents at Anahuac and tried to disarm the colonists at Nacogdoches. The settlers from Ayish Bayou, in response, came to town, captured the Mexican colonel, and sent him packing to Bexar. In 1835 President Antonio López de Santa Anna consolidated power in Mexico City and became a virtual dictator. The Mexican congress voided the Constitution of 1824 and states lost their representation.

Reinstatement of customs taxes at Anahuac and the arrest of several suspected smugglers roused William Barret Travis, a hot-headed young lawyer from Alabama, and others to forcibly free them. This led to a demand by General Martín Perfecto de Cos for an arrest of the "criminals," and to back his command Cos marched from Copano Bay to Bexar with five hundred men in September 1935. He neglected to reinforce the presidio at Goliad, and it was shortly taken with a thirty-minute skirmish by Texans led by George M. Collingsworth. This cut off reinforcement for Cos from the coast.

Colonel Domingo de Ugartechea, meanwhile, in command at Bexar, ordered in early October 1835 that a patrol seize the six-pound cannon used for Indian defense at Gonzales. The Texans refused, flew a flag that said "Come and Take It," and exchanged gunfire. The patrol, without orders to attack, retired to Bexar. Cos reached town on October 9, took command of the 647 men, and briefly engaged a part of the Texas army that was probing for a closer position to town.

A contingent of Cos' force fought a thirty-minute battle at Mission Concepción in which the Texans, led by James W. Fannin, Jr., and James Bowie, took a defensive stand in the curve of a wooded river bottom. Here, the Texans avoided the lances of the Mexican cavalry, deadly on open ground, and used the accuracy of their Kentucky long rifles to pick off the gunners as they stood up to fire their cannons. The long rifles could kill at 200 yards; the Mexican musket was effective at 70 yards. The rebels lost one man and the Mexicans seventy-six before the Mexicans moved into the town. Juan Seguín, an alcalde of San Antonio who had joined the revolutionaries, formed a mounted unit of Tejanos (Mexicans born in Texas) to help patrol the perimeter of the town. Bexar, now generally known as San Antonio, thus became a city under siege.

Confused citizens, meanwhile, called for a "consultation," or convention of representatives to discuss goals, governing, and leadership. Preliminary meetings at San Felipe in 1832 and 1833 led to the Convention of 1836, which declared Texas independence on March 3, wrote a constitution, and chose Sam Houston as the military leader. Delegates met at the village of Washington, later called Washington-on-the-Brazos, which had developed as a supply place where the La Bahia road crossed the Brazos River. Andrew Robinson, one of the original settlers of the Austin colony, ran a ferry at that point, and his son-in-law, John W. Hall, laid out city lots and streets in 1833 on the bluffs above flood level. It was named by Asa Hoxey, one of the town's salesmen, after his hometown in Georgia.

The promoters shrewdly rented an unfinished building as a free meeting place in order to attract the consultation. This was an early Texas effort of town boosting for the benefit of landowners. Although the small inn was inadequate, the village of one hundred served as the capital for the Texas revolt until it was abandoned in front of Santa Anna's advancing troops.

In San Antonio, before the declaration of Texas independence, Cos barricaded the streets of the city and prepared the presidio and the Alamo for battle. After a month of inconsequential siege the Texans just about gave up despite the arrival of the New Orleans Greys—two companies, about 120 men dressed in gray uniforms, recruited and equipped by Adolphus Sterne, a Texan patriot from Nacogdoches. A captive, however, told the rebels that Cos was about to quit, and the "grass fight" confirmed the desperate nature of the Mexican force. Mexican soldiers with pack animals precipitated a skirmish between Mexican and Texan cavalry. Texans mistakenly thought they were reinforcements, but it was only a foraging party. After attack and counterattack the Mexicans lost their mules and escaped back into the town. The captured pack animals carried only newly cut grass to feed the starving Mexican horses.

Ben Milam, a forty-seven-year-old former Indian trader and scout, rallied the indecisive Texan troops with, "Who will go into San Antonio with old Ben Milam?" This started five days of close house-to-house urban fighting with breaking down doors, dropping through rooftops among startled residents, chiseling holes through adobe walls with crowbars and axes, and Mexican snipers shooting from the San Fernando bell tower. Mexican cannons raked the streets with a cross fire, and both sides dug trenches for protection. Isolated rebels in a contested stone house depended upon a tough ox and a wandering rooster for something to eat.[1]

For city combat the Texan long flintlock rifles, comparatively harder to load, were at a disadvantage compared to the short-range muskets of the enemy. Shotguns, pistols, and Bowie knives were the best choice for the close fighting, but both sides used sharpshooters. Milam, one of four

Texans killed, was shot through the head by a Mexican sniper who in turn was knocked out of his tree along the river and into the water by Texan rifle balls. Mexican captives were immediately paroled and released under promise to quit fighting. There was no one available to guard them.

Cos desperately sent a cavalry patrol, some two hundred men, to search for anticipated reinforcements outside of town, but finding none, the men deserted, all of them, and headed for the Rio Grande. The reinforcements finally arrived on confiscated horses from Laredo, but the soldiers were largely Mexican convicts who saw little need to die in remote Texas for officers who had impressed them into service. As the Texans closed in on the presidio, Cos surrendered.

San Antonio was left a wreck, with piles of stone and dirt, smoldering wooden breastworks, dead animals, cannon balls littering the ground, and plaster broken off the outside of houses.[2] Cos and his men were paroled after they promised to cross the Rio Grande and never return. This was a promise not kept, but the Texans thought that the war had been won and many of the volunteers, including the commanding general, Edward Burleson, headed for their homes. The Texans had lost 18 men (killed and wounded); the Mexicans had lost 150.[3]

Santa Anna thought otherwise about the outcome of the fighting. He was determined to avenge the defeat of Cos, his brother-in-law; to establish a base in San Antonio, which he perceived to be sympathetic to Mexico; and to crush the rebellious province. He gathered his forces at Monclova, marched them through snow and mud, and entered Texas from San Juan Bautista with six thousand men and twenty-one cannons. The army was badly funded, ill fed, and poorly motivated. Many soldiers were peasants who had been conscripted and who had never fired a gun in battle. Dependents—women and children—followed the men. There were no doctors or priests. Since Santa Anna expected the army to live off the land, the troops—even in Mexico—pillaged and looted along the road. Fifty yoke of oxen died in their traces, but they were too gaunt to eat. Six soldiers froze to death. Desertion was common and local Indians saw no need to help.

With forced marches and half rations, the hungry army nevertheless entered San Antonio with its band playing. Its appearance was no surprise. The remaining Texans had taken refuge in the Alamo with water and supplies extracted from a town that had been recently ravaged twice by occupying soldiers. There was not much left.

The military story of the dramatic storming of the Alamo and Santa Anna's pursuit of Sam Houston across South Texas to meet Mexican defeat at San Jacinto on April 21, 1836, has been well described, memorialized, and debated. It does not need to be retold in this study.[4]

In the fight for San Antonio, however, Santa Anna had needlessly lost six hundred of his best soldiers. Departing Mexican soldiers blew up the Alamo and San Antonio purportedly was left with only six people in it; Gonzales, San Felipe, and Harrisburg had burned; Texas' only operating newspaper press had been cast into Buffalo Bayou; and the Texan government had fled to barren Galveston Island to be ready for a quick escape to New Orleans.[5] After Santa Anna signed the surrender paper following the Battle of San Jacinto, which included a command for Mexican forces to retire to Bexar, the second in command, General Vincente Filisola, began a retreat. There were still some four thousand Mexican soldiers left in Texas and fighting might have continued, but Filisola, burdened with dependents and wounded men, ran into a "sea of mud" after several days of pelting rain along the retreat route.

José Enrique de la Peña, an officer of the campaign, wrote:

> Today I had to dismount, sinking up to my knees in the mud, falling and getting up, finally taking off my boots and continuing thus.... All around one could see groups at a distance one from the other. The artillery remained stuck up to the axles two or three miles away from the point of departure. The load of ammunition, provisions, and equipment were left scattered along the road and the individual who at great sacrifice was able to bring up his corresponding equipment found it useless. Many loads were lost, many mules were ruined, and the troops could not have mess [meals] because it never reached them.[6]

Napoleon famously observed that an army marches on its stomach. The Mexican army—weakened by Texas weather, disrupted by the loss of Santa Anna along with the best of the soldiers, and confronted with an already looted countryside—lost the ability to fight. After their victory at San Jacinto Texans returned to their farms and sniped at Mexicans stealing food from their fields.[7] Filisola continued the retreat across the Rio Grande to Matamoros, where he faced a court-martial to explain his actions. Although he was exonerated, the war was not renewed and the Rio Grande became the de facto southern boundary of Texas.

★

PART TWO

The Dirt Road Frontier, 1836–1900

6

MAJOR EVENTS

From the end of the Texas Revolution through the end of the century, three major events shaped the development of Texas cities. Foremost was the extraordinary one-hundred-fold growth of population, engendered by the remarkable agricultural and urban opportunity. People overflowed into Texas from the population expansion of the United States and Europe. In every decade Texas grew faster than the United States. "Gone to Texas," abbreviated "GTT," supposedly was carved into the front doors of abandoned cabins in the southeastern United States by those who had left for a better place.

The second major event was the Civil War. Although Texas experienced only minor battles, it contributed its share of soldiers to the Southern cause. Its towns stagnated and its western settlements shriveled in the face of opportunistic Indian raids. A great loss of capital resulted from the investment in the Confederate States government, absence of business, and the emancipation of slaves.

David G. Mills of Brazoria, for example, owned three hundred slaves and possessed a fortune in 1860 of $614,000. In 1870 it was $50,000. His neighbor John McNeel had 136 slaves, and his fortune dropped from $317,000 to nothing. Almost everywhere in the countryside there was a shortage of labor, a lack of capital, and substantial debt. The eighth census (1860) revealed 263 Texans with wealth of $100,000 or more; the ninth census (1870) showed only 58.

Profound was the decline in the number of wealthy planters and farmers, from 65 percent of the wealthy rank in 1860 to 17 percent in 1870. Equally impressive was the increase in the number of wealthy merchants, from 16 percent to 40 percent. The three richest Texans in 1870 were cattleman Richard King of Duval County and merchants John Sealy and J. J. Henley of Galveston, who possessed fortunes of over $500,000.[1]

The war shifted wealth and influence from the countryside to the city, from the plantations to the banks and merchant houses. In a survey of occupations of Texas governors from 1865 to 1900, only two—Andrew J. Hamilton and Sul Ross—had any genuine farming experience. The other governors were lawyers and professional politicians with town locations and occupations.[2] Although the majority of Texans remained rural in residence and thought until the 1940s, the shift of money, mind, and power to the cities began in the 1860s.

The third major event was the extraordinary growth of the railroads, which lifted cotton commerce out of the mud, transported cattle from West Texas grasslands to eastern markets, redirected the wealth of the cities to corporate business, and introduced a complex transportation technology from the eastern United States. It was the inauguration of a modern, capitalistic, market-oriented economic system for Texas.

The arrival of the rail lines assured the success of some towns, such as Dallas and Fort Worth, and doomed others, such as Washington-on-the-Brazos and Castroville, when the railroad passed them by. It was a matter of access for urban places. Although the railroads often went bankrupt, overbuilt, and created pollution, they also brought information, employment, attention, growth, excitement, and people of ambition to the places that embraced them. The towns that rejected the railroads declined.

The population of Texas thus increased and the land began to fill.

The United States Census mapped cities with over ten thousand people with each ten-year census. No place in Texas in 1860 reached ten thousand—Galveston was the largest at seven thousand. In 1870 Galveston and San Antonio were recognized on the map, and in 1880 Houston and Austin made the list. By 1890 the addition of El Paso, Denison, Laredo, Dallas, and Fort Worth largely set the urban pattern and made apparent the urban spine of central Texas cities from Dallas to San Antonio. It was the beginning of dominance by large places in a hierarchy of cities.

TABLE 6.1. Population of Texas, 1850–1900

YEAR	NUMBER
1850	213,000
1860	604,000
1870	819,000
1880	1,592,000
1890	2,236,000
1900	3,049,000

Source: Elizabeth Cruz Alverez, ed., *Texas Almanac, 2010-2011* (Denton: Texas State Historical Association, 2010), p. 418.

This spine was reflective of the topography and the economy. The curve of major cities followed the border of the Coastal Lowlands with the eastern Great Plains. This was a major division line of rainfall and soil. It was also the historic demarcation between East and West, between cotton land and cattle country. More precisely, the division followed the Balcones Escarpment, an area of desiccated chalk hills some 300 feet high, several miles wide, and 200 miles long that marked the uplift of the Great Plains landform. Underground water seeping from the plains to the lowlands came to the surface at the escarpment by artesian pressure and provided springs of fresh water to nourish the young towns planted along this natural boundary.

The sequence of census maps also confirms the frontier movement of American civilization from east to west, the slower settlement of the arid Great Plains, the heritage of the Spanish Empire, and the significance of central cities. The word "frontier" is elusive in meaning, but usually relates to a limit, or boundary. Generally, in American history it refers to an area of settlement activity where ranchers, farmers, and townspeople clashed with earlier native users of primal land. The newcomers wanted to use the resource in a different manner. Historian Frederick Jackson Turner looked at settlement patterns based upon the density of population. In a different manner in nineteenth-century Texas, the interconnection of people on the land and in the towns through a network of dirt roads marked out the actual settlement pattern of this frontier land—a dirt road frontier.

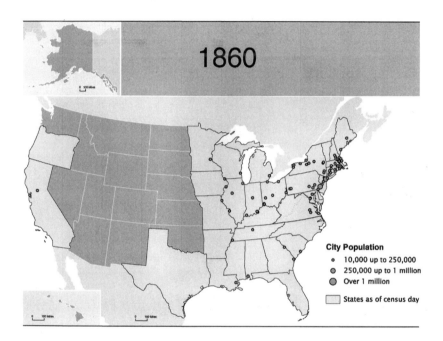

(ABOVE AND FOLLOWING PAGES) *City population of the United States, 1860-1900. When looked at in a series, the maps reveal the rapid urban growth of the United States. For Texas, the maps show the development of an urban spine of larger cities following the Balcones Escarpment from north to south in the latter part of the nineteenth century. That urban line divided the culture and economy of East and West Texas. Source: U.S. Census Bureau, "Growth and Distribution of Cities, 1790-2000," www.census.gov/history/www/reference/maps.*

MAJOR EVENTS   53

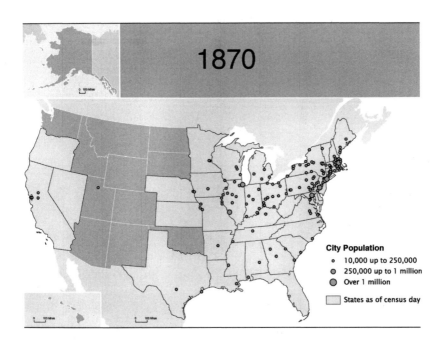
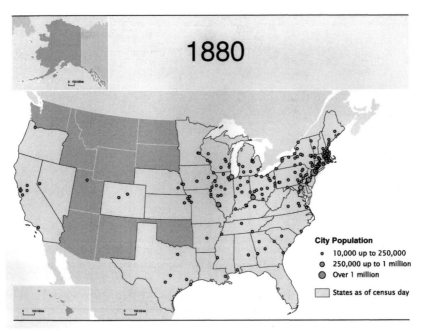

THE DIRT ROAD FRONTIER, 1836–1900

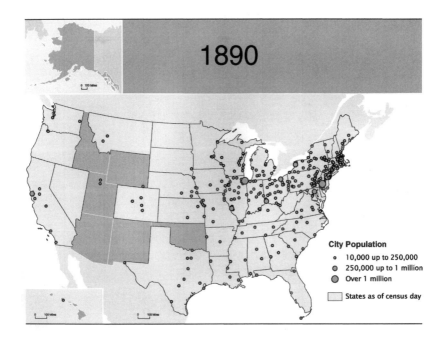

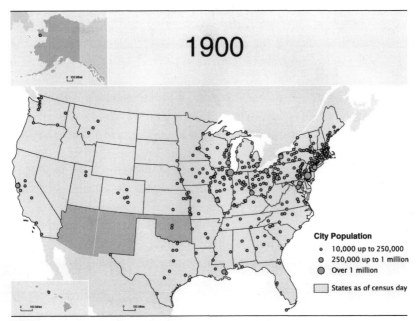

MAJOR EVENTS

7

THE DIRT ROAD

In the Spanish and Mexican periods people moved between the towns on paths defined by hoofprints, but without pavement or bridges or maintenance. Frederick Law Olmsted (1822–1903), who traveled on horseback through East Texas and Louisiana in the mid-1850s along the immigrant route of the old Camino Real, said, "The road could hardly be called a road. It was only a way where people had passed along before. Each man had taken such a path as suited him, turning aside to avoid, on high ground, the sand, on low ground, the mud. We chose, generally, the nontrodden elastic pavement of pine leaves, at a little distance from the main track."[1]

Roads lacked permanence. Still, roadways were the arteries of commerce, the veins of information, and the hope of the heart. Some pathways disappeared while others persisted and improved, with stump removal, ferries, and temporary log bridges. The Spanish tried to avoid steep hills and irritating insects while following a dry path with resources of drinking water and grazing. As historian Jesús F. de la Teja noted, the Camino Real was really "Caminos Reales" as variant branches emerged.[2]

Most of the roads converged on Bexar and then described a gentle northeastward arc, with more alternatives to reach Nacogdoches and Los Adaes in Louisiana. The Camino Real required a laborious and

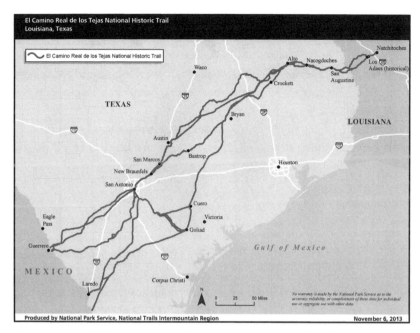

El Camino Real de los Tejas National Historic Trail. National Park Service, National Trails Intermountain Region, Santa Fe, New Mexico, 2011.

The dirt road into Texas. Photograph by author.

THE DIRT ROAD

dangerous fording of rivers that frequently cut at right angles across the direction of travel. After Texas independence the road system shifted to follow the rivers to newly founded ports on the Gulf of Mexico. By the Civil War, the Camino Real had largely been abandoned, and today only bits and pieces coincide with the modern highways like Texas 16, 21, 57, 81, 90, and IH 35.[3]

Following the Spanish and Mexican periods the wagon road became much more common with its characteristic two tracks carved by the wagon wheels into the dirt, and grass or weeds growing in the median. These roads led into the towns and lingered until the advent of the automobile and paved highways.

THE TECHNOLOGY OF THE STREET

Among the earliest vehicles used on the crude roads were the two-wheeled Mexican carts pulled by oxen or mules. It was of simple and ancient design that utilized two large, thick wooden wheels; a large box-like wagon bed tied on the axle with rawhide; and a long pole extending in front to a yoke of oxen. Since the wheels rotated around the stationary

Most Mexican wooden carts disappeared long ago. This is a replica from the International Heritage Center in New Mexico. Photograph by author.

axle, the carts made an awful squeaking noise that could be heard for miles. The only palliative was a paddle of grease on the rubbing parts.

Americans looked upon the primitive two-wheeled cart as a symbol of Mexican backwardness and preferred the wagons of the United States.[4] These four-wheeled vehicles all had in common a front axle that would pivot so that the wagon could turn corners easily; lightweight, spoked wheels; and fixed axles with the wheels attached to a hub. Front wheels were often smaller to allow turning without the wheel hitting the body of the vehicle.

There were many wagon makers in the United States—Studebaker, Shuttler, Milburn, John Deere. Seven such establishments were listed for New Braunfels alone. After the Civil War a good wagon cost $150 to $200; the wagons could be made more comfortable with springs under the seats, or wagon bed. The U.S. Army widely utilized a wagon called an ambulance that had springs between the axles and bed, a permanent canvas top, and benches along both sides that could be used to transport men, wounded or not. Concord stage coaches became popular after 1820.

Motive power included horses, oxen, donkeys, and mules. The wisdom of the road held that oxen could pull heavier weights, forage along the roadway, and were slow. Horses and mules were faster, but required grain to eat in order to maintain their strength. Donkeys could be used as pack animals, but were too lightweight for wagons.

The best draft horses, like Percherons or Clydesdales, were sweet-tempered, blocky, and deep chested, with heavy bone and muscle. They could pull large loads at a steady walking gait, and could trot if necessary. Such breeds came to the United States after the Civil War, but they were too large for hot fieldwork and so were generally assigned to the cities. The "workhorse" of Texas, comprising nearly half the draft-animal population, was the lowly mule.[5] It would not labor unto death like a horse; insisted on a break time; and could bray in protest like its father.

ROAD AMBITIONS AND THE TOWNS

The politicians of the Texas Republic had ambitions beyond their means to improve the road system. They created postal roads in 1835 that had irregular weekly service over thirty-six routes by 1840, but failed to build a national road.[6] The dirt roads nonetheless linked the towns together, and wagons concentrated in the streets. Stables, blacksmiths, tack, drivers, corrals, hay, grain, and water had to be provided for the animals as well as burial when they died. An adult horse, moreover, can urinate five and a half quarts and defecate forty pounds of manure per day. The feces piled along the sides of streets produced odor and attracted flies. Animal discharges were ground into the soil of the streets, contributing to the dust of summer and the mud of winter.

8

MIGRATION

GONE TO TEXAS

Travelers tramped along the Trammell Trace, a trading trail scouted by Nicholas Trammell in 1824 that linked Nacogdoches and the Red River settlements of Arkansas and followed the old Spanish route through Louisiana, St. Augustine, and Nacogdoches over the Camino Real. Adolphus Stern, who was a German-Jew townsman in Nacogdoches, recorded in his diary in 1840, "Emigration pours in, *en masse*." Two years later, he wrote, "A Mr. Dupree from Georgia Passed through to day with 96 negroes [slaves]—hurrah for Texas!"[1]

Cultural geographers Terry G. Jordan, John L. Bean, Jr., and William M. Holmes point out that before the revolution the migrants came mainly from the upper South—Tennessee, Kentucky, Missouri, and Arkansas. These people, of Scots-Irish, German, and English descent, were mainly small farmers with few slaves who drove their cows, mules, horses, and pigs into the new country. They were the people who fought for independence in the Texas Revolution, people like Davy Crockett, and they liked living on isolated farms in the rich blackland prairies of East Texas.[2]

Following the revolution immigration from the lower South, with its cotton-plantation-slave culture, moved into eastern and southeastern Texas. Slaves amounted to 12 percent of the Texas population at the time of the revolution; by the Civil War they amounted to 33 percent. This portion remained the area of black concentration until the economic upheaval of the 1930s. The Hispanic population, in contrast, dwindled to a low of 4 percent of the population in 1887 while maintaining a core of culture in San Antonio, El Paso, and Laredo.[3] Until the bonanza of the Spindletop oil well in 1901, cotton growing in the east and cattle raising in the west dominated the Texas economy.

WOMEN, FAMILIES, AND THE CITY

Part of the reason for all the hard drinking in the dirt road frontier was the excessive concentration of males. Frontiers required male physical strength and also a certain recklessness. The Spanish-Texas frontier had an overabundance of males, and the early empresario towns, such as San Felipe, had an excess of males who used drinking as a form of recreation. Although difficult to prove, it would seem from the currents of history that it was the increasing presence of families who needed nurturing—protection, education, and religion—that brought sobriety and civilization to the rowdy towns. At least, that is what happened.

A rough measure of the change can be seen in the gender ratio of the settlers. After all, no females, no families. The United States census of 1850, the first reliable accounting, reported that the towns of Galveston, Houston, New Braunfels, San Antonio, and Nacogdoches had a range of 6 to 16 percent more males. The state had 8 percent more males. This disproportion leveled out to a near fifty-fifty ratio by the end of the century.[4]

The imbalance meant that men needed to be attentive to their wives if they wished to keep them, since men were readily replaceable.[5] In the first divorce in Dallas, Charlotte M. Dalton paid the cost of the suit, won the case, and within a few hours married Herndon Crouch, who was the foreman of the jury that granted the divorce. This example perhaps raises more questions than it answers, but it does suggest that women were not powerless.[6]

Civilizing was a joint task of male and female, although the males, usually in a position of power, often got more credit for institutions such as libraries and schools. In the dirt road frontier there arose no female political, military, or religious leaders. Under English law, unlike Spanish, a married woman could not make a contract, own property, write a will, or sue in the courts. Each sex had traditional gender roles: men cleared land, plowed, planted, built houses, fought intruders, took care of livestock, and voted. Women raised vegetables, took care of milk cows and chickens, nurtured children, made clothing, nursed the sick, and cleaned the house. The work, however, was interdependent and the sexes aided one another.[7]

In the towns the roles were somewhat altered: men operated various mercantile businesses, set up saloons, ran livery stables, labored at construction projects, moved freight, and engaged in politics. Women who moved to town did much as they did before, but with greater opportunity for establishing female friendships, doing millinery work, running a boarding house, cooking and waitressing, doing laundry, and engaging in prostitution, which was an occupation that prospered in places with an excessive male population. Historian Elizabeth York Enstam in her study of women in Dallas in the latter part of the century found increasing opportunities for employment in teaching, basic housework, and department stores. Women made up 26.1 percent of the Dallas labor force in 1900.[8]

Eventually urban life brought increased freedom to women and family size declined, but not during the period of the nineteenth-century dirt road frontier. Ann Patton Malone, an early feminist writer of Texas history who studied the lives of women, including Indian females, soberly concluded, "Both women and oxen were essential in the building of a frontier community, and both, ideally, were expected to be not only strong and hardworking, but also docile and silent." It gave truth to the frontier proverb, "Texas is a heaven for men and dogs, but it is hell for women and oxen."[9]

Thus the lure of the town was not only for making money or recreation, but also for the rearing of a family. When Shapley P. Ross, a ranger and Indian fighter, took his family to Texas from Missouri in 1839 a relative commented: "Ah well, let him go. In a few years he will come back from Texas in an old cart drawn by a crop-eared mule, and he will be followed by a gang of yellow dogs covered with mange. In that cart, and walking behind it, will sit a set of ignorant boobies, who would not know a schoolhouse from a hog pen or a schoolmaster from a Hottentot." In 1845 Ross decided to sell his wilderness land and move to Austin in order to educate his children. When informed of the reason for the move, his wife tersely replied, "You have been a long time coming to that conclusion."[10] Their fourth child, "Sul" Ross, became a governor of Texas and a champion of education.

9

THE EVOLUTION OF SAN ANTONIO

Following the revolution, San Antonio changed in important ways. Initially the town suffered two raids by the Mexicans and continual Indian troubles that worsened its condition. In an attempt to lessen tensions and arrange a peace, twelve chiefs and fifty-three Penatekas Comanche Indians brought several captives to San Antonio—a few Mexican children and sixteen-year-old Matilda Lockhart, who claimed to have been tortured by the Indians. They met with Texas commissioners and soldiers in the Council House on the east side of the Main Plaza.

Lockhart said that there were other prisoners that the Indians failed to bring, and the commissioners demanded the remainder. The chiefs explained that the prisoners belonged to other tribes, and the commissioners replied that they would hold the chiefs captive until the other prisoners were delivered. At this moment armed Texas Rangers entered the room and the Council House Fight of 1840 exploded as the insulted Indians unleashed their weapons and tried to escape to the river.

Mary A. Maverick witnessed an Indian cutting through her back yard; her black cook protected the children by holding up a large rock and saying, "If you don't go 'way from here I'll mash your head with this rock!"[1] The Indian fled and was shot trying to cross the stream. In the melee of gunsmoke and screams all the chiefs died along with eighteen others; six

Texans also perished and ten were wounded. The Texas Rangers imprisoned the remaining Penatekas and sent an Indian woman to inform the tribe to send the rest of the captives.

The demand backfired. At their encampment the Indians went into a frenzy of mourning, sacrificed horses, and killed thirteen prisoners—some tortured by roasting. Shortly, the young, nearly naked chief Isimanica rode by himself with weapons and warpaint into the Main Plaza, circled his horse, screamed curses, shook his fist, challenged the inhabitants to battle, and left. Thus began twenty-five years of unmitigated Comanche warfare that included raids east of San Antonio, down the Guadalupe River Valley to the coast.

Meanwhile, a macabre side event of the Council House Fight illustrates the lack of respect between the antagonists. A Russian surgeon in San Antonio, a Dr. Weidman, took two of the Indian bodies, boiled them in a soap kettle to obtain the skeletons for study, and dumped the remainder of the pot into the "esequia" that ran in front of his home. This ditch provided the drinking water of the town and was protected by city ordinances. When the townspeople realized what he had done, they crowded into the mayor's office with men talking loudly and women rolling their eyes and vomiting. They thought that they had been poisoned, but the offal had all drained away. There was no danger. The doctor simply laughed and paid a fine.[2]

In 1842 two Mexican invasions took place based upon the Mexican denial of Texas independence, the failure of a Texan expedition to capture Santa Fe, and the weakness of Texas defenses. In March Mexican troops under Ráfael Vásquez occupied Goliad, Refugio, Victoria, and San Antonio without fighting and then quickly retreated before the Texans reacted. It was mainly a plundering expedition.

In September General Adrian Woll captured San Antonio for a week and then, facing Texan opposition with a brief battle, retreated to Mexico. These raids drained the city of supplies, prompted the frightened population to flee, and inspired the fruitless Texan retaliatory expedition to Mier. William Bollaert, on a tour of Texas in 1843, observed: "San Antonio has been the theatre of so many revolutionary scenes and skirmishes, that not a house has escaped the evidences of strife. The walls and houses on all sides are perforated by balls, and even the steeple of the church bears evidence of rough usage from cannon shot."[3]

During this period, shortly after the victory at San Jacinto, land speculators flooded into Texas. Soldiers had been paid in land script that they readily sold; there was good land with faulty titles to be stolen; and some landholders were happy to leave. Noah Smithwick, who served in a Texas Rangers unit, received three land certificates in payment—1,280 acres per twelve months. "No one cared anything for land those days," he said. "I gave one of my certificates for 1,280 acres for a horse which the Indians relieved me of in less than a week."[4]

In the San Antonio area six years after the war, thirteen Anglo buyers purchased 1,369,000 acres from 358 Mexicans, while fourteen Mexicans bought 279,000 acres from 67 Mexicans.[5] One of the most prominent land speculators was Samuel Augustus Maverick (1803–1870). He arrived in Texas in time to help defeat General Cos in San Antonio and to sign independence at Washington-on-the-Brazos. Taken ill with chills and fever, Maverick went home to Alabama. In 1838 he returned with a new wife and baby son to establish a home in San Antonio and to practice law and trade in land. He was mayor in 1839, a short-time captive of General Adrian Woll, and a member of the Texas Congress. After a sojourn at DeCrow's Point, an early resort area on the coast of the Matagorda Peninsula, Maverick and his family returned permanently to San Antonio in 1847.

He left behind a small herd of cattle at DeCrow's Point that was allowed to wander, untended and unbranded. He was no cattleman, didn't care much, and sold the herd in 1856. Maverick left his name, however, as an enduring label for such loose, independent animals. He eventually acquired 300,000 acres, mainly through the purchase of headrights and bounty certificates. In the Texas legislature, Maverick worked to develop fair land acquisition laws and to oppose Reconstruction after the Civil War until his death in 1870.

In the bitterness of the Texas Revolution, hatred was born, and thereafter Mexican communities, especially those along the San Antonio and Guadalupe Rivers, experienced the blanket prejudice against all Mexicans implied in the battlefield cries of "Remember the Alamo!" and "Remember Goliad." There was little protection for Mexicans or Tejanos, even for those who fought for the freedom of Texas.[6]

The most poignant individual story of this miserable time is that of Juan Nepomuceno Seguín (1806–1890). He was the son of a prominent San Antonio family who joined the Texans in the revolution. He organized a vaquero cavalry that helped defeat General Cos at San Antonio, escaped death at the Alamo when he was sent out as a courier, led a Tejano unit that fought at San Jacinto, became the military commander at San Antonio who buried the cremated dead of the Alamo, twice served as mayor of his home city, and was the only Tejano in the Texas Senate.

He lost favor at home by opposing Anglo squatters on city land, protecting Mexicans against the land sharks, and supposedly betraying San Antonio during the invasion by Vásquez. Much about Seguín is yet to be known, but murder threats drove him with his family to Mexico into exile with others.[7] There, he was arrested as a traitor to Mexico and given the choice of life in prison or service in the Mexican army of Adrian Woll. He soon returned to his hometown as an officer of an invading force and later fought against the United States in the war with Mexico. To his detractors this proved his perfidy.

The embers of Anglo versus Mexican enmity continued to smolder in the Rio Grande region, where they flared into flames around Brownsville during the Cortina Wars (1859-1860, 1873-1875), and in West Texas near El Paso with the Salt War (1877). Competing claims to land and livestock brought a condition of distrust and simmering conflict between armed Mexicans and Texas Rangers that lasted over fifty years. Juan Seguín, however, returned to Texas after an exile of six years, settled down near his father's ranch, and peacefully became involved in Wilson County politics. He died in Nuevo Laredo in 1890, and his remains came home to Texas in 1974 to be interred at Seguin, Texas, a town named in his honor and in memory of Tejano patriots.

Following a population decline to about eight hundred in 1846, San Antonio experienced a surge that made it the largest city in Texas at the census of 1860. Anglo-American population growth from 1850 to 1900 outpaced Mexican American growth in Bexar County by three to one.[8] Significantly, the city started a free public school system for girls and boys in 1853, the first in Texas. This was an indication of urban maturity. It was recognition both of the importance of education for society and the need for equality among citizens.

Close urban living was not without hazard, however. Just as coastal towns suffered from yellow fever, so San Antonio was plagued by the scourge of cholera, a severe bacterial infection spread through polluted water. Victims suffered vomiting and diarrhea, and died within days from dehydration. Mathilda Wagner, who moved to the city in the mid-1850s as a girl, remembered carts coming to the doors of houses in the early morning with men calling, "Any dead here?" Wrapped in sheets, the dead were buried in long trenches in the overburdened cemeteries.

No one knew the cause or cure, but it was said that a storeowner on Alamo Street opened a whiskey barrel and attached a tin cup on a string for anyone who wanted a drink. There was a bucket of water beside the barrel for fastidious people to wash the cup. This was probably not a good idea, but Mathilda thought that if nothing else, the drink gave people courage; the disease struck almost every family.[9]

The population grew, nevertheless, and Frederick Law Olmsted, who walked through the town in the mid-1850s, recognized the elements of change. During the war with Mexico the town became a supply point for the United States Army, which allowed contractors to accumulate capital. Military goods came by wagons from Matagorda Bay for distribution as the United States built a line of forts to control the Indians and to protect argonauts on the way to California.

Olmsted estimated the population at 4,000 Mexicans, 3,000 Germans, and 3,500 Americans. "The money-capital is in the hands of the Americans, as well as the officers and the Government," he wrote. "Most of the mechanics and smaller shopkeepers are German. The Mexicans appear to have almost no other business than that of carting goods."[10]

Olmsted had glimpsed the future of San Antonio as a military outpost for its new nation, a purpose for the city that has endured into the twenty-first century. He also saw that the Mexicans would live on the margin of a dominating white society, as they did for the remainder of the nineteenth century.[11] They had lost political power. In 1837–1847 there were 31 non-Mexican aldermen and 57 Mexicans as recognized by their Spanish surnames. From 1848 to 1857 there were 82 non-Mexicans and 17 Mexicans. The number of Mexican aldermen had dwindled to zero by 1895.[12] Mexicans also lost cultural power when the 1849 city council banned fandangos, nude bathing in the rivers, and cockfights, and placed restrictions on Catholic Church celebrations. Proclamations were to be printed only in English.[13]

Still, like others, Olmsted fell under the charm of San Antonio—the romance of the ruined missions and the Alamo, the acequias, and San Pedro Springs. The river had always invited bathing, and the New Yorker commented that Mexican women were excellent swimmers and fond of "displaying their luxurious buoyancy."[14] He wrote, "The favorite dress appeared to be a dishabille, and a free-and-easy, loloppy sort of life generally, seemed to have been adopted as possessing, on the whole, the greatest advantages for a reasonable being."[15]

But life had become more modest. Ferdinand von Roemer, a German scientist who traveled Texas to study geology and natural life in 1846, commented when he reached San Antonio, "It was quite a startling spectacle to see here just above the bridge in the heart of the city, a number of Mexican women and girls bathing entirely naked. Unconcerned about our presence, they continued their exercises while laughing and chattering, showing themselves perfect masters of the art of swimming."[16] The censorious Abbe Domenech, who complained about almost everything, stayed in a nearby mission garret and wrote, "My window was in view of all their gamboling; I was, therefore, obliged to keep it closed during the day."[17]

Such exposure was also too much for Mary Maverick, who lived on the northeast corner of the Main Plaza on the river, but she was not immune to the pleasure of a bath. She wrote:

> During the summer, the American ladies led a lazy life of ease.... We fell into the fashion of the climate, dined at twelve, then followed a siesta, (nap) until three, when we took a cup of coffee and a bath. Bathing in the river at our place had become rather public, now that merchants were establishing themselves on Commerce Street, so we ladies got permission of old Madame Tevino, mother of Mrs. Lockmar, to put up a bath house on her premises, some distance up the river on Soledad Street.... Here between two trees in the beautiful shade, we went in a crowd each afternoon at about four o'clock and took the children and nurses and had a nice lunch which we enjoyed after the bath. There we had a grand good time, swimming and laughing, and making all the noise we pleased.[18]

She presided over the American families as San Antonio experienced a population surge of Germans, French, Irish, English, Poles, and Americans that gave the city a lasting cosmopolitan complexion. The housing distribution shifted. The Spanish and Mexican upper-class citizens built their houses on the west side of the San Antonio River. San Pedro Park was on that side. Dating to 1718 it was the first such declared recreational area in the city and also, incidentally, the second in the United States.

With the influx of Americans, Germans, and the Irish, who were attracted to jobs at the U.S. Army depot at the Alamo, the east side began to change. The Germans gathered along the Acequia Madre, an east side irrigation ditch that ran north to south, while Americans, including black Americans, scattered across both sides. Two-thirds of the Germans and one-fourth of the Mexicans lived on the east side at the time of the ninth census in 1870. By sampling heads of households historian David R. Johnson calculated that the leading ethnic groups of San Antonio were American and German. Mexicans had slipped into third place.[19]

The resourceful Germans moved into a twenty-two-block area along King William Street just south of the business district and built houses in high Victorian style designed by the best San Antonio architects. It was declared a historic district in 1968. The Germans established breweries—twenty-seven in Texas by 1880. Adolphus Busch of St. Louis started the first Lone Star Brewery in 1884, which distributed beer in Texas, Mexico, and California. William A. Menger (1827–1871) built the first Texas commercial brewery and the best-known hotel adjacent to the Alamo. He used the cool water of the Alamo acequia to chill and age his lager beer in a stone cellar at the hotel.

The Menger Hotel, still in operation, attracted a wide patronage of famous personalities to its cherrywood bar with its mint juleps, rum toddies, and chilled beer, and to its upscale rooms, which included baths. Theodore Roosevelt supposedly recruited his "Rough Riders" contingent for the Spanish-American War from the bar at the Menger. He certainly enjoyed its hospitality over the years. The hotel was also the gathering place of many West Texas ranchers, who stayed there while doing their banking in the city and arranging cattle drives to the Kansas railheads after the Civil War.

In 1870 the Texas Department of the Army moved to 50 acres of donated land and built a major infantry post in the northeastern segment of the city that eventually was named Fort Sam Houston. It expanded piecemeal with cavalry, artillery, and hospital until 1940, by which time it was the largest army post in the United States. San Antonio thus became the mother of the United States Army.

A building boom started in 1877 with the arrival of the Galveston, Harrisburg and San Antonio Railroad (the "Sunset Road"). When it arrived the *San Antonio Express* exuded, "San Antonio can now take a position in the great family of first class cities and more grandly on to that greatness and prosperity that could never have been reached without the aid of the iron horse."[20]

The Quadrangle of Fort Sam Houston, the "Mother of the U.S. Army." Photograph by author.

Banker George W. Brackenridge and local construction contractor John H. Kampmann, although on opposite sides of the Civil War, led the drive to approve $300,000 in county bonds to encourage the railroad, which had been bankrupted, sold, and reorganized. Major Kampmann received the first freight delivery of lumber, and San Antonio hosted a two-day celebration for the arrival of a passenger train five days later. Brackenridge and Kampmann then worked together to complete a waterworks for the city. August Belknap of New York built the first street railway, from Alamo Plaza to San Pedro Springs, in 1878.[21] The springs, already the second oldest city park in the nation, thus became the first amusement park in Texas. The city gained eight thousand residents per decade and was the largest city in Texas in 1900.

The railroads ruined the Mexican freighting business, and the Mexican population experienced downward mobility. They sold their choice business sites around the plazas and moved westward across the San Antonio River. The city thus split into two societies, one white and the other brown, with San Pedro Creek being the dividing line.[22]

The flirtatious chili queens of Military Plaza maintained a Mexican flavor for a while by selling food from clay pots nightly at open-air tables. This was the place to go for entertainment—chili, tamales, tacos, dancing, accordion music, and cockfights. People of all colors and backgrounds sat and ate together at the long tables with no discomfort. Like the fandango, however, this too came to an end. The city plopped down its new city hall in the middle of the plaza in 1891.[23]

Most significant for the tourist trade, though, was the preservation of the Alamo. The state bought both the Alamo and the San Jacinto battleground site in 1883 and placed custody of the Alamo in the hands of the city. Ten years later schoolteacher Adina De Zavala (1861-1955), granddaughter of the first vice president of Texas, founded the local chapter of the Daughters of the Republic of Texas and began collecting money for the restoration of missions.

In 1903 a proposal to sell the Alamo "convento," the historic barracks that would be cleared away for a hotel park, brought her into alliance with Clara Driscoll (1881-1945), a well-educated rancher's daughter from Corpus Christi who bought the land to preserve it. The embarrassed legislature reimbursed Driscoll the following year, and in 1905 placed the Alamo and the grounds in the hands of the Daughters of the Republic of Texas. Unfortunately, the restoration of the "convento" split Driscoll and De Zavala, but the property had been saved for the future.[24]

10

THE GERMAN TOWNS OF TEXAS

The Republic of Texas granted headrights and continued the Spanish and Mexican use of empresarios to encourage occupation of the land to raise revenue for the struggling nation. In 1841 the republic made a grant to twenty American and English investors for settling the land south of the Red River in North Texas. Known as the Peters Colony, it expanded its boundaries four times and eventually attracted 1,787 settlers, mainly non-slave-owning Anglo farmers from the upper South. Confusion over land titles, headrights, and the expiration of the contract in 1848 led to mass meetings, petitions, and ten legislative adjustments over twenty years to finally straighten out the mess.[1]

In 1842 the republic also gave two grants west of San Antonio and along the Rio Grande below Laredo to Henri Castro (1786–1865) for six hundred families. He recruited from France, particularly from the German border province of Alsace, and in the first year sent 2,134 people. In spite of their suffering from Indian raids, cholera, and drought, the immigrants formed Medina County in 1848 and established the town of Castroville in 1844. It was modeled after a European village with narrow streets, town squares, and two-story houses of stone on the first floor, timbered second floor, and steep, thatched roofs. The frugal German-Catholic citizens who lived in town prospered during the Civil War, when

Castroville served as a way station for Texas contraband sent to Mexico. They later suffered when the Southern Pacific Railroad bypassed the town because its citizens refused to produce a bonus for the railroad.

At the same time as Castro, Prince Carl of Solms-Braunfels (1812–1875), a leader of the "Adelsverein," an investment association of Prussian noblemen, promoted German immigration to Texas. He traveled extensively in Texas and led the first settlers to the well-watered and fertile land between the Comal and Guadalupe Rivers. In 1845 he founded New Braunfels, a town that quickly became the central commercial target for German immigrants.

Both Solms-Braunfels and Castro sought to impress their recruits with aristocratic accouterments. Castro dressed stylishly and drove an impressive carriage, while the prince traveled with a retinue. Castro, who demanded half the property of his recruits in payment for his services, lived a comfortable life in Texas, while Solms-Braunfels returned to a military career in Germany.

The prince disproved the folk statement used to demonstrate the equality of males, "All men put on their pants one leg at a time." At DeCrow's Point revenue officer Alexander Somervell, to his immense amusement, observed two attendants lift the prince into his pants both legs at once.[2] Not all men were equal after all.

Settlers from the Adelsverein and New Braunfels established Fredericksburg on the old trail to San Saba in 1846. Named for Prince Frederick of Prussia, the town imitated villages of the Rhine River, with a long main street parallel to Town Creek. Each immigrant was given 10 acres of farmland and a town lot. The town benefited from Fort Martin Scott, two miles away, and from the California gold rush. It was the last place before El Paso on the immigrant road to the West.

Residents with bitter memories of Confederate martial law carried out a postwar determination to eschew politics and to speak only their native language. It was not until after 1900 that the public schools hired teachers who did not speak German. Interestingly, this stubborn German attitude contributes to the tourist attraction of Fredericksburg over a century later.

The antebellum German population in Texas reached about twenty-four thousand and colonized a wide "belt" from Galveston and Houston to San Antonio and Kerrville. Although interrupted by the American Civil War, the immigration of ethnic Germans continued until the 1890s.

Most were ambitious farmers who settled in the German belt, with notable populations gathered in San Antonio, Galveston, and Houston.

They differed among themselves in dialect, physical features, religion, and attitudes about slavery. Indelible in their culture, however, were tidy farms, half-timbered homes, rock walls, community centers, the polka, singing, gymnastics, sauerkraut and sausage, and the ability to make superior beer, such as Pearl, Lone Star, and Shiner. As historian Glen E. Lich commented, "The German immigrant showed his busy Anglo-American neighbor how to relax after toil, since what marked the German perhaps most of all was his passion for 'organized fun.'"[3]

11

THE COASTAL PORTS

Most of the German immigrants entered into Texas through the new ports along the Gulf Coast. Castro directed his people to Galveston, for example, while Solms-Braunfels established Indianola on Matagorda Bay as the entry point for his group. Earlier, Stephen F. Austin had used the small landings of Velasco and Quintana at the mouth of the Brazos River. Immigration and commerce demanded the establishment of port towns along the Gulf coast. They were the earliest stew pots of Texas culture.

For greater distances of shipping on the Gulf of Mexico, shipping magnate Charles Morgan (1795-1878) of New York opened regular steamship service between New Orleans and Galveston in 1837. He expanded this to Matagorda Bay in 1848, Corpus Christi and Rockport in 1868, and to other ports around the Caribbean Sea and Mexico. His reach extended to the control of the Houston and Texas Central Railroad in the Houston area, effectively creating a transportation monopoly. Morgan steamships and those of competitors were twice as long as river steamboats, narrow-hulled for ocean transit, and deep drafted.

Propellers replaced paddle wheels and iron hulls replaced wood in the 1870s along the Texas coast. Even so, sailing vessels dominated Texas harbors until early in the twentieth century.[1] The steamboats and steamships, however, provided Texas improved access to the wider world of

New Orleans, Mobile, New York, and Europe. News, people, and products traveled three to four times faster with steam engine technology than with wind.

GALVESTON

The most important of the ports was Galveston. Although it was located on a sand barrier island that was only 27 miles long, 1.5 to 3 miles wide, and 8 feet high, the town possessed the best harbor between New Orleans and Vera Cruz. Scooped out by the natural currents of Galveston Bay, the harbor on the eastern end faced the mainland, two miles distant.

Late in 1836 Michael B. Menard and nine partners put together a complicated land purchase from the Republic of Texas for the eastern end of the island to be paid for by the sale of city lots. Menard and his associates organized the Galveston City Company, divided the town in gridiron fashion with alleys, and began to sell lots. People used the generous back yards for privies, cisterns, stables, kitchens, and gardens.[2]

In Texas the sale of city plots was another way to make a fortune. In the first year they sold seven hundred lots at an average price of $400. In 1839 the Congress granted incorporation status, which permitted the election of a mayor and city council. Male property owners could vote, but in 1845 the franchise was changed to all white, male taxpayers who had been residents for a year.

Merchants such as Thomas F. McKinney from Kentucky and Samuel May Williams from Rhode Island built wharves and warehouses to trade cotton to New York, New Orleans, and Great Britain in exchange for a great variety of imports to meet the needs of South Texas farmers. The British consul reported in 1840 that Galveston had grown from three houses to six hundred in three years and that the population neared four thousand.

The island suffered during the Civil War from a Union blockade of the port, and experienced the most interesting battle in Texas during the conflict. To break a token occupation of the city by northern troops, General John B. Magruder coordinated a land and sea assault in 1863. Confederate soldiers crept over an early railroad bridge and lined up through the city while two small steamboats armored with cotton bales sailed among the five Union ships anchored in the harbor.

One northern ship blew up, another was captured, and the remaining three fled to New Orleans. Yankee soldiers marooned on a wharf had no choice but to surrender. The battle was of little consequence—Magruder fortified the city and the U.S. Navy reestablished the blockade. This stalemate continued until Captain Benjamin F. Sands of the blockading squadron landed to raise the U.S. flag over the customshouse to announce the end of the war in June 1865. On June 19 (Juneteenth Day), Major General Gordon Granger issued an order confirming the emancipation of the slaves in Texas.

Within a month citizens who had fled returned to rebuild; the railroad began to run; Confederate soldiers were paroled; several thousand Union soldiers arrived; and riverboats began to bring in cotton for export as the town sprang back to life. Galveston society adjusted to the new social order with martial law and the Freedmen's Bureau, a federal agency that tried to help both races. Free blacks, young and old, moved to town, went to school, worked for the U.S. Army, confirmed their marriages in the courts, tested their right to vote, and joined the integrated crowds at saloons.

George T. Ruby (1841–1882), a black man born and educated in New York, traveled to Galveston as a representative of the Freedmen's Bureau. He joined the Union League, which organized the black vote, supported the Republican Party in the state, and was president of the Texas branch in 1868. Ruby was deputy collector of customs in Galveston in 1868–1872 and a state senator 1869–1873. His influence waned as Democrats regained power, and he moved to New Orleans in 1874. Ruby nonetheless left behind a legacy of workable biracial politics.

Norris Wright Cuney (1846–1898), the educated son of a white Brazos Valley planter and a black mistress, took up the cause of black justice as a leader in the Republican Party and as an elected alderman in Galveston from 1883 to 1887. He organized black dockworkers and became the customs officer of the port after the election of Republican Benjamin Harrison. This well-dressed, friendly politician provided the community with an example of a competent black person. Cuney commented: "Negroes are human beings and should be considered from that standpoint, if people would understand them as a race. In their actions and manner of life, they are prompted by very much the same motives actuating others of the human family."[3]

The jumble of humanity in the port at this time resulted in the evolution of a sin district of prostitutes, variety theaters, and saloons near the docks on Post Office Street that welcomed all comers and endured into the 1950s. The expanding clutter of new people, however, particularly the young northern soldiers, were susceptible to mosquito-born yellow fever. Galvestonians had suffered before from "Yellow Jack," which hit during the summer months and lasted until the first frost killed the mosquitoes. No one knew the cause until it was proven by Walter Reed in Cuba in the early twentieth century.

Yellow fever spread from the port cities as far as 200 miles inland, and the only effective action at the time was a strict quarantine of places where it broke out. The death rate was 20 to 25 percent of the people who caught it, but victims would have immunity for life if they survived. Yellow fever could decimate a population, and the fever years of 1866 and 1867 were particularly hard for the Island City with all of its recently arrived population.

During times of contagion there was always a scramble to clean up the streets and alleys. Like other places, Galveston used free-roaming pigs to clean up garbage and human excrement, but they were declared a nuisance in 1869. Citizens were responsible for cleaning their own property and they hired private contractors to haul the trash away. Service and adherence to the law were irregular, however, and people swept the dirt of their stores into the streets and dumped the offal from outhouses into the alleys. The city designated a dumpsite in 1879, and the product of privies was supposed to be hauled away in barrels at night and dumped into the Gulf.

Open ditches served from the beginning to drain the sand and shell streets, but since the grade was so slight, every street became a pond when it rained. Worse, some building owners in the 1870s began to flush toilets into the ditches. This malodorous situation continued until the city in 1886 gave the Galveston Sewer Company the right to lay pipes, charge for connections, and drain the sewerage into the Gulf.

That helped, but there remained a problem of fresh water for drinking and water to fight the inevitable fires of a city built largely of wood. For drinking water people caught rainwater from roofs and stored it in large wooden barrels. The city provided some street cisterns for firefighting and encouraged volunteer fire brigades. With the growth of the city this became insufficient; cisterns went dry in 1870 and 1879.

Local insurance underwriters raised the fire insurance rates 10 percent in 1880 and another 25 percent in 1882. This caught the attention of the business community, and the city council contracted to install a saltwater system to provide water from the bay through eight miles of pipes and 110 hydrants. The aldermen, in addition, created a professional fire department in 1885, just in time for the worst fire in city history. It started in a foundry, and a stiff northwest wind carried flames and sparks across the wooden buildings. The department and the hydrants were inadequate, and the city lost 568 homes in forty-two blocks. The insurance underwriters raised their rates again and condemned the water supply system.

Attempts to drill for artesian water on the sand barrier island produced only brackish results, but across the bay at Hitchcock, wells produced wholesome water for ranchers and railroads. Galveston authorities contracted for a thirty-well field west of Hitchcock. A 30-inch main placed in a trench below low tide between the mainland and the island then transferred fresh water to a pump house, standpipe, and a network of water pipes in town. The system was completed in 1895 and resolved the problem of fresh water for the city.

Galveston developed meanwhile into a significant cotton export port—third in the nation in 1878, fifth in 1882. Led by cotton magnate William L. Moody and attorney Walter Gresham, both born in Virginia, a Deep Water Committee succeeded in 1890 in gaining federal aid to deepen the harbor and protect it with stone jetties. Consequently, in October 1896 the largest cargo ship in the world tied up to the Galveston wharves. Ocean access had been attained. Galveston had become the number one cotton port in the United States by the end of the century.

It was also the largest city in Texas for the census of 1870 and 1880—and the richest. Eleven of the fifty-eight Texas estates worth over $100,000 in 1870 were located in Galveston County. The men involved were all merchants, eight of them born in the northeastern United States.[4] They did not come from simple southern yeoman or plantation stock, and their business transactions tied them to New York City. These townspeople were different not only in occupation but also in mentality from the majority of Texans living as farmers, planters, or ranchers.

They were also the first to receive information. The mail arrived by packet from New Orleans and then Postmaster Peter J. Menard, the brother of the founder of the city, distributed it to the interior of Texas. The first telegraph wire, strung under a bridge, came from the United States in 1859; the *Galveston Daily News*, Texas' oldest surviving newspaper, began in 1842; Alfred H. Belo, the owner of the newspaper, installed the first telephone of the state in 1878 after witnessing a demonstration at the 1876 Centennial Exposition in Philadelphia. As a result of such information the citizens were among the first to benefit from electric lighting in 1882; electric streetcars in 1891; and pavement of streets with wooden blocks bound together with hot tar in 1871. The establishment of the state medical school in 1881, iron-front business buildings, and elegant homes testified to the power and wealth of the city.

Galveston's greatest import was its immigrant population—those who entered through the port, glimpsed the city, and departed for interior Texas places. They came at a rate of about four thousand per year, but in January 1871, a high point, that many came in one month. As a boy in Galveston Jesse Ziegler witnessed the disembarkations at the time, which to him seemed like a circus. People were tagged with destinations and herded along by immigration officers. He saw Russians wearing fur coats in July; women in native costume from Switzerland; Irishmen with short pipes clamped in their mouths and knapsacks on their backs; Scotsmen with bagpipes; and frail women trailed by children and loaded with household items carrying pans, plates, and cooking utensils.[5]

INDIANOLA AND PORT LAVACA

To the southwest of Galveston along the coast was Matagorda Bay, the place mistaken by René Robert Cavelier, Sieur de La Salle, as the mouth of the Mississippi River. His ill-fated colony Fort St. Louis in the northwestern tip of the bay, which lasted but a historical blink, jolted the Spanish into East Texas exploration and mission founding. The offshore depth was deep enough for sailing vessels and close enough for the use of lighters. During the war with Mexico it served as an army supply depot, and Samuel Addison White and William M. Cook, the owners of the land, surveyed the site to sell lots in 1846.

With twenty-three blocks of bay front property for warehouses and wharves, the town expanded down the flat beach for three miles, changed its name from Indian Point to Indianola in 1849, and became the county seat of Calhoun County in 1852. Fresh water for steam engines and drinking, however, was in constant shortage. The only source was rainwater collected in cisterns, and residents used salty bay water for kitchen and water closets. Refuse and garbage were picked up each Saturday by a cart employed by the town's hospital committee and taken to a dump. Slop buckets of leftover food were emptied into barrels and fed to pigs in pens beyond the city limits.[6]

Indianola prospered as the wholesale point at the eastern end of a military road that reached San Antonio, Austin, and San Diego. It was the shortest overland route to the Pacific Ocean. Charles Morgan, who had selected Indianola as a terminal for his New York steamship company in 1849, returned to business after the war and in 1869 sent the world's first shipment of refrigerated beef to New Orleans. A telegraph line reached the town in 1871, the same year that a 15-mile railroad tap, part of the Great Western Texas and Pacific Railway, was completed that connected the port with Victoria.

Indianola was at a peak of prosperity, with about five thousand people in 1875, when the first of two major hurricanes tumbled up the bay and flooded the town with a 15-foot storm surge. The storm filled the marshes and lakes behind the town and prevented the escape of the inhabitants. After the hurricane moved inland, the pent-up water rushed back through the town to the bay with a flushing action. More than a hundred buildings were washed away; only twelve remained. The storm left 270 corpses, and in the following days ships found bits of furniture, trees, animal corpses, and pieces of buildings floating in the Gulf.

Most of the survivors wanted to move, but the Morgan Company, the town's most important enterprise, refused aid for a change of location. Charles Morgan was not known for his philanthropy. The town reluctantly rebuilt on a smaller scale, and in 1886 a second hurricane struck. This time a lantern fell over, exploded, and downtown buildings flamed in the wind and rain as the water rushed through the streets into the countryside and then out again with the same powerful flushing action. Almost everything was ruined or carried out to sea as new drainage bayous cut through the city. Enough was enough. The survivors gave up the county seat, abandoned their railroad, discontinued the post office, and moved away. Indianola became a ghost town.

Port Lavaca, 12 miles away and located on higher ground, survived. It had been established in 1841–1842 as a point of refuge after the Comanche attacks on Linnville and Victoria. The county seat had been located there before being moved to Indianola, and returned after the storms. The hurricanes, however, dampened forever the ambitions for Matagorda Bay, and Port Lavaca has remained a small fishing and vacation town to the present time.

CORPUS CHRISTI

Farther to the west, in the Coastal Bend of Texas at Corpus Christi Bay, Henry L. Kinney (1814-1862), a glib land speculator from Pennsylvania, and a partner, William P. Aubrey, set up a trading post atop a shell bluff on the west shore in 1839. The site encompassed a long beach area that developed as a harbor and a high bluff that later became a place for expensive mansions. The region to the north was cattle country.

The two traders purchased the land from an angry, displaced Mexican rancher, carried on an illegal trade of cloth and tobacco with Mexico, fended off Indian raids, and opened a post office. It was in a no-man's land between Texas and Mexico. Kinney explained his success: "When Mr. Mexican came, I treated him with a great deal of politeness, particularly if he had me in his power. When Mr. American came, I did the same with him, and when Mr. Indian came, I was also very frequently disposed to make a compromise with him."[7]

By the mid-1840s a small village of about fifty families had gathered around the trading post. Then Kinney got lucky and the war with Mexico broke out in 1846. In preparation for fighting, President James Polk ordered General Zachary Taylor to establish a base near the Rio Grande, and Taylor moved an army of four thousand men to Kinney's trading post.

Captain W. S. Henry commented, "The scene was charming, and the soft, refreshing sea-breeze, cooling the atmosphere to the temperature of an October's day, made one exclaim in the enthusiasm of the moment, 'It is god's favored land—the Eden of America.' When the enthusiasm subsided, it was not exactly *that*, but it certainly is very beautiful." Experience with northers, humidity, bad water, dysentery, and rattlesnakes reduced Henry's original exhilaration.[8] The army camped on the beach for seven months before moving on to the battles of Resaca de la Palma and Palo Alto near the Rio Grande. It left behind two thousand camp followers at Corpus Christi. Kinney served as an aide to Taylor for his Monterey campaign and then returned to his home.[9]

He tried to promote the town as a state representative and by organizing a fair in 1852. He imported a circus from New Orleans and sponsored a bullfight to attract attention and encourage real estate sales. The fair was a success for the 2,500 visitors, but Kinney lost money. His personal life, bedeviled by his roving eye and drinking, fell into disarray. He floundered in starting a colony in Nicaragua and died mysteriously at 3:00 a.m. in Matamoros in 1862, possibly caught in a crossfire of political factions, maybe shot by an irate husband.

Corpus Christi became a jumping-off place for people going to the California gold rush, and in 1852 it was incorporated as a city. It was also the county seat. The census of 1850 counted a population of 689 people plus 47 slaves and 151 houses. Half the population was Mexican. The town was not significant in the Civil War, but it was twice bombarded by a blockading squadron, and it was ravaged by the same yellow fever epidemic that struck the Texas coast at the end of the war.

During the cattle boom of the 1870s and 1880s, Corpus Christi became a shipping point and processing place for hides and tallow. Through the urging of local commission merchant Uriah Lott (1842–1915), the Corpus Navigation Company dredged an eight-foot channel through Aransas Pass at the opening of the bay to the docks in 1874. It eventually eroded and the Army Corps of Engineers saw no need to keep it open. The resources of the federal government went to Galveston.[10]

Lott also promoted the construction of a narrow-gauge railway, the Texas and Mexican, to Laredo. Because of erratic service it was locally known as the "Mañana Line." The irrepressible Lott became involved in three other railroads and died penniless. By the mid-1880s Corpus Christi had a population of 4,200, three banks, an ice factory, two newspapers, railroad machine shops, stockyards, meatpacking houses, cattle baron mansions on the bluff, and five varieties of Christian churches.

The future of Corpus Christi, however, was clouded by poor accessibility to the sea and to fresh water. Large vessels had to stop at Aransas Pass. The sand bar that piled up at that crucial point shifted between 7 and 18 feet below the surface as the pass itself crumbled and migrated to the south. Lighters, shallow draft barges, transported cargo over the bar and through a twisting channel to the docks at Corpus Christi.

Dredges, jetties, dikes, revetments, and riprap ultimately failed to direct the tidal flows to deepen and prevent the sandbar. The Rivers and Harbors Act of 1899 finally authorized a jetty system to open the pass. It achieved success twenty years later. The deepwater passage assured that a permanent ship channel access be maintained and the port of Corpus Christi opened in 1926. Whew.

The second major problem was water supply. Kinney had been unable to locate a good source, and the town depended upon rainfall and cisterns, the pools on Blucher Creek (favored by the local pigs), and the water vendors who hauled water in barrels from the Nueces River. Saltwater for firefighting came from fire trucks that ran onto the wharves and sucked it from the bay. Efforts to find artesian water failed.

Late in the century, in 1888, however, Elihu Harrison Ropes (1845-1898?), from New Jersey, arrived with grand schemes to make Corpus Christi the "Chicago of the Southwest." He was a former advertising manager of the Singer Sewing Company, and he envisioned a grand resort hotel on the bluff, a ship channel through Mustang Island, streetcars, and a railroad line to run from Corpus Christi to South America. He organized a company capitalized at $5 million, bought a dredge, and commenced with the construction of the 126-room, three-story Alta Vista Hotel on the bluff. Then the national financial panic of 1893 struck. Ropes abandoned the hotel after an opening ball; the streetcar line was dismantled; the railroad scheme evaporated; the dredge broke down; and Ropes left for New York with his secretary, a Miss Woodcock, never to return.[11]

Ropes was not a charlatan. He was a dreamer and a booster who failed and died impoverished. While he was trying to make his dreams come true Corpus Christi doubled in size, to a population of nine thousand, and his promotion allowed the city to sell its sluggish water bonds. In 1893 the Corpus Christi Water Supply Company completed a pump house, three-and-a-half miles of mains, and a standpipe that brought water from the delta of the Nueces River. The water was somewhat brackish, and in 1898 the Calallen diversion dam succeeded in keeping out the salty tidal water.[12] The dam was the first impoundment of that historic river. Without fresh water and the eventual opening of Aransas Pass, Corpus Christi would have remained a poor coastal village.

12

THE RIVER PORTS

In 1829, a few decades after Robert Fulton's demonstration of steam power in 1807, a boat with a similar sidewheel design called the *Ariel* explored about 300 miles of the Rio Grande and its tributaries before it finally wrecked on a Brazos River sandbar. Although financially unsuccessful the *Ariel* demonstrated both the feasibility and danger of steamboat transport on fickle Texas rivers.

Small, shallow-draft wooden steamboats subsequently became common along the near coast and rivers during the middle decades of the nineteenth century. The fragile wooden boats suffered frequent difficulties with low water, sandbars, fires, and snags. Loose tree limbs that floated downstream could lodge in the stream bottom and lance through a wooden hull or shatter a paddlewheel. "Snagged and sunk" was a common newspaper epitaph. Consequently, a boat's lifetime was short, four to five years.

The boats used high-pressure wood-burning steam engines with paddle wheels on the side or stern. Side paddles allowed greater maneuverability; stern paddles avoided damage from floating logs and could be reversed if the boat ran aground. The small, shallow-draft steamers, with two decks and a pilothouse perched on top, dominated river traffic until the latter part of the century, when their work was taken over by railroads.

The stern-wheeled steamboat St. Clair *loads cotton at Allen's Landing on Buffalo Bayou in Houston, about 1868. Photograph courtesy of the Houston Public Library, HMRC.*

HOUSTON

Houston, the adjunct of Galveston, located across Galveston Bay on Buffalo Bayou, was basically a "port for a port," so to speak. The location was as far as could be reached by the small river steamboats of the day. At Allen's Landing, Houston cotton brought by oxcart from the interior could be loaded and sent to Galveston. Farming and urban supplies as well as immigrants could be exchanged and dispersed into the countryside. Two brothers, Augustus C. and John K. Allen, started the town in August 1836, named it for the hero of the moment, offered lots and buildings to the government, and hoped to profit from the sale of city lots. The legislature selected their site as the temporary capital until 1840. When President Sam Houston arrived in April 1837 he found one hundred houses and 1,500 people.[1]

Within a few years the capital transferred to Austin, but Houston survived as a trading town, mainly as a conduit for cotton to reach Galveston.

THE RIVER PORTS   87

It was a place of mercantile establishments, including in 1860 retail groceries, dry goods, hardware, commission merchants, and three bookstores. The trading hinterland reached 90 to 100 miles to the west and northwest, where small farmers swapped honey and animal skins for powder, lead, coffee, calico, and castor oil for the children. Larger farmers and planters exchanged cotton, hides, lumber, corn, and livestock for clothing, groceries, weapons, tools, books, and medicine bought on credit. Auctions periodically sold livestock, land, "segars," books, and slaves. The trading season lasted from September to April. In the summer off-season the merchants traveled to New York, Boston, Mobile, and New Orleans to replenish their stocks, arrange credit, and set up shipments through Galveston.

Although Houston possessed sawyers, brickmakers, millers, and craftsmen to cater to the local populace, it largely failed at manufacturing, as did much of the South. To escape being a place that simply supplied others with raw materials, a colonial situation, Texas and Houston had to use those materials to make their own products for sale to a larger market. In 1869 and the next year or two, textile mills opened that used cotton and wool from the countryside, but they did not last. The wealth of the town remained in mercantile operations. In 1870, Harris County was the second richest county, behind Galveston County, based mainly upon its trade.[2]

Thomas W. House (1814-1880), as a business example, arrived in 1838 from England, became a candy maker and dry goods merchant, and evolved into a cotton factor, banker, and investor in public utilities. During the Civil War he eschewed Confederate currency, put his money into gold reserves in England, and avoided the United States naval blockade by running cotton to England through Matamoros. He died in 1880 with a fortune of $1 million. In similar fashion William Marsh Rice (1816-1900), from Massachusetts, arrived in 1839, established a general store, became a cotton factor and investor, and made a fortune avoiding the blockade by sending cotton through Mexico. He retired to New York in 1863, during the war, but remembered the town of his good fortune by funding the establishment of Rice University through a bequest.

The Texas Legislature granted incorporation to Houston and sixteen other places in 1837. The charter gave the city the power to sue or be sued, own property, pass laws, tax, establish schools, maintain streets, and elect a mayor and aldermen. A new charter in 1839, supplemented in 1840, designated a boundary of nine square miles, four wards, and an electorate of white male inhabitants who had resided in Houston for six months, possessed $100 of real estate for three months, and were citizens of Texas. Before 1860 the main sources of city income were wharfage charges, licenses, bonds, and special taxes; after 1860 the major source of city revenue was ad valorem taxes on property. Chief expenses before the war were streets, salaries, and the city hospital; afterward they were for city indebtedness.

Since the Bayou City was a commercial town, the leading merchants were sensitive to the conditions of transportation, particularly on the roads into the hinterland and on the bayou that connected them with Galveston. Teamsters brought cotton by ox team, one yoke of oxen per bale, at the end of the growing season during the rainy months. In good weather a round trip from fields in the Brazos River country, 60 miles or so, to Houston took seven days, but in bad weather it took twice that long. Wagons sank to their axles in black mud and had to be unloaded and double-teamed to be pulled out.

The solution to this miserable situation in the countryside was the railway. In 1850–1851 promoter Sidney Sherman, allied with Boston capitalists, William Marsh Rice of Houston, and others, acquired the nearby town of Harrisburg, including its railroad charter from the Texas Republic, and began construction of the Buffalo Bayou, Brazos and Colorado Railway (BBB&C) to the west with the idea of cutting off Houston and becoming the inland port for Galveston.

Sherman, from Massachusetts and Kentucky, was a hero of the Battle of San Jacinto who settled nearby on San Jacinto Bay. The first 25-mile segment opened for traffic in 1853 with an imported locomotive, the 10-ton *Sidney Sherman*. Texas granted the line 887,000 acres of land and a loan from the state school fund. The legislature set the rates.

The BBB&C, using slave labor and imported iron rails, reached the Brazos River in 1856 and became the first operating railroad in Texas. Anxious Houstonians then voted an ad valorem tax on bars, billiard halls, and grocery stores to finance a seven-mile line to intercept the BBB&C, as the original charter allowed, in order to divert the cotton traffic to Houston. After successful completion the "tap" was sold by vote of the property owners to a group of Brazoria planters, who extended the renamed Houston Tap and Brazoria into the sugarcane area to the south. This resulted in an initial shipment of molasses and sugar to Houston over the "Sugar Road" in 1859.

Houston commission merchant Paul Bremond (1810–1885), meanwhile, began to construct the Houston and Texas Central Railroad (H&TC) to the northwest in 1853 with funds from investors like Thomas W. House. It began hauling freight while under construction and reached a 50-mile mark in 1858. Galveston investors attempted to tap the H&TC by building the Galveston, Houston and Henderson Railroad starting in 1853. The Island City completed a railroad bridge to its docks in early 1860, which made it possible for upland cotton to remain on the trains and bypass Houston.

Abram Morris Gentry (1821–1883), a Houston merchant from Indiana with New York funding, began building the Texas and New Orleans Railroad (T&NO) from Houston in 1857. It connected with Orange to the east in 1862 and was useful in transporting soldiers for the Confederacy. Yankee gunboats patrolling the Mississippi River and the occupation of New Orleans by the North in the same year made further construction pointless. The T&NO nonetheless raised the future possibility of moving trade east and west and leaving Galveston out of the commercial flow.

Consequently, by the time the Civil War disrupted rail development in the state, Houston had become the center of railroading in South Texas. Houstonians had eagerly embraced the new technology. It was an answer to the mud of the roadway; it provided quicker, safer access; and it enhanced the prospects of the city. A writer to the *Tri-Weekly Telegraph* in Houston recalled a 35-mile trip in 1854 that, after ten days of rain, took a day and a half, including an overnight stay. A similar trip in 1857 on the Houston and Texas Central took one hour and forty minutes.[3] Ox teams transporting cotton gradually disappeared from the streets as farmers took their produce to upcountry rail depots. Cross-country railroads thus began to take over the dirt road frontier.

The city supported the Confederate States, contributed soldiers, held prayer meetings, suffered shortages and inflation, and endured eventual occupation by northern soldiers. Railroad building took up afterward with the help of William E. Dodge, the president of the National Temperance Society, who was impressed with Houston's Sunday closing laws. He secured enough capital to start the northward construction of the Houston and Great Northern in 1866. It became a part of Jay Gould's southwestern system in 1873.

At the time of the Civil War there were 1,069 slaves in Houston and 8 free blacks—22 percent of the population. With release from bondage, the number of blacks in Houston increased to 39 percent in 1880. At first blacks lived scattered across the city's five wards, with places of concentration such as "Freedmantown" on the outer edge of the fourth ward, west of downtown. By 1875 residential and social segregation was affirmed and Houston was a white-black city. In the first unrestricted election, however, Houston voters in 1872 elected two blacks as aldermen.

City debt increased after the war with money spent for sidewalks, a new market house, sewers, roads, and bridges. This debt was made worse by the national depression of 1876 as well as the burning of the new market house. The greatest irritation for the town, however, was mud and dust. Citizens held mass meetings, but little happened due to lack of money and good ideas. Merchants built wooden or brick sidewalks and laid white oyster shells on Main Street in 1858.

The shells provided a smooth surface, but when the shells were ground by wagon wheels and dried out, the dust was unbearable. The *Tri-Weekly Telegraph* newspaper, which had suggested the shells in February, recorded in September: "We have dust everywhere. Dust in the street, dust in the air, dust in the houses. The streets are filled with dust. We eat dust, breathe dust, walk in dust, sit in dust. Dust rises in clouds on every puff of air, and floats about as though it has no gravity. It settles on everything."[4]

Taking advantage of the rails already in town, trolley companies began to send mule cars for passengers over the tracks as early as 1868. They traveled no faster than a walk, but in Houston, the streetcars provided relief during the humid, blistering summers as well as in the muddy winter. That helped. In 1890, finally, an Omaha company purchased the mule lines and converted them to electric trolleys.

Mud within the city, meanwhile, remained a challenge. About 1874 Jesse A. Ziegler, a young cotton merchant from Galveston, visited rainy Houston for the first time and observed:

> I contemplated the street in amazement. Reared in Galveston, I never had seen such a vast amount of mud; it was not only deep and morass looking, but stretched in both directions as far as I could see. Over at what is now J. C. Penney's corner, at Texas and Main, some jokingly inclined wag had driven down a four-by-four post with a sign on it declaiming "No bathing, please!" An hour later I passed it again. The original sign had been taken away; a stovepipe hat had been placed on the post, and a new

sign announced to mildly surprised pedestrians, "Don't kick me—I'm down here on horseback, trying to get out!"

I noticed also in parts of town where no sidewalks existed, that the pedestrians would make their way by frequently hanging to the picket and rail fences, gaining foothold on a firmer but smaller piece of ground just beneath the fence, or sometimes on the bottom rail or footboard. Occasionally I would see their feet slip, and down they would go into the sticky mire over their shoetops or halfway up to the knees....

In the middle of the streetcar track was a narrow board walk on which the mule drawing the streetcar would walk. In rainy weather pedestrians always used these walks. They provided excellent footing until the mules came along. Then, there was no alternative but to step off into the deep mud![5]

It is no wonder that women hiked up their long skirts, men tucked their pant legs into their boots, and the name of the first Houston baseball team was the "Mudcats." During a campaign to pave the streets the *Houston Daily Post* described the town as "a huddle of houses arranged on unoccupied lines of black mud."[6] In 1882 property owners paved two blocks of Main Street with limestone squares set on a gravel base. The stone was hard on horses' hooves and threatened to sink into the mud. Nonetheless, in the downtown area gravel, cypress blocks over a sand-and-gravel base, asphalt, macadam, brick, and planking resulted in 26 miles of pavement by 1903. That was a relief, but mud and dust remained a nuisance.

The quest for fresh water in Houston became entangled with the needs for public health, fire control, and a ship channel. Early Houstonians gathered drinking water from rainfall in cisterns and from Buffalo Bayou. They also drained their sewerage into the bayou at a time before germ theory explained their frequent complaints of "bowel trouble." In 1878 the city bought fire hydrants and authorized James M. Loweree of New York to build a waterworks to supply the town from Buffalo Bayou. The system failed to provide water for fire protection or good health. Inspections revealed the rank pollution of the bayou and live catfish in the water mains. The city finally took over the system in 1906, flushed it out, and began to pump pure water from the artesian wells that had been discovered in 1887.

Buffalo Bayou, meanwhile, had become the main sewer of Houston, and Major A. M. Miller, who inspected the bayou in 1895 as a potential ship channel, pronounced that Houston could expect no federal aid until it was cleaned up. The city, therefore, contracted with nationally known engineer Alexander Potter for an elaborate $250,000 sewer system that would collect the sewerage with a series of mains and pumps, and filter it through sand and charcoal. The effluent then drained into Buffalo Bayou. It was one of the best systems in the country. So confident was Potter in the purity of the treated water that at its completion he scooped up a glass of the effluent and drank it.[7]

Having resolved the problem of mud, fresh water, and sewerage, the city merchants focused their attention upon improving water transportation on the bayou. It was an old dream—to dig a ship channel and create an inland port. The city of Manchester, England, had done it. Already small vessels from Houston were transferring cotton bales to blue-water ships at Bolivar Roads, thus avoiding the monopolistic dock fees of the Island City. A ship channel was an enduring vision that would be fulfilled in the early twentieth century.

JEFFERSON

Perhaps the most interesting illustration of river port success and demise is the history of Jefferson in Marion County, East Texas. Named for Thomas Jefferson, the town started on Big Cypress Creek in 1842. It was the westernmost port of the Red River. The first sternwheeler, winding through the bayous and Caddo Lake, reached the site in 1843. The boat had a folding smokestack and a 12-inch draft. Within a few years steamboats regularly delivered cotton to Shreveport and New Orleans and returned to Jefferson with manufactured goods and immigrants. Jefferson became the county seat in 1846.

Leaders made an effort to build a rail line to Marshall, Texas, and Shreveport, but the Civil War interrupted construction. During the war the town operated a slaughterhouse for the Confederacy to produce canned meat, boots, and shoes. Afterward, commerce revived and only Galveston shipped more cotton than Jefferson. The town prospered and all was well. With a population of 7,300 Jefferson boasted of the first use of artificial gas lighting and commercial ice making. But then a distant engineering triumph brought about Jefferson's collapse.

The Red River raft was a long-established, 100-mile logjam that started about 25 miles above Natchitoches. A tangled mass of uprooted trees, brush, debris, and dirt clogged the riverbed and caused streams and tributaries to back up. Thus, Caddo Lake and Big Cypress Lake became navigable. Earlier attempts to remove the raft failed, but in 1872-1873 Captain W. W. Howell tried again by exploding canisters of nitroglycerine at the bottom of the pile. The mass loosened, the raft broke up, a channel opened, the river rose rapidly, the bayous drained, and Jefferson was left high and dry.

The railroads, thrusting into East Texas by this time, took over cotton shipping, the main business of the river steamboats. The destruction of the Red River raft was dramatic and aided almost every port along the Red River—but not Jefferson, which was located inland. Jefferson's population dwindled to about three thousand, and the town gradually wrinkled with age to become a curiosity and tourist destination.[8]

THE RIO GRANDE

Following the war with Mexico, steamboats made an entrance on the Rio Grande. In the Treaty of Guadalupe Hidalgo, the United States promised Mexico protection from Indian raids and set up a string of posts along the river. The soldiers were supplied from the military depot at Brazos Santiago, south of Padre Island, with the use of steamboats. Through collusion with the assistant quartermaster, Mifflin Kenedy (1818-1895), Richard King (1824-1885), and Charles Stillman (1810-1875) obtained a government contract that gave them a monopoly of trade on the lower Rio Grande. Below Presidio a chain of rocks blocked further upstream passage of the steamers.

During the Civil War, Texas cotton taken to Laredo was shipped downstream on Kenedy boats under Mexican registry to the neutral Mexican port of Bagdad at the mouth of the river. Waiting offshore were eager English ships ready to circumvent the United States blockade of the Confederacy to take the cotton to the factories of Manchester. In 1862 the partners posted a profit of 131 percent on 636 bales. They were paid in cash.[9] They poured their profits into land purchases for their expanding ranch in South Texas. After the war Kenedy and King gradually retired from river shipping to concentrate on ranching. Stillman suffered a stroke in 1866 and spent the rest of his life in New York.

Upstream irrigation, meanwhile, gradually lowered the amount of water in the river, and railroads reached Laredo in 1881 to take over the trade with Mexico. *Bessie*, the last of the river steamers, was lashed to a dock at Brownsville in 1907 and allowed to fall apart.[10] Today, the waters of the Rio Grande are so absorbed by agriculture that the stream never reaches the gulf. Such was the fate of the fourth longest river of the United States. The economic and environmental loss is worth pondering.

13

THE POLITICAL TOWNS

As a structure for political control the legislators of the Republic of Texas, relying upon their inherited experience from the United States, converted the twenty-three Spanish "municipalities" into counties and instituted English common law. New counties could be formed when one hundred males lived in 900 square miles. Once a county had been approved by the legislature, the citizens could elect commissioners, who became justices of the peace, sheriffs, coroners, and clerks. The county could appoint a tax assessor and surveyor. The purpose was to uphold local law and safety, collect taxes, record legal documents, and build roads.

Boundary lines were drawn as square as possible, and the county seat was located close to the center. Although not a bad idea, no record exists of the folk belief that a farmer should be able to ride to and from the courthouse in a single day. Texas patriots contributed the most popular county names. These rules of county building guided the formation of new counties with little change as settlers marched across the expanse of Texas.[1]

Selection as a county seat almost guaranteed success for a town since the designation carried a political purpose. Lawyers, courts, judges, and merchants came to the site. The county seat, consequently, was important to land speculators and the designation was an issue worth the struggle.

Shackelford County Courthouse, Albany, built 1883-1884. Photograph by author.

Commonly, a town promoter donated land in a public square for the governmental offices and jails. The buildings were constructed at first of local materials, but with increasing population in the 1850s the log cabins were replaced by structures of more durable stone. The courthouse thus became a point of pride, an honored place of civic authority, a place of justice, protector of precious records, and a location for memorial statues and plaques. It represented the values of the community and was bound to the state in a network of roads and law.

In the latter part of the nineteenth century patriotic citizens often erected expensive edifices of Victorian elegance in their town squares that endure to the present day. As a mark of progress the courthouses contained lavatories, steam heat, and electric lights. The clock towers, a common feature, provided an explanation point of orientation for the town and a constant reminder of an American culture that prized the rule of law and the significance of time.

Under Spanish and Mexican control, the governments planned settlements, but with the freedom of the Texas Republic and the United States any property owner could start and plat a town. Incorporated cities that allowed the citizens to select their own leaders, however, at first required approval of the state. For most places a variant of the old Alcalde system occurred when male citizens elected a town mayor and council. As it worked out, the councilmen, or aldermen, represented either the city as a whole or specific districts (wards).

Power varied between weak and strong mayors and their right to veto legislation and appoint subordinates. An 1858 law allowed a village of three hundred free white inhabitants to gain incorporation through a county court. Such a town would be led by an elected mayor, constable, and five aldermen. If it had 1,500 inhabitants it could gain status as a city governed by a mayor and city council of nine aldermen. This essentially democratic, aldermanic system predominated until the end of the century.

The Constitution of 1876 explicitly permitted incorporated places to collect taxes and sell bonds for civic improvements. The republic granted about fifty such charters, and by the end of the century there existed around two hundred incorporated towns, less than the number of counties at the time.

For small and medium-sized places the county government was most important for the enforcement of law.[2] As places became larger during the century, however, city governments became increasingly important for the administration of fire, police, water, and public health. City offices began to crowd the courthouse square. Nonetheless, as the state expanded in population the county system provided a fundamental network of towns interconnected with roads. County government was generally reliable, consistent with state law, and understood by the people.

AUSTIN

The most important political city was the state capital of Austin. The idea of Austin as the capital began with general discontent about the raw temporary seat of government in muddy Houston and a specific pique of Mirabeau B. Lamar. He loathed Sam Houston, and when he followed Houston as president of the republic he resented serving in a capital named for his predecessor. He quickly moved for a change.[3] There was no love lost between the two leaders. Houston wrote to his wife about Lamar, "He is too base to be respected and too imbecile to be trusted!"[4] Lamar referred to Houston as "a bloated mass of inequity."[5] Interestingly, in the passage of time the city of Houston became a creative economic powerhouse while Austin became the most beloved of Texas cities.

During the war there had been temporary meeting places of government—Washington-on-the-Brazos, Harrisburg, Galveston, Velasco. Columbia was capital of the first elected Texas government for three months before Houston was selected as a temporary capital late in 1836. The Bayou City then served until 1839, when the Texas government moved to the village of Waterloo on the edge of the western frontier. The Texas Congress renamed the town in honor of Stephen F. Austin, the Anglo "Father of Texas."

The site selection commission followed the recommendation of Lamar, who had seen the beauty of the area and approved of its location regardless of its vulnerability to Indian or Mexican attack. The commission purchased 7,735 acres along the Colorado River, nestled in the chalk hills of the Balcones Escarpment, and laid out a new town under the direction of Edwin Waller, a patriot, planter, and politician who became the first mayor. Descriptions of the first roads to the new capital of Austin claimed that they were "impassable—not even jackassable."[6]

With his surveyors, nonetheless, he designed a fourteen-square-block grid with each block divided by an alley. Congress Avenue, 120 feet wide, which stretched northward from the river to the four square blocks of Capitol Square, bisected the town. Waller put up temporary buildings and log cabins to be ready for the Texas Congress in November 1839, including a one-story capitol on a hill at Eighth Street. Waller offered city lots for sale and the government officials arrived to a twenty-one-gun salute. By 1840 the town had 856 inhabitants, including diplomats from France, England, and the United States.

Austin had a tough time. When Mexican troops took over San Antonio in 1842, Sam Houston, once again president of the republic, ordered the government moved, first to Houston and then to Washington-on-the-Brazos. Houston sent a company of Texas Rangers to save the archives, but citizens of Austin looked upon the public documents as the soul of the capital and resisted. The Texas Rangers quietly loaded their wagons in the early morning with ten boxes from the General Land Office, but as they drove away innkeeper Angelina Eberly, a widower, set off a loaded town cannon that peppered the Land Office with grapeshot and aroused a vigilance committee. The Austinites chased down the Texas Rangers for 18 miles, retrieved the documents without bloodshed, and returned them to the town. They packed the papers in tin boxes and put them under guard in a log storehouse, where they waited until Austin became the capital once again.

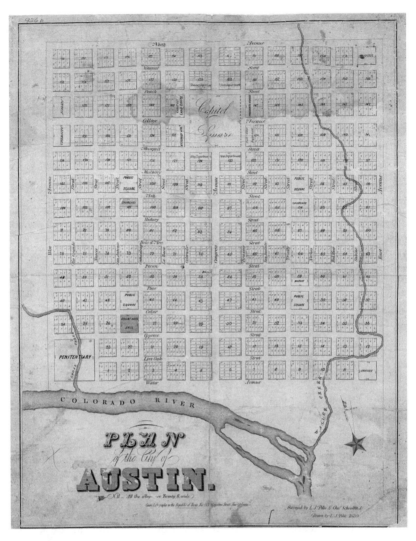

Plan of the City of Austin, 1839. Courtesy of the University of Texas Libraries, University of Texas at Austin.

With no political significance and repeated Indian attacks, the town deteriorated and lost population over the next three years. Wandering Englishman William Bollaert reported in 1843 that the president's house was falling to pieces and that the capital was "the abode of bats, lizards and stray cattle." The buildings, he noted, were constructed of green wood and as they dried the plaster peeled off.[7] A constitutional convention in Austin in 1845 approved annexation to the United States and confirmed Austin as the capital until 1850. The city obtained a majority vote as capital in 1850, and then again in 1872 when it permanently triumphed over Houston by sixty-three thousand to thirty-five thousand votes. The population surged from 850, including 225 slaves, in 1850 to 4,400, including 1,600 blacks, in 1870.

The state government erected permanent buildings, including a capitol at the head of Congress Avenue, in 1853 and the Governor's Mansion in 1856, as well as asylums for the deaf, blind, and mentally ill on the outskirts of town. A variety of Christian churches appeared as well as houses for city leaders. The Civil War dominated life in this political city from 1861 to 1865, although the majority of people in town and in the county voted against the conflict. Archivist David C. Humphrey commented, "When reading letters written by Austinites during the war and the newspapers published locally, one is struck by the frequent expression of themes like the sense of isolation from the rest of the Confederacy, frustration at the sea of misinformation, anxiety over the safety of Texas and Austin, and pride and sadness at the fate of Austin men in arms."[8]

Reconstruction brought Union troops, an appointed governor, a small Mexican community west of lower Congress Avenue, and a flood of freed blacks that would soon amount to a third of the population. The blacks settled into enclaves around the town—Masontown, Wheatsville, and Clarksville. The center of Clarksville, west of downtown, was the Sweet Home Missionary Baptist Church, which has occupied a wooden gothic building from the 1880s to the present. It is "well-proportioned, simple, and truly sweet," according to architectural historian Kenneth Hafertepe.[9] In 1977, Clarksville became the first black neighborhood in Texas to be listed on the National Register of Historic Places.

After a statewide contest in 1881, Austin won possession of the University of Texas for undergraduate and graduate education. The medical school was assigned to Galveston, where, supposedly, the flux of mariners would give fledgling doctors lots of disease and injuries to work upon. These educational institutions gave their host cities a lasting purpose and a stream of income from the state and from students.

The state assigned the University of Texas 40 acres north of the capitol and an endowment of 2 million acres of West Texas scrub land to build a university "of the first class." This land, which was the last of the public domain, however, was so worthless that even the railroads did not

Sweet Home Missionary Baptist Church. Photograph by author.

want it as a subsidy. To feed a single steer required at least 25 acres. The university, consequently, suffered, limping into the twentieth century. This arid land, however, possessed a hidden subsurface resource that later would transform the university into the richest public institution of higher learning in the nation.

At the same time as the establishment of the university, the state constructed a new capitol that has since become the most recognized building in Texas. Ignited by a faulty stovepipe, a fire destroyed the old capitol in 1881. The 1876 Constitution, however, had reserved 3 million acres of Panhandle land in ten counties for funding another.

The Capitol in Austin. Photograph by author.

A Capitol Board selected the design of Elijah E. Myers of Detroit following an architects' competition. The construction contract fell into the hands of the Illinois firm of Taylor, Babcock, and Company, which subcontracted the work to Gustav Wilke, a builder from Chicago. Difficulty working the red granite stone donated from a quarry near Marble Falls led to the controversial use of Texas convict labor and stonecutters from Scotland. A union boycott and federal lawsuit resulted in an $8,000 fine in labor violations for Wilke. He and assistant George Berry bought peace with the union for $500 each. The structure reached completion in 1888 with the placement of the "Goddess of Liberty" standing on top of the dome and a weeklong celebration.[10]

The Texas Capitol copied the Renaissance Revival design of the remodeled National Capitol (1863), with a 311-foot central dome and separate wings for the two branches of the legislature. The dome was constructed of wrought iron, with galvanized sheet iron painted like stone on the outside. Electric lights replaced the inside gas and arc lights in 1899. The grounds were decorated with sculpture evocative of Texas history, and the inside was lined with imaginative paintings of the Texas Revolution. The capitol mixed the mythic themes of a rural and revolutionary Texas into a building reflecting national patriotism and civic virtue.[11]

The syndicate that accepted the contract for the capitol took the Panhandle land and formed the XIT ranch to use for cattle until the land could be sold. Since the ranch touched on parts of ten counties, the idea has grown that XIT meant "Ten in Texas." It is one of those charming legends that ought to be true, but there is no historical evidence to prove it. The name was probably just a convenient brand, not easily copied.

With the ebb and flow of the all-male legislature and the closeness of the western frontier, Austin developed a reputation for gambling, drinking, and carousing. The city had eighty saloons by the 1880s. They lined Congress Avenue and tempted patrons with cool beer, choice whiskey, Havana cigars, free lunches, and private gaming rooms. The professional gambler and gunman Ben Thompson (1842-1884), for example, ran the Iron Front Saloon at Sixth Street and Congress. He was elected town marshal, and after he gunned down Jack Harris, another saloonkeeper, in San Antonio, Thompson's admirers greeted him at the train station, unhitched the horses of his hack, and hand-pulled the vehicle in adulation to the steps of the capitol.[12] In addition, Austin was known for a notorious red light area called Guy Town that supported one hundred prostitutes. The madams hired extra women when the legislature was in session. All of this faded at the end of the century and Guy Town closed in 1913 as the city matured into a place for families and churches.[13]

Even though two railroads—the Houston and Texas Central in 1871 and the International and Great Northern in 1876—reached Austin, the city failed to develop commerce and manufacturing. The rail lines diverted

The "Moonlight Tower" in Zilker Park. Photograph by author.

trade to other towns, and an attempt to attract factories with cheap electricity failed. Inspired by Alexander P. Wooldridge (1847–1930), a local leader in banking, politics, and education, the city in 1891 constructed a 60-foot-high dam across the Colorado River as a scheme to attract businesses with cheap water and electricity. The electricity was used to power a streetcar system and light the city with thirty-one 165-foot-tall "moonlight towers." Manufactured in Fort Wayne, Indiana, the steel towers with vertical truss assembly and guy wires used carbon-arc lamps at the top to flood the city with light enough to read a pocket watch. Equipped later with mercury-vapor lamps, fourteen of the unique "moon" towers have lasted into the present time.

The dam, however, did not, nor did it produce as much electricity as anticipated. Manufacturers and factories did not come. Lake McDonald, a recreational site behind the dam, silted up, power shortages occurred, and on April 7, 1900, after a big rainstorm, the dam collapsed. Eight men drowned as the flood washed away houses, barns, and livestock. Austin thus failed for the time to develop industry. At the turn of the century, with twenty-two thousand population and Capitol Avenue still unpaved, the sixth largest city in Texas remained noted mainly for its political and educational purposes.

14

THE MILITARY TOWNS

As a part of annexation Texas ceded all property of public defense to the United States. The Treaty of Guadalupe Hidalgo (1848), which ended the war with Mexico, in addition obliged the United States to halt Indian incursions across the Rio Grande. To stop the Indians, defend settlements, and protect westward-moving pioneers, the U.S. Army established military posts along the Rio Grande and on the line of settlement in 1849-1852. This line extended from Brownsville to Eagle Pass on the river and north past Fredericksburg to Fort Worth. When the settled areas caught up to the installations in a few years, the posts closed and moved in a ragged line farther west to points near Abilene, San Angelo, and Belknap. Fort Davis and Fort Stockton were meant to constrain Indian activities in the Big Bend; Fort Bliss in El Paso guarded the route westward to California.

It was a leaky defense against an estimated thirty thousand mobile Indians. During the Civil War General David E. Twiggs surrendered the installations to the Confederacy. Opportunistic Indians, mainly Apaches and Comanches, pushed back on the defenses until U.S. Army troops returned after the war. Fighting with the Indians continued until they were forced onto Oklahoma reservations in the mid-1870s.

The military effort on the Texas frontier brought army exploration,

Officers' quarters at the restored Fort Davis. Photograph by author.

wagon roads, supply contractors, towns, telegraph wires, and injections of cash into local economies. In the 1850s Texas had the greatest number of military installations in the entire Southwest; from 1846 to 1890 the army commanded thirty-five forts. The army used its surveyors to find the best routes and its soldiers to construct the roads.[1] Stage lines, cattlemen, and merchants used these roadways, and towns often formed close by the forts along the route.

The townspeople, like those who followed Taylor's army into Corpus Christi, were basically camp followers who offered various services to the soldiers, such as laundry washing. They often had access to the camp. Mainly, though, the towns provided recreation, with saloons, gambling places, and bawdy houses. They were a curse to the camp commanders, and a relief to the soldiers. When buffalo hunter Dick Bussel watched soldiers at work unloading one hundred wagons to build Fort Elliot in the Texas Panhandle in 1875, he noted that opportunistic employees of a supply company, Lee and Reynolds, were erecting a nearby tent. They had a bar in operation by mid-afternoon of the first day.[2]

MILITARY BOOMTOWNS

These military towns were the first boomtowns in Texas. Boomtowns are characterized as transient, exploitive of a single resource (in this case, soldiers), rowdy, male dominated, and deficient in women, children, families, and old people.[3] In American history they include mining towns and cow towns. If the resource disappears, such as the soldiers being ordered to go elsewhere or the exhaustion of a mine, the boomtown usually disappears unless it finds some other purpose for its existence. On the current Texas road map there are eight places with "Fort" in their name. They endured somehow, but there are many more with a fort in their history.

Historian Robert Wooster reasoned about life in such places:

> The mixed collection of servants, traders, gamblers, farmers, craftsmen, thieves, and laborers, and the families they in turn often brought with them, rounded out the inhabitants of the forts and nearby towns. The diversity of their backgrounds encompassed both good and bad, both pillars and scourges of the American scene. Most important, their presence prevented the soldiers they accompanied from becoming completely isolated from nineteenth-century American society.[4]

JACKSBORO

Among the most notorious of the military towns was Jacksboro, an Indian-ravaged village that boomed to a population of some eight hundred in 1871. Nearby Fort Richardson (1868-1878) was the anchor of Indian defense in North Texas and had the largest garrison of the United States in 1872. It was the staging point for the Red River War, which eventually brought an end to Indian conflict in Texas.

The town was a center for bidding on army contracts and for auctions of surplus army equipment. It was also the county seat. Infamous, however, were the tents and shacks that lined the half-mile road to Fort Richardson, such as "Mollie McCabe's Palace of Beautiful Sin" and "The Last Chance." Twenty-seven saloons were available for the enjoyment of the troopers. Predictable decline, like wilting wildflowers, came after the closing of the fort, but railroads at the end of the century revived the town as an agricultural shipping point.[5]

BROWNSVILLE

During the war with Mexico General Zachary Taylor ordered construction of Fort Brown, across the Rio Grande from Matamoros, as a part of his war preparations. It was made of dirt with nine-foot walls and a ditch around its 800-yard perimeter. Mexican forces that intercepted supplies intended for the post precipitated the opening battles of the war. Bombardment of the fort from Matamoros killed Major Jacob Brown, and the post was renamed in his honor. A permanent garrison was left after the war as a part of the effort to contain the Indians, but the army built a brick wall to separate the post from the town that had grown up nearby.

Land for the fort had been purchased from the heirs of José Salvador de la Garza. At the end of the war Charles Stillman bought a segment of Garza land for a town from the children of José Narciso Cavazos and his first wife. The children of Cavazos' second wife, led by Juan N. Cortina, however, claimed legal title. This led to a long series of court battles that the United States Supreme Court finally settled in favor of Stillman in 1879. The court battles, meanwhile, fueled the Cortina wars of the countryside. For two days in late September 1859 Cortina and his men galloped through the streets of Brownsville shouting "Death to the Americans"; they killed five men.

Stillman—dour and puritanical—and his partner, Samuel Belden, surveyed a town site and began selling lots. It was bad timing because in 1849 half the population of three thousand promptly died of cholera. Stillman, however, explained to his relatives, "There's nothing down there but the Rio Grande. There's nothing across the Rio Grande but Matamoros. There is nothing in Matamoros but the gateway to all Mexico for cotton, hides, and gold."[6] Since Stillman, along with Mifflin Kenedy and Richard King, owned a monopoly of steamboat shipping on the Rio Grande, the town flourished. It became a county seat in 1849, gained incorporation in 1853, and established public schools in 1855. John W. Audubon, the second son of bird artist John James Audubon, passed through the town in February 1849 and observed:

> Brownsville is one of those little places like thousands of others in the Southern states; little work and large profits give an undue share of leisure, without education or refinement. The river here is narrow and rapid and crossed by two ferry boats swung on hawsers in the old fashioned

way, stretching from bank to bank of the great "Rio Grande del Norte." They do a thriving business, as Matamoros contains many Mexicans who do both a wholesale and retail "running business," that is, smuggling.[7]

Audubon thought the land was of poor quality and could not understand why anyone would want to stay there. This opinion was confirmed by Helen Chapman, an army wife, who wrote, "The prosperity of Brownsville depends mainly on success in smuggling, and this seems to me a very uncertain basis for real advancement."[8] The postmaster said of the men at Brownsville, "They embrace every class—merchants, shop keepers and clerks, traders and boatmen, professional men and loafers, politicians and blacklegs—and of this number not more than thirty have families to protect or interests to defend."[9]

The port absorbed the river traffic and became the most important trade outlet for northern Mexico. During the Civil War, Union troops trying to interdict cotton smuggling briefly captured the town after the Confederate soldiers blew up Fort Brown and withdrew. The 8,000 pounds of gunpowder used in the explosion hurled firebrands into the town and set a ferryboat afire in the river.

The United States took over after the peace and undertook a massive rebuilding of the fort—seventy new buildings by 1869. Although river traffic dwindled, Brownsville slowly recovered. The town restarted its public schools in 1875 and hosted several banks, a cotton gin, an icehouse, and a newspaper. There was an easygoing respect for Mexican and American culture from the Spanish, French, English, American, and Mexican population, and half the newborn children were the result of mixed marriages. At the end of the century Brownsville had a population of six thousand but needed a bridge to Mexico and national rail connections. The Rio Grande by this time had been lost as a river of transport.

SAN ANGELO

Fort Concho (1867–1889), in mid West Texas near the geographic center of the state at the juncture of the North and Main Concho Rivers, replaced Fort Chadbourne, which lacked an adequate water supply. The soldiers served as a police force that fought skirmishes with Indians, furnished troops for the Indian campaigns, escorted survey parties, protected stagecoaches, built roads and telegraph lines, and held Indian prisoners.

About forty structures, left unprotected with no stockade, appeared slowly, built by the soldiers on rented land with materials brought by ox-wagon from the Gulf Coast and from locally quarried limestone. Water was abundant from springs and streams, and local farmers provided meat and grain. It was the regimental headquarters of the black Tenth United States Cavalry, later known as the Buffalo Soldiers, from 1875 to 1887. As a post it was notably uncomfortable, replete with cold, heat, dust storms, hail, tornadoes, scorpions, snakes, fleas, centipedes, and bats.[10]

In 1870 San Angelo, at first called Santa Angela, formed across the river from the fort. Its major purpose was to provide entertainment for the men. The town had its birth in sin. Lawless, with gambling, drinking, and prostitution, officers would not leave the fort after dark, and women from the post were not allowed to go to town without a military escort. Racial conflict fueled the drunken fights between whites and black troopers, Texas Rangers and soldiers, and men in general. A sheepman observed:

> Saint Angela is over run with drink saloons, gambling dens and dance houses of the very lowest class. It is the most immoral town I was ever in. Gambling is carried on in broad daylight… The gamblers and saloon keepers get most of the Nigger's money as pay day comes and every little while we hear of a soldier being killed, shot or stabbed without any cause whatever.[11]

Yet, the town became a meeting point for ranchers from the west and farmers from the east. Longhorns heading to market were fed and watered along the Concho River. Sheepherders found a means to get their flocks to market after the arrival of the Santa Fe Railroad in 1888. Telegraph wires came with the fort and telephones appeared in 1899. San Angelo, thus, established communication access at a place of agricultural and ranching convergence.

15

THE RAILROAD TOWNS

The history of railroad construction in Texas is exciting, important, damning, and confusing. Two hundred seventy-four railroads recognized by the Texas Railroad Commission eventually emerged from seven hundred charters. Over time railway companies merged, went out of existence, never started, suffered mismanagement, became bankrupt, fell into receivership, changed names, and endured as pieces of larger networks.[1] The railways nonetheless dictated the urban spread of the state, with towns strung like beads on an iron wire. Texas had 9,700 miles of track by the end of the nineteenth century and was the leading railroad state in 1905.

Railroad construction required survey teams and work crews of men to locate and prepare the roadbed, lay the crossties, and place the rails using mules and drays. It was hard work, and expensive. The Texas and Pacific (T&P), for example, in 1880 ordered 500,000 crossties, 10,000 tons of rails and fastenings, 20 locomotives, 350 cars, and food for eight thousand men and countless mules.[2] When Walter Justin Sherman directed the building of the Gulf, Colorado and Santa Fe in 1886-1887, intending to construct 300 miles in three hundred days, he stood by at the end of the day to ladle out a rewarding dipperful of whiskey to the sweating men.[3]

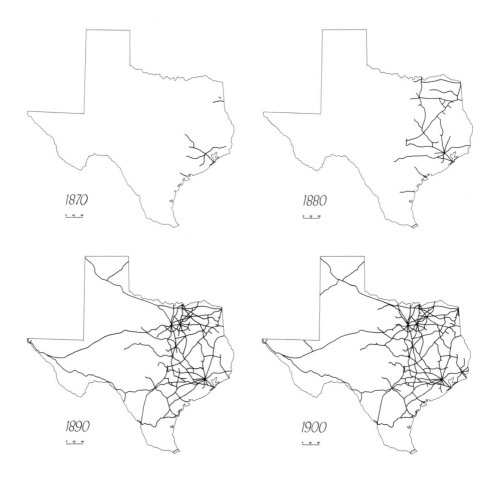

Railroad trackage, 1870-1900. This series of maps illustrates the dramatic expansion of railroads in Texas from after the Civil War to the end of the century. The railways introduced a new transportation technology, a city-oriented capitalism, and thousands of people carrying hopes and ideas. The railroads spread telegraphs and clocks, which together changed Texas culture and society forever. Reprinted with permission from Charles P. Zlakovich, Texas Railroads *(Austin: Bureau of Business Research, University of Texas at Austin, 1981, pp. 108-111).*

Engines became larger and more powerful. The "iron horse" could pull increasingly greater loads—as much as 500 tons on a level track. Headlights, bells, whistles, safety valves, steam gauges, air compression brakes, and cowcatchers to nudge reluctant pigs and cattle off the unfenced track became standard equipment. Better passenger and freight cars evolved. Although coal gradually replaced wood as fuel, clean water for boilers remained essential. Tank towns for water and fuel and ice were required every 20 to 30 miles.

Money for railroad building came from personal investment and gifts, especially in the early years; from the bonds of cities and counties (illegal after 1876); and mainly from state land grants and loans. Railroads in Texas borrowed from the Special School Fund, at $6,000 per mile of track, and following the example of the United States received land grants from the public domain as generous as 20 sections per mile of track. The average was 16 sections. The idea was that settlement, trade, and investment would be encouraged by the land grants. The rail lines would use the land to sell to farmers and leverage the grant to raise capital from investors. Various estimates of land given away range from 27 to 39 million acres; this stopped in 1882 when no more land was available. The average resale was less than $1.50 per acre. The state loaned $1,816,000 at 8 percent interest and got back $4,272,000. A bargain.[4] Thus, Texas spent its patrimony of public lands.

It would seem that for most Americans the railroad was a cultural as well as an economic experience. John S. Spratt recorded about the railroad at Thurber, Texas:

> A huge steam locomotive, either coal or oil burner, represented awesome majesty. Poised at the head of a train, freight or passenger, this giant iron monster emitted latent power in every jet of steam spewing from an injector as it forced water into the boiler, and the regular cadence of subdued puffs bounced gently from the smokestack. Every whistle on these iron horses had its own distinctive blast. The sounds ranged from high soprano to resonant low basso. When an engineer opened the throttle, the monster came alive, producing chuggings that exploded balls of black smoke skyward. With steam spewing from its exhaust valves, every person in sight and hearing recognized that a dragon was roused into action.[5]

The arrival of the first train in town was a time of celebration—dancing and frivolity. In 1858, when the Houston and Texas Central reached Hempstead, 50 miles from Houston, the newspaper promised a grand occasion:

> The entertainment will consist of oratory of the highest order, the fare of roast beef of the best kind, and terpsichorean exercises to consist of waltzes, polkas, schottisches, flings, etc. Then there will be pyrotechnic works, to consist of congreave and sky rockets, chasers, snakes, Roman candles, Greek fire, whirligigs etc. There will be oratory, beef, dancing and fireworks to suit the most fastidious tastes.[6]

The various railroads aimed for the larger cities, bullied smaller towns along the way for concessions, enjoyed enormous welcomes, spawned supply towns, and took up urban space with switching yards and repair shops. They brought employment and thousands of immigrants, opened the door to distant markets, founded new towns, and introduced Texans to a modern technology that met their need for speed and provided relief from the mud.

To be sure, the Texas railroads suffered from mismanagement, poor construction, and the greed of distant corporate owners. The local nickname of the Houston East and West Texas Railway (HE&WT) was "Hell Either Way Taken"; the Waco, Brazos, Trinity and Sabine (WBT&S) was known as "Wobblety, Bobblety, Turnover, & Stop"; the Texas and New Orleans (T&NO) was "Time No Object"; the Marshall and East Texas (M&ET) was "Misery and Eternal Torment." When Sam Bass, outlaw and train robber, was asked why he didn't rob the Dallas and Wichita Railroad, he replied: "Well, I would have pulled it, but the poor thing was bogged up in Elm bottom, and I'd as soon hit a woman as to tap it. Besides, if I had, I'd have had to rob the sick thing on credit, and that won't do in our business."[7]

It was a love-hate relationship between railways and patrons. Farmers complained about unfair rates and monopoly. Many did not understand that for a railroad it cost more per mile for a short haul, with the expense of loading, switching, and connecting, than for a long haul, where the same expenses were spread over a longer distance. So, short distance rates were higher, which was an offense to common sense.

The Texas Constitution of 1876 reflected the frustration of the farmers'

Grange, which inserted all sorts of regulations into the document, including one that required interstate carriers to maintain an office in the state. Finally, in 1891 Governor James Hogg set up the Texas Railroad Commission, with jurisdiction over railroad rates and operations. With the extension of its power over oil and gas pricing in the twentieth century, the commission became one of the most powerful regulatory agencies in the United States.

RAILROADS, TIME, AND TEXAS URBAN CULTURE

The railroads transformed the culture as well as the economy. They established forty-two county seats. The depot became a common piece of urban architecture, and wherever rails crossed roads there was a question of safety and privilege. Moreover, the railway warped time and space. For cities along the route, the far became near while unconnected towns remained as remote as ever. The measurement of time changed.

Time no longer was counted by the change of seasons, the flooding of rivers, or the place of the sun in the sky. Time was no longer measured by a rural rhythm of "from can see to can't." It was measured precisely to the second with the tick of a mechanical clock; all hours and minutes were of the same length. Large timepieces, their faces bravely displayed in four directions from the new county courthouse towers, marched westward across Texas with the railways to proclaim the new order.

Although the English and Swiss crafted pocket watches and mantel clocks in the eighteenth century, they did not become popular until the end of the nineteenth century, when the "American system of manufacturing" (the use of standard and interchangeable parts) provided cheap mechanisms. The Montgomery Ward catalogue advertised a mail order, Waterbury stem-wind pocket watch for $1.35 in 1895; Sears Roebuck in 1908 offered a pocket watch for fifty-nine cents.[8] The precise measurement of time, the most fundamental element of modernity, thus reached Texas cities with the iron rails. It became a virtue to be "on time."

Railroad technology, moreover, demanded a precise schedule, not just for the convenience of customers, but also for safety. It was not wise to have trains on the same track headed toward each other. Timing was important, and in 1883 the lines all adopted standard time, a suggestion of Professor C. F. Dowd, the principal of the Temple Grove Seminary for Young Ladies at Saratoga Springs, New York. This set up four time

Caldwell County Courthouse, Lockhart, built 1894. Photograph by author.

belts running north to south across the nation so that everyone could be on time. In recognition Dowd received free annual passes on all railroads of the country. Ironically, he was killed by a train at a crossing in Saratoga in 1904.

THE TELEGRAPH

The telegraph played a crucial role of coordination. Samuel F. B. Morse of New York in 1841 perfected a rugged telegraph transmitter that used an electromagnet to send dots and dashes over a wire, a moving paper tape to record them, and a code to correspond to letters of the alphabet. The device provided instantaneous information, and soon the Western Union Telegraph Company dominated the industry. It was shortly noticed that sharp-eared telegraphers could translate the messages without the paper tape at a rate of thirty to forty words per minute without error. This opened a new urban job for women.[9]

Telegraph lines strung through treetops arrived in Marshall in 1854, but the first permanent line followed the Galveston, Harrisburg and Houston Railway in 1860. The telegraph office, usually housed at the train station, provided not only the information needed for the safety of railroads but also news for the communities. Newspapers improved with "telegraphic communication," and cotton distribution points such as Dallas and Houston could become "spot" markets of instant supply and prices. The telegraph lines paralleled the rails and also linked the military establishments in West Texas. Consequently, precise time measurement and telegraphic communication traveled hand-in-hand to provide revolutionary access to the cities.

MARSHALL

Railroads organized themselves into large segments that supervised 200 to 300 miles of track with scheduling, switching, maintenance, and repairs. The division town was the point of changeover of train crews. Harrison County provided the T&P with a $300,000 bond subsidy to locate its division offices and shops in Marshall. This brought a permanent influx of railroad workers that almost tripled the population in the 1870s. The workers, skilled and unskilled, worked for wages on a tight schedule under factory conditions. Although Marshall became the marketing center for cotton in East Texas, the town population was no longer dedicated to farming. The rail men and their families and their dreams were linked directly to a distant corporation that reminded them of their loyalty with a shrill morning factory whistle. This was a different sort of life.[10]

DENISON

The T&P built westward to establish the new town of Longview, bypass Tyler, connect with Sherman, and prepared to pass to the south of Dallas. The voters of Grayson County saw no need to meet the demand of $150,000 from the Missouri, Kansas and Texas (MKT), which was poised to jump the Red River from Indian Territory. It was no idle request, however. The voters did not understand that the Katy could open their whole trading territory of North Texas to eastern markets.

The MKT consequently bought a town site on the Texas side, built a bridge, and crossed the river to Denison, the "Gate City of Texas," on Christmas Eve 1872. Named for George Denison, a vice president of the company, it rapidly became a railroad boomtown. A writer from *Scribner's* wrote in July 1873, "All around us was Babel—a wild rush of business, a glory in affairs, an unbounded delight in mere labor, which at once oppressed and appalled us."[11] The riffraff of the Indian Territory poured in—Cherokee Joe, Monte Jack, prostitute "Dirty Legs" Kitty—to gamble, drink, whore, and run whiskey to the Indians. Two other railways joined the melee and five more were chartered to connect with other places in North Texas.

Denison had three thousand residents in 1873. The town incorporated, established a free public school in 1873, obtained a water supply system in 1886, installed two cotton compresses, and became a regional shipping point for cotton routed to St. Louis. An opera house opened in 1884, a post office in 1886, and a newspaper in 1889. Denison had ten thousand residents by the end of the century, and the lawlessness had been confined to Skiddy Street, across from City Hall. This "red light" area, taxed for the benefit of the town, remained in operation until World War II. Denison retained its rowdy reputation, and when William B. Munson, one of the founders of the town, married in 1876, his bride refused to live there and resided instead 20 miles away in the more sedate town of Sherman.[12]

DALLAS

John Neely Bryan (1810-1877) of Tennessee established Dallas with a store 10 by 12 feet, at a rocky ford on the east bank of the Trinity River in 1841. He sold gunpowder, lead, whiskey, and tobacco. Bryan as a town promoter persuaded other people to build nearby, served as postmaster of the Texas Republic, operated a rope ferry across the river, helped to organize Dallas County in 1846, and worked for the selection of his town as the county seat in 1850.

He platted a reasonable gridiron site facing the Trinity River, but a rival claim by John Grigsby cut a diagonal line across the plan and forever skewed the Dallas street pattern. Bryan sold his interests in the site, briefly searched for gold in California, fled to the Creek Nation for six years after shooting a man, fought briefly in the Civil War, returned to Dallas and his family, pushed for the completion of the Houston and Texas Central, and promoted the construction of the first iron bridge across the Trinity. He died in the State Lunatic Asylum in 1877.

The origin of the city's name has been a long-standing mystery. Perhaps it was named for naval hero Commodore Alexander Dallas, but newspaperman Sam Acheson said that Neely's son claimed his father named it for George M. Dallas, the vice president under James K. Polk. "He was always a Democrat as I have been," said the son. "We are Methodists too."[13]

Alexander Cockrell, from Kentucky and the Indian Territory, in 1852 bought Bryan's property in the town for $7,000, built a sawmill, began a hotel, and replaced the ferry with a covered wooden bridge. The town incorporated in 1856 and portly Samuel Pryor, doctor and druggist, became mayor. He was gruff, outspoken, and said to have been old when he was born.[14] At the same time some two hundred French settlers set up a utopian village, La Reunion, three miles away, across the river. They were urban folk—tailors, shoemakers, jewelers, artists, weavers, stonemasons, dancing teachers, milliners, musicians—and only two were farmers. Their fate was predictable. The colony gradually fizzled and its population drifted into Dallas to fertilize the frontier town with French culture.[15]

Dallas County voted for secession, and sent soldiers and money for the war effort. Reconstruction brought bitter opposition to a local Freedmen's Bureau office and its effort to protect blacks. The first administrator was forced to leave town and the second was murdered.

Nevertheless, freed blacks flocked to the city in search of jobs and settled on the outskirts, particularly on the eastern part of Elm Street, which became known as "Deep Ellum."

Business in dry goods, blacksmithing, wagon making, brick making, and cotton gins blossomed while leaders harbored dreams of making the Trinity River navigable. They experimented, and failed. Their hope thus turned to the coming railroads. The Houston and Texas Central was planning to go to McKinney, eight miles east of Dallas, but Dallas voters offered $5,000 in cash, 115 acres of land, and right-of-way on Main Street (now the Central Expressway). With such inducement the H&TC bent its course to Dallas. That was excellent; it meant good business.

Now, if the Texas and Pacific could be attracted to Dallas, where the east-west line would intersect the north-south railway, the city could win economic dominance in North Texas. Texas and Pacific officials planned to build 50 miles south of Dallas, but they needed right-of-way permission from the state. It was typical that such routes would go near clean water sources, such as springs, for the use of the engines. John W. Lane, the state representative from Dallas and former mayor, quietly inserted into the contract with the T&P that it had to pass within one mile of little-known "Browder's Springs."

Everyone was in a hurry, the bill passed, and no one noticed until after the legislature adjourned that "Browder's Springs" was one mile south of the Dallas courthouse! Texas and Pacific officials were hopping mad at the trick, but calmed down when Dallas voters offered $5,000 cash, $100,000 in bonds, right-of-way into the city, and land for a depot.[16]

On July 16, 1872, preceded by a telegraph wire, an H&TC train of flat cars carrying lumber and a single passenger car huffed into Dallas and was greeted by a throng of cheering people and an afternoon of barbeque and speeches. The T&P arrived one year later, just before the Panic of 1873 and the choking depression of 1873–1877. Railroad construction halted as rail companies went bankrupt, with Dallas at the end of the line.

People preparing to move west went as far as they could and disembarked at Dallas and Dallas County. The city population subsequently popped from 3,000 in 1870, to 10,000 in 1880, to 38,000 in 1890, to 43,000 in 1900—over a thousand people per year. It was the fastest-growing city in Texas, and the largest in 1890. Merchants who had followed the rail construction settled down in Dallas. A prime example was Sanger Brothers dry goods merchants, who followed the H&TC northward and set up

Dallas in 1872. From Wikimedia Commons.

stores in Millican, Bryan, Hearne, Calvert, Bremond, Kosse, Groesbeck, Corsicana, Dallas, and Sherman. After consolidation due to the Panic of 1873, the Dallas store, with 650 employees, became the flagship.

The brothers, Philip and Alex, organized the store by departments, extended credit to customers, bought goods wholesale in New York, and provided home delivery. They sold an expanding inventory that included plows, dress goods, needles, pins, and groceries. Alexander Sanger (1847-1925) became a civic leader who supported the State Fair, the Dallas Public Library, the first synagogue, and the building of the T&P to Dallas.

Dallas dealers built the first grain elevator in Texas and Dallas became an inland cotton market. In the final three decades of the nineteenth century, East Texas cotton became a commercial cash crop for almost everyone due to the railroad. In 1874 the T&P hauled 102,000 bales; four years later it moved 351,000 bales. In thirty years the railroad freight rate declined to an estimated 5 percent of the cost of an ox team. With the burgeoning Texas population, the number of bales produced had increased sevenfold by the end of the century.[17] The crop-lien system became prevalent after the Civil War, when everyone needed capital. Illiterate farmers, with no knowledge of credit, pesticides, or crop rotation, and with the bad luck of weather, caterpillar worms, fungus, and the boll weevil, fell permanently into debt.

Town merchants bought their cotton, sold supplies, invested in compresses and gins, and prospered. Bills of lading as well as warehouse receipts could be used as collateral for bank loans. Farmers' organizations such as the Patrons of Husbandry, however, erroneously blamed the merchants for farm poverty and denounced cities as "plague centers" of "debasing pleasures."[18]

Dallas factors provided cotton gins, compresses, and storage, and they used telegraphic data about the Liverpool market. A local factory in 1888 employed 250 employees to spin cotton into thread and cloth, and sold red flannel underwear all over North Texas. This action, a portent of the future, indicated a mature manufacturing process for clothing—from fiber to a finished product. By the turn of the century Dallas possessed thirty factories producing finished cotton materials.

As might be expected, banking and insurance emerged to enhance the growth of business. The first banks were private affairs with rich individuals lending money to others. In 1868, for example, William H. Gaston (1840-1927) and A. C. Camp opened a bank with $40,000 capital, a dry goods box as a counter, and their pockets as safe deposit boxes. The first state-chartered bank came in 1873, and by 1893 ten banks faced the panic of that year. Five of them failed.

During the same period Dallas began to develop insurance companies, with fourteen agencies operating by 1886. In 1899 the Modern Order of Praetorians, a fraternal organization with headquarters in Dallas, began to offer life insurance. This nucleus attracted other insurance companies to Dallas in the early twentieth century, including Southwestern Life Insurance Company, which was organized in 1903. With their premiums these companies possessed resources to invest in the city.

Dallas started a primitive water system with wooden pipes to pump drinking water from Browder's Springs in 1873. The first telephone connected the downtown fire station with the springs in 1880. Gas lighting began in 1874 and electricity came in 1882. After a tax levy passed in 1881, public schools started, with a separate school built for blacks the next year. A weekly newspaper that would later become the *Dallas Herald* began in 1849, struggled through the Civil War (once printed on tissue paper), and became a daily newspaper with the arrival of the telegraph. The *Dallas Morning News*, a sister of the *Galveston Daily News*, started in 1885 and shortly purchased the *Herald*. A town of twenty-five thousand could not support two large morning newspapers.[19]

A growing, boisterous place like Dallas provided residents and visitors with a variety of attractive recreation activities unavailable in the countryside.[20] To the usual frontier fare of drinking, gambling, whoring, and eating was added iced drinks, candy, and freshly brewed local beer. To the usual sports of horse racing, cockfighting, and dogfighting were added boxing matches in the 1880s, roller skating in 1885, tennis in 1886, professional baseball in 1887, bicycle riding in the 1890s, football in 1891, and golf in 1896.

John W. Thompson in 1872 opened a variety theater that offered food, drink, and crude burlesque—jigs, dances, and songs. The Black Elephant, a black variety theater, copied the Thompson Theater until the city council banned all such places. Variety theaters followed a pattern that originated in New Orleans and were the progenitors of today's strip clubs.

As a counterbalance, J. Y. and Thomas Field built the Field Opera House on Main Street in 1873, and in 1879 John A. Moniger presented the "legitimate theater" productions of traveling troupes at the Craddock Theater, located over a wholesale liquor store. The Dallas Opera House Association, composed of twenty-two members, opened, in addition, the Dallas Opera House in 1883; it seated an audience of 1,200 to view the traveling operas and shows of the impresario Henry Greenwall of New Orleans. Greenwall presented the greatest acting of the time, from New York City to Texas audiences. Edwin Booth's presentation of *Hamlet*, for example, was sold out a week in advance.

Most significant for Dallas and recreation, however, was the establishment of the State Fair of Texas in 1886. Other places—Corpus Christi, Houston, Fort Worth—held fairs to attract attention, provide recreation, and to show off the fruits of the land. In 1859, with a population of only 175, Dallas hosted a three-day fair. The Civil War and Reconstruction intervened in its annual continuation, but the idea revived with the coming of the railways.

In 1886 a private corporation led by businessmen William H. Gaston, Thomas Marsalis, and John S. Armstrong organized a fair on an 80-acre tract in East Dallas. An implacable rival group, however, promoted a competing fair north of town. Racetracks and exhibit facilities were built at both sites, and both failed to make a profit. In 1887 they sensibly merged and expanded the East Dallas site.

Thousands of visitors came each year to view livestock, balloon ascents, parades, gardens, machinery, and horse racing; to compete in baking, needlework, and fruit preservation; to listen to concerts and oration; and to eat ice cream, watermelon, and raw oysters. Despite public interest, the finances of the fair bumped along and came to a halt in 1903, when the state banned gambling on horse racing, which was the main source of revenue.

The fair corporation sold the property to the city. Reorganized under a municipal park board, the fair continued into the new century.[21] The State Fair of Texas, thus, grew to be a major entertainment event for the city, a tourist attraction, and an informal statewide holiday.

FORT WORTH

Thirty miles to the west, initially separated from Dallas by the eastern branch of the Cross Timbers, Fort Worth languished after missing the railroad rush of the 1870s. The town had begun as part of a defensive line of nine forts set up against Indian attack after the war with Mexico. In June 1849 Major Ripley S. Arnold established a post on the banks of the Trinity River and named it Camp Worth in honor of the general who proposed the defense. Prompted by floods, Arnold shortly moved the camp to a bluff overlooking the mouth of the Clear Fork of the Trinity.

Settlement had already caught up with the defensive line, the Indians were not much of a threat—no attacks, just taunts and yelling—and the army closed the fort in September 1853 to move farther west. When the soldiers abandoned the site the small civilian community that had grown up around the fort moved into the empty cabins and set up a store, hotel, saloon, schoolhouse, and homes. They used the parade ground as a public square and as a place for a future courthouse. Fort Worth amounted to about one hundred people.[22]

Fort Worth grew but slowly, until it wrested from Birdville, Texas, perhaps with the help of whiskey and imported voters, the designation as the Tarrant County seat in 1860. The town split over secession; sanguine young men went off to war; families moved fearing Indian attack; and the population shriveled from 350 to 175. The new courthouse, started in 1860, remained incomplete, with only rock walls to the first floor. The stores had empty shelves and locked doors. There were more houses than people; there was no post office; there was no saloon. When disheartened

Confederate veteran Khleber Miller Van Zandt arrived he observed, "Fort Worth, as I first saw it late on an August afternoon in 1865, presented a sad and gloomy picture."[23] Van Zandt nonetheless stayed, opened a dry goods store, and became a leader of the town's revival.

Recovery came slowly, but Fort Worth was blessed with an adequate river water supply and a location that bordered the extensive prairie land of the Great Plains. The northern demand for beef after the Civil War, the nearby supply of cheap longhorn cattle, and a branch of the Chisholm Trail called the McCoy Trail that came through Fort Worth saved the town. The first herd arrived in 1866; 360,000 animals passed through in 1871 alone. Fort Worth consequently became a cattle boomtown with a cowboy reputation.

Fort Worth was the last major stopping place before the railheads, and cowboys used it for supplies and recreation, both going to Kansas and coming home. A red light area of bawdy houses, dance halls, and saloons known as "Hell's Half-Acre" flourished on the south end of town. Buffalo hunters, in addition, mingled with the cowboys and used Fort Worth as an accumulation point for hides until the southern herd of bison was eliminated at the end of the 1870s.

At the Red Light Dance Hall a man paid a dollar for a drink, fifty cents for a dance, twenty-five to fifty cents for dinner, and seventy-five cents to a dollar for a trip with his partner to a back room. The women made three dollars per night.[24] Town officials, of course, clucked about the debauchery on the one hand and taxed the bawdy houses for the good of the town on the other.

Black cowboys worked the trails (a number of 4 percent is only a guess), and integrated black saloons thrived in Hell's Half-Acre. Black railroad workers and former farmhands seeking the freedom of city air formed the town's first black neighborhood in this disreputable south end of town. Blacks, along with Asians and Hispanics, were for the most part a small, invisible minority in this segregated town until after the turn of the century.

Fort Worth incorporated in 1873 with a mayor-council government. The first ordinances (unenforced and ineffectual) prohibited gambling, prostitution, and the wearing of guns. The leaders looked forward to the coming of the T&P, gone to ground by the depression 16 miles away at Eagle Ford. The anticipatory population dwindled by 75 percent to 1,100, and a Dallas reporter, like a teasing older brother, said life was so slow in Fort Worth that a cougar was observed napping undisturbed in the middle of Main Street.[25]

The lasting jealousy of Dallas' success dates from this time, with "Big D" portrayed as urbane and Fort Worth as "Cowtown." The developing rail linkages in Dallas reached eastward and in Fort Worth they extended westward. The towns came to represent a regional and cultural divide. When Dick Ware, a Panhandle banker, was asked by a friend to move to Dallas in the 1930s he replied, "I told him if I ever left Amarillo I'd probably take Fort Worth. I would not care to live in Dallas for in that big shot town, it's a sin to be poor."[26]

After several extensions the legislature imposed a deadline of completion upon the distressed railroad to reach Fort Worth by July 20, 1876. In the early part of the month the track was still nine miles away and the anxious residents turned out—men, women, children, and mules—to help prepare the roadbed. The city council extended the city limits by a quarter-mile and placed the depot on that edge of town. There was no time to build a trestle, so they used a horse and wagon bridge. Rainy weather did not help. On July 19, nevertheless, gandy dancers spiked down the last piece of track as a work train crawled into town at 11:23 a.m. to the loud rejoicing of a twelve-piece brass band and an all-night jubilee.

Other railways followed, such as the Katy in 1881; the Gulf, Colorado and Santa Fe in 1887; the Fort Worth and Denver City in 1888; and the Rock Island in 1893. All received a bonus for locating in Fort Worth. The town, for instance, raised $75,000 and gave a right-of-way to the Santa Fe. Fort Worth thus became a rail center with a yard in the south end that included space for the T&P to house shops and a terminal. Feeder stagecoaches reached out to nearby prairie communities. The T&P pushed through and on to Weatherford, and challenged the Southern Pacific in a building race to El Paso.

The town set up a mule-driven streetcar line for a mile along Main Street between the courthouse and the T&P station that allowed strong men to ride free; they could boost the trolley back on track when it went amiss. A slaughterhouse shipped out an experimental boxcar of beef quarters on ice in 1877, and local entrepreneurs built the 258-acre Union Stock Yards in 1888.

The town also hoped to control its drinking, gambling, and violence by electing gunman "Longhair Jim" Courtwright (1845-1887) as marshal in 1876-1879. He wore two six-shooters, holstered butt forward to allow a right hand draw from the right hip. He was moody, overbearing, hard drinking, mean, and fast. After serving as marshal Courtwright tried to force proprietors to pay him protection money, and this led to one of the few genuine face-to-face gunfights in Texas history.

Luke Short (1854-1893) managed the upstairs gambling casino of the elegant downtown White Elephant Bar. He refused Courtwright's shakedown and the former marshal, drunk, confronted Short on the street in front of the saloon. As Courtwright began to pull one of his big pistols, Short surprisingly moved toward him, whipping out a small revolver from a specially made leather-lined rear pocket. He shot five times at point-black range and left Courtwright sprawled, dead and bleeding, in the doorway of a neighboring shooting gallery. Officials issued no indictment of Short for his self-defense, but this marked a zenith of the Wild West in the Texas cities. Such a death was now a shock to city folk. Short was shunned, and violence from the saloons slowly dwindled after this point.[27]

Typhoid in 1881 and smallpox in 1882 and 1886 prompted city officials to install wooden sewer lines to empty into the Trinity River and to franchise a waterworks to pump raw river water to businesses and homes in 1882. Before this, water had come from springs, wells, and water wagons. The city purchased the private water company in 1885, drilled supplementary wells, and began to purify the water in 1890.

Other urban amenities came in the early 1880s, when the city replaced its free-roaming pigs with a city scavenger, installed police and fire protection, and put gravel on the two main streets. The Fort Worth Gas Light Company installed eighty-six gaslights around town. In 1889, when the gas light company merged with the Fort Worth Electric Light and Power Company, the city street lamps and streetcars converted to electric power.

Anglo males dominated politics and business, but Anglo women were noted for the establishment of the Fort Worth Library Association in 1892. Their efforts led directly to the building of a Carnegie library in 1901. The local leader, Mrs. D. B. Keeler, asked every man to donate the price of a cigar per day to the library. She even asked Andrew Carnegie for the same tariff, and he agreed. On the effort for a public library, Fort Worth was ahead of its Dallas rival, although Fort Worth was but 60 percent as large.

A telegraph line from Dallas arrived in 1874 and long-distance telephone service in 1882. An independent public school system that segregated children by sex and race began in 1879, and the Methodist Episcopal Church chartered Texas Wesleyan College in 1881. The Panic of 1893, however, placed undue pressure on city finances, and the bankrupt government defaulted on its bonds in the last five years of the century. The city finally worked its way out, but a suspicion of insolvency haunted Fort Worth as late as 1927.[28]

WACO

Somewhat similar to Fort Worth was Waco Village, founded in 1849 70 miles south of Dallas along the Balcones Escarpment fault line, the future spine of Texas urbanization. It was located at a hard bottom ford of the Brazos River on the site of an ancient Waco Indian village. It became the county seat of McLennan County, which was organized in 1850, and became incorporated as the town of Waco in 1856. By that time it possessed a new courthouse, a newspaper, and two Protestant churches. The First Baptist Church started in 1851 and spawned fifteen others. Surrounding cotton plantations insured success for the 749 residents. The town wholeheartedly contributed to the Civil War, with seventeen companies of soldiers and six generals for the Southern cause. Afterward, as might be expected, Reconstruction was difficult for the community, and race conflict occurred in the late 1860s.

Like Fort Worth, Waco recovered from the ravages of warfare by way of cattle drives going through town and across the Brazos River, following a branch of the famous Chisholm Cattle Trail to Fort Worth and Kansas. Waco served as a supply and recreation place for the cowboys.

The town particularly boomed with the opening of a suspension bridge across the river in 1870. At the time it was the only bridge spanning the Brazos River. Led by local citizens, the Waco Bridge Company hired Thomas M. Griffith of New York and commissioned the use of innovative steel cables from John A. Roebling and Son, the company that later built the Brooklyn Bridge. It operated as a toll bridge until it was purchased by the county in 1889. Thereafter, with various repairs it was free to vehicular traffic until 1971, when it was reserved for pedestrians as a National Historic Site.

A reporter of the *Waco Daily Advance* described the early traffic as it funneled across the bridge:

The Waco Suspension Bridge. Photograph by author.

First there comes tearing by with a spanking team of grays and an elegant road wagon, one of the Waco bloods out for an evening drive. Next a party of cowboys, mounted on Spanish ponies, wearing the regular "snake" hats, long angling spurs, lareats [sic] and whips, followed by a pack mule loaded down with their camp equipage. Anon, we have an immigrant wagon, drawn by three mules and a horse, the stalwart Missourian who trudges beside it being the proprietor of the team. The dog under the wagon and the group of chubby, tow-headed children, whose heads peep out from under the canvas cover show they are bound for the West and a home. May they have Godspeed in procuring it. The sleek and portly old party who now ambles by, with the queer-shaped saddlebags, is a country doctor, and carries his apothecary shop in those same saddlebags.[29]

As might be expected of a place nicknamed "Six Shooter Junction," a red light district of saloons and bawdy houses called "Two Street" developed near the bridge. The town gave prostitution legal recognition and regulated it with licenses, fees, and medical inspections until the early twentieth century. The Waco and Northwestern Railroad was built into the city in 1871, and later, in the early 1880s, the Katy and the St. Louis and Southwestern railways joined the rail convergence to enhance the shipping of cotton—fifty thousand bales in 1884.

Hot artesian water discovered under the center of town resulted in a natatorium and a sanitarium that advertised a cure for rheumatism, sciatica, lumbago, gout, blood poisoning, syphilis, epilepsy, alcoholism, and hysteria. Waco thus became a spa, made delightful with a local soda fountain drink, "Dr Pepper," first served in 1885 at the Old Corner Drug Store. A theater district, including two opera houses and variety theaters, presented song, dance, plays, and minstrels from 1877 to 1916. The city hosted a county fair from 1894 to 1930 in November to celebrate the cotton industry.[30] The end of the century counted 20,700 residents, the largest woolen mill in the South, grain elevators, six banks, bottling works, a water system supplied by artesian wells, the beginnings of a park system, and new electric streetcars.

Most important was an emphasis upon higher education, which gave Waco a claim as the "Athens of Texas," although the schools often projected the religious ideas of their founders. Waco Classical School started in 1860, became Waco University the next year, and merged with Baylor University when it moved to town in 1887. The African Methodist Episcopal Church moved Paul Quinn College to Waco in 1877. It taught practical skills such as carpentry and saddlery. Smaller private and sectarian schools abounded, including Add-Ran Christian University, which moved to Waco in 1895 and became Texas Christian University in 1902 before it was tempted to move to Fort Worth.

Adding sparks to this intellectual mix was newspaper editor William C. Brann (1855-1898) of the *Waco Daily News*, who revived a newspaper called the *Iconoclast* in 1895. In this newspaper Brann neither straddled an issue nor defended the status quo. His words stung and attracted a circulation of one hundred thousand. "Waco, we would have you know," he wrote, "is the religious storm-centre of the Universe, and one of the few places that license prostitutes—a fact for the consideration of students of cause and effect."[31]

Brann referred to Baylor University and its Baptist Church affiliation as a "chronic breeder of bigotry and bile," and said that its students took but two baths in life—once when they were born and the other when they were baptized. He outraged just about everyone and was shot down in the street in 1898, hit in the back precisely where the suspenders crossed his shirt. People still remained angry and his gravestone thereafter became a target of drive-by shootings.[32] Even today, after a century, Waco has an odor of religiosity, a chipped grave marker, and the highest concentration of Baptist Churches (about one hundred) in the state.

ABILENE

As the Texas and Pacific moved westward a mile per day into Taylor County on a line to El Paso, local ranchers Claiborn W. Merchant (1836-1926), his twin brother John Merchant, John N. Simpson, John T. Berry, and Sam L. Chalk met with the T&P town locator, H. C. Withers, and arranged to have the railroad bypass the county seat of Buffalo Gap and cross their land. The deal was to have ranchers provide the land for a depot, siding, cattle pens, and half a town site. Buffalo Gap had been the county seat since 1874, when it was the only town in the county and at the time had about 1,200 residents with dreams of being the "Athens of the West."

The T&P established headquarters in the new town of Abilene, however, and the population of Buffalo Gap began a slide from which it never recovered. It lost the county seat to Abilene in 1883, but refused to give up the records. A judge in Buffalo Gap ruled in favor of Abilene and rushed to the new town with his family for safety. Disgruntled neighbors in the old town who showed up with tar and feathers thus missed him, but in vengeance they built a fire in his yard, caught his chickens, and ate them.[33]

Promoted by the T&P as the "Future Great City of West Texas," Abilene, named after the leading cattle town of Kansas, initially became an unruly cowboy and railroad worker tent city. Residents celebrated the arrival of the tracks by "firing an anvil." Two anvils were faced together with gunpowder in between them. When set off with a trail of powder it sounded like a cannon. One hundred thirty-nine town lots sold on the first day in 1881; the town incorporated in 1883; and as planned, it became a shipping point for cattle. A rancher explained, "You can get two things in Abilene—a train ticket to get away, and a drink to make you willing to stay."[34]

The early churches (Baptist, Church of Christ, Methodist) and the women of Abilene did their best to tame the excesses and establish schools. The first public school, established in 1881, involved about a hundred segregated students, and was considered by teachers more like "herding" than teaching.[35] The first women's clubs and organizations began in 1883 and eventually acquired a Carnegie library.

An effort to abolish drinking succeeded in 1887 and Abilene, remarkably, remained dry until the 1960s. Drinking alcohol could be prescribed through drugstores and bought outside the city limits. Electricity came in 1891 and telephone service in 1895. The greatest difficulty, however, was the shortage of water in a land with a 24-inch annual rainfall. In 1897 the city, unable to sustain itself with the flow of several small creeks, dammed Lytle Creek to form a lake and began a long-term construction of surface reservoirs for the municipal water supply. Water was delivered through redwood pipes.

AMARILLO

The history of Amarillo is similar to that of Abilene except that the railroad was the Fort Worth and Denver City Railway (now Burlington Northern), which was built northwestward from Fort Worth to Wichita Falls through the Panhandle in the 1880s with no state subsidy except right-of-way. A group of Colorado City, Texas, merchants promoted it as a site for their stores, and bought land along the right-of-way at the point of a cattle watering hole. The merchants gave one-fourth of the town site to the railroad as an inducement.

Led by James T. Berry and supported by the LX Ranch, the town was selected as the county seat in 1887. Originally called Oneida, by majority consent it was renamed Amarillo ("yellow" in Spanish), perhaps for the yellow soil, or maybe yellow wildflowers. In celebration, most of the first houses were painted yellow.

The railroad rejected Tascosa, a rip-snorting Panhandle cattle town, and doomed it to oblivion. The FW&DC also passed by Clarendon and Mobeetie. "Old" Clarendon was a prissy Methodist town where a newcomer had to take a temperance pledge in order to purchase real estate. The cowboys called it "Saint's Roost," a good place to die but not to have a good time. A "New" Clarendon arose along the railroad line, where the saintly attitude evaporated in the heat of sin.

Amarillo, consequently, boomed as the major cattle shipping point with its new railroad, holding ground, and pens for the herds of the cattle frontier. In the 1890s the cattlemen loaded one hundred thousand steers per season. Also, buffalo bones left bleaching on the ground from the slaughter of the bison herds fetched $6 per ton for fertilizer. Hundreds of people scavenged and picked the prairie clean as the cattle trails ceased.

Henry B. Sanborn (1845-1912), part owner of the nearby Frying Pan Ranch, warned that the site was too low and subject to flooding. Sanborn and his partner, Joseph F. Glidden, of barbed wire fame, bought land to the east on higher ground, dug wells for a water system, and offered to trade lots from the original site. Sanborn built an elegant hotel that became a social center and business place for ranchers. People slowly had begun to relocate when a prophetic flood covered the old location in 1889. That confirmed Sanborn's prediction and hastened the move. The FW&DC chose a second location with the old depot and courthouse standing for five years by law at the old site. The Pecos Valley and Northern Texas Railroad joined the Santa Fe in Amarillo in 1895, and the Rock Island came to town in 1903. These railroads made Amarillo a Panhandle crossroads that has lasted to the present time.

By the 1890s Amarillo had three newspapers, three churches, public schools, and a population that reached 1,400 by 1900. A red light area briefly flourished in the early twentieth century. It was a time, according to Mary H. Turner, wife of a Santa Fe executive, when men wore unbuttoned vests, big white hats, high-heeled boots, and spurs, and rode cow ponies on the streets. When she arrived from Chicago in 1902 she observed "no sidewalks, no trees, no nothing, and no conversation except 'cattle, cattle, cattle.'" Amarillo had no herd law, and she watched a black bull wander the town, opening gates with its nose and eating the flowers. Taking frequent trips away, she thought, was the only way to make living there possible.[36]

EL PASO

In 1859 Anson Mills (1834-1924), the district surveyor for Forts Quitman, Stockton, Davis, and Bliss, drew up a map for a settlement that had been called variously Ponce's Rancho, Franklin, and Smithville. Mills called it El Paso and the name stuck, although it caused confusion with El Paso del Norte until the Mexican city changed its name to Juárez in 1888. The plat, a compromise between six landowners, revealed two major sections of irregular rectangular blocks, divided for alleys, colliding at a 35-degree angle with San Francisco Street. This resulted in a number of odd-shaped angular blocks at the juncture.

The street names indicated the trading ambitions of the town builders—San Francisco, San Antonio, Overland, Chihuahua, Santa Fe, Oregon, Utah, Kansas. It had a large public square (now San Jacinto Plaza), a small plaza (now Pioneer Plaza), and an acequia from the Rio Grande running eastward that carried drinking water to the inhabitants. A plank in the plaza served as a community bulletin board.

A high protective tariff imposed by Mexico brought a commercial decline on the American side, but in 1858 John Butterfield's 2,700-mile stagecoach line from St. Louis to San Francisco opened with a station at the joining of Oregon, Overland, and El Paso Streets. It took twenty-five days for a stagecoach carrying mail and six passengers to travel from Missouri to San Francisco. This was six days faster than travel by sailing ship around the Horn of South America. El Paso thus became an important way station, with a population of 428 in 1860. The Butterfield line represents the zenith of transportation development for the dirt road frontier.

A list of registered voters in 1867-1869 indicated that all but 82 of the 741 residents were Mexican American.[37] In 1873 El Paso incorporated as a city, elected barkeep Ben Dowell as mayor, and selected six aldermen from three wards. Their first ordinances addressed the care of the acequias—no bathing, no dumping, no watering of dogs or cattle, and one day labor in maintenance by males over eighteen. They also set up fines for swearing in a saloon, drunkenness, stealing, playing marbles for keeps, and creating a disturbance.

In addition, they sought to capture the county seat, which had been moved from San Elizario to Ysleta in 1873. With El Paso gaining population, Ysleta called for an election in 1883 to confirm its position. El Paso rigged the election by importing Mexicans to vote and otherwise stuffing the ballot box. Writer Owen P. White observed that one man voted twelve times for El Paso by changing his clothes and progressively trimming his whiskers from full beard to clean-shaven to alter his appearance. El Paso was thought to have only 300 votes, but it counted out 2,200 and the county seat passed to El Paso. This marked the ascendancy of Anglo political rule. Before 1883 there were five Mexican American county judges, but none afterward.[38]

The most transfiguring event in El Paso history, according to historians C. L. Sonnichsen and W. H. Timmons, however, was the arrival of the railroad. Four major railroads descended on the town in a matter of a few months. El Paso was the target of a race between the Southern Pacific from California and the Texas and Pacific from Fort Worth. With the help of 1,600 Chinese laborers, the Southern Pacific reached the town first, on May 19, 1881, and was built through the heart of the city.

The Southern Pacific continued eastward to meet the Galveston, Harrisburg, and San Antonio, which was being built westward, and to join the Texas and Pacific at Sierra Blanca in December. The Santa Fe Railroad was not far behind, and the Mexican Central was starting construction into Chihuahua from Juárez. Celebration for the Southern Pacific came on May 26, 1881, with roaring cannons from Fort Bliss, bunting in American and Mexican colors, the shriek of the train's whistle, black smoke burping from the stack, oratory, toasts, a banquet, and dancing until midnight.

James P. Hague, who had donated 30 acres for a right-of-way, gave a speech: "The Lone Star, in the splendor of her course, shall now enter the portals of the Golden Gate; the Nereid of the Pacific shall now add to the wealth of her dominion, the chief jewel that once adorned the diadem of the Montezumas." No one understood what he said, but he sounded impressive and everyone thought he was a fine speaker. The crowd applauded with enthusiasm.[39]

The railroads pushed a wave of exploitative humanity into the town—bankers, real estate dealers, merchants, railroad men, cattlemen,

The Southern Pacific built eastward from El Paso and bridged the mouth of the Rio Pecos, where it entered the Rio Grande. This photograph was taken in the 1890s and has been cropped from the original scan. Photographed by Charles B. Turrell, Southern Pacific Sunset Route Photographs, di_03367, the Dolph Briscoe Center for American History, the University of Texas at Austin.

THE RAILROAD TOWNS   137

gamblers, miners, dance hall girls, saloon keepers, and prostitutes. Society was divided into two equal parts for the remainder of the century—the gentility, who wanted a peaceful and improving life, and those who had not come to teach Sunday school.

El Paso became a noted sin city with many saloons—one for every two hundred people—that sported female entertainers who hustled drinks and sat on laps. El Paso was convenient. If there was trouble a miscreant could be across the river into a foreign country within ten minutes. On Utah Street (now South Mesa) a line of bordellos and cribs provided sexual entertainment as well as money from licenses, fines, and taxes for the community. It was impossible for the righteous city officials to forgo the income, and so El Paso abided an uneasy tolerance.

The city hired gunman Dallas Stoudenmire (1845–1882) as marshal in 1881 to keep the peace. The justice who swore him in said, "Do you know what you are expected to do?" Stoudenmire replied, "Yes, and I will do it."

Three days later the six-foot, two-inch marshal engaged in a gunfight that left four people dead in five seconds. One was an innocent bystander. Three days later he gunned down an assassin who tried to kill him with a double-barreled shotgun. This left the town rowdies momentarily quiet. A year later, after he had resigned his El Paso job but while acting as a U.S. deputy marshal, he was killed in a fight with two brothers. The inquest said that it was a fair fight and no prosecution took place.[40] The town breathed easier—this was too much law enforcement—and continued its depraved activity.

The town grew with railroad, army (Fort Bliss), and mining businesses. It jumped from seven hundred to ten thousand residents between 1880 and 1890. "Lungers"—people suffering from tuberculosis—arrived to find health from the dry, desert air. Two newspapers started in 1881, a smelter for New Mexican metals began in 1885, a mule streetcar line started in 1882, and the El Paso Water Company was organized in 1881. Its goal was to provide better water than that of the muddy Rio Grande, which flowed through the main acequia. The company settling tanks failed to clear the mud, however, and the pipes lacked enough pressure to fight fires.

Nevertheless, lumber and brick replaced adobe, an ice company started in 1882, a telephone system began the same year, the first four Protestant churches were organized and shared a tent in 1882, and forty arc electric lights gave the downtown a blaze of light in 1885. A public school district began in 1882, and Miss Mary I. Stanton, a beloved teacher, started an eight-hundred-book library for boys. So many women wanted to use the library that she opened it to the public and moved it to City Hall.[41]

Surprising in this rough border culture was the McGinty Club, of some one hundred male musicians, which lasted through the 1890s. It began in 1889 when H. F. Heckelman, a mandolin player, taught his ebullient partner in the assay business, Dan W. Reckhart, to play a guitar and they began to play duets on their porch. Others joined and they began to have regular drinking parties that featured their signature tune: "Down Went McGinty." They began a club that charged one dollar and banned anyone who talked about politics.

The club sponsored grand parties, performed at civic occasions, marched in parades, and spawned subgroups of quartets, choirs, fife and drums, and banjos. It fed members into a symphony orchestra and counterbalanced the wickedness of the city with joyous and spontaneous fun.[42] It celebrated the advent of electric streetcars in 1902, for instance, by giving old, gray "Mandy," the last working mule of the mule cars, a ride in a special coach with a twelve-piece McGinty band.[43]

At the end of the century a surge of immigration due to unemployment and dislocations in Mexico gave Hispanics a majority of the population. The population totaled sixteen thousand and included three hundred leftover male Chinese rail workers who had remained behind to open laundries and restaurants. They lived in seclusion and contributed opium dens to the attractions of the sin city. Once the Chinese Exclusion Act of 1882 took hold, El Paso became a major smuggling point for Chinese immigration through Mexico to San Francisco and New York City.[44]

Some blacks lived in the city after the Civil War, but a black man in army uniform was a target of abuse. There were 466 blacks in the city according to the twelfth census, in 1900. The excessive number of males of all colors, often found in a frontier town, was only 3 percent at this point. El Paso was becoming more concerned about families, and this spelled doom for the overt sin of the city in the new century.[45]

16

THE LUMBER TOWNS

Sash mills with a single blade that moved up and down, held in a frame and powered by water or animals, existed in early Texas, and Santa Anna at Harrisbug destroyed the first steam-powered sawmill in 1836. Such mills, cutting only on the down stroke, produced but one board at a time. After steam-driven circular saws were introduced at the end of the Civil War the lumber mills could produce 25,000 board feet per day. As the forests of the North and the white pine trees of the Great Lakes region became scarce, the yellow-pine timber of East Texas, northeast of Houston to the Red River, became important. Lumberjacks floated logs down the Neches and Sabine Rivers to small sawmills, but rail access into the forests created the first great bonanza of the region in the last two decades of the century.

Early Houston promoters had built the Texas and New Orleans Railroad east and west from Beaumont to connect Houston with Orange near the Louisiana border in 1862. The founders had originally thought to tap into the lumber market and reach New Orleans, but the Civil War intervened. The line served instead for military transport, suffered poor maintenance, and eventually sank into receivership. It was restored in 1876 and purchased by Collis P. Huntington for the Southern Pacific in 1881 as a part of his southern transcontinental system. At Beaumont, founded

Logging provided an East Texas bonanza at the end of the century. Photograph courtesy of the East Texas Photographic Collection, the Dolph Briscoe Center for American History, the University of Texas at Austin.

as a small lumber town in 1840 on the Neches River, the railroad stifled a promising steamboat development as the locomotives hauled away all the products of four large sawmills. A zero census population was recorded for 1880; two decades later it was 9,400.

ORANGE

Lumbering also brought prosperity to Orange, on the Sabine River. It was originally called Green's Bluff, after a river boatman, then Madison after President James Madison, and then, to avoid confusion with Madisonville, it was named Orange when incorporated in 1858. It was selected as the county seat when the new county of Orange was created in 1852. The name derived from a local orange grove.

The town stood on the southern edge of the Piney Woods, and when the T&NO reopened in 1876, lumbermen Henry Jacob Lutcher and G. Bedell Moore, both from Pennsylvania, visited. Their eastern trees were diminishing, and the two established a sawmill at Orange the following

THE LUMBER TOWNS   141

year. They set a high standard for their products, produced as much as 100,000 board feet per day, and triggered the yellow-pine boom that engulfed the region.

By 1890 Orange had a population of 3,200, with five churches, a weekly newspaper, public schools, two banks, four hotels, an opera house, waterworks, a fire department, and a lumber exchange. Although Orange shipped cotton, rice, and livestock, shingles and lumber remained the chief industry. In 1897 Arthur Stilwell's Kansas City, Pittsburgh and Gulf Railroad (KCP&G) arrived. It was on its way to establish Port Arthur, with deepwater access through Sabine Pass.

The lake was formed by the confluence of the Sabine and Neches Rivers with a pass to the sea through a five-mile-long tidal outlet replete with shallow sandbars. Stilwell had platted Port Arthur on the western shore of the lake in 1895 and it was incorporated in 1898 with a mayor-council form of government. Viability as a port required, however, the dredging of an expensive canal to deep water at Sabine Pass that was not completed until 1899. At that point Stilwell lost control of the project to promoter John W. Gates.

THE TRAIN WHISTLE IN THE PINEY WOODS

Meanwhile, Paul Bremond (1810–1885), a successful merchant of Houston who had helped start the Houston and Texas Central Railroad in 1855, pursued an interest in penetrating the underexploited Piney Woods. With local financing and state support of 16 sections of West Texas land per mile, Bremond started the narrow gauge Houston East and West Texas Railway (HE&WT) in 1875. Bremond thought that the narrow gauge would be cheaper and more efficient even though the cars swayed on the narrow base. Using log trestles over the rivers, the route ran to the northeast from Houston to Cleveland, Livingston, Lufkin, Nacogdoches, and crossed the Sabine River to connect with Shreveport in 1886. It passed into receivership at Bremond's death in 1885, underwent reorganization, converted to standard gauge in 1894, and in 1899 became a part of the Southern Pacific.

Poor landowners looked upon the pines as an impediment to agriculture and readily sold them as "stumpage," the right to cut marketable trees, usually for less than $2 per acre. Lumbermen established temporary company towns, called "nameless towns" by historians Thad Sitton and James H. Conrad, with a sawmill, quarters for workmen and their families, a commissary, and a tramway into the forest.

Work groups—Anglo, black, Mexican, immigrant European—were segregated. They were poorly paid at $2 per day, ruled by the superintendents, and regulated by the shrill whistle of a mill that called the men to work at dawn and released them at night. With steam-powered machinery the whirring, screaming saws could convert a 30-inch diameter log into 2 × 4 lumber within minutes. It was exhausting, dangerous work at a 25 percent injury rate, but the men neither complained nor unionized. They simply moved on to another job.[1]

As sawmills were being established in the Piney Woods region, John Henry Kirby (1860–1940), a Houston lawyer from Tyler County, successfully combined fourteen companies into the dominating Kirby Lumber Company in 1901, which came to control 320,000 acres of pinelands, 900,000 acres of stumpage, and thirteen sawmills. It was said at the time that the sun did not rise until this vigorous, handsome "Prince of the Pines" rolled over in bed and opened his eyes.

In thirty years, however, the pine forests were gone, the land was barren, and John Henry Kirby was impoverished. Smaller trees had been damaged in the cutting and dragging of the large ones to the flat cars of the tramways. Few at the time thought much about sustainable growth or conservation. That had to wait for the response of the Civilian Conservation Corps and the Great Depression.

17

THE END OF THE DIRT ROAD FRONTIER

One of two major points of consideration about Texas cities at the end of the nineteenth century is that size of population made a difference. According to the census map of 1900, none of the Texas cities measured as much as 250,000, but the urban spine along the Balcones Escarpment was apparent as well as the prominent outliers of Houston, Galveston, and El Paso. All had an economic purpose; all were political centers; some possessed military posts; others had gained educational status; and all were crisscrossed with railways. Larger size made it possible to buy or attract urban amenities that pushed them along to a greater level of complexity and attraction. Population growth with a balance of the sexes generally meant families and a dampening of sin city characteristics.

From the history of Texas cities in the nineteenth century can be deduced some of the results of size. It is an old principle that the larger a nation or city, the greater the division of labor.[1] Yes, and a certain level of population also was needed to finance taxes and bonds. In general, a population of 20,000 was needed to support a fire department; 5,000 for a professional police department; 10,000 for a waterworks; 5,000 for an opera house; 3,000 for a public school system; 15,000 for electric street lights; 22,000 for streetcars; 29,000 for a sewer system.

Weekly newspapers sprang up like dandelions, but daily papers

This train station at Paris, Texas, demonstrates the new locus of the cities. The train stations demanded urban space, influenced architecture, provided shelter for telegraphers, and created a point of access for the cities. Photograph by author.

Trains were exceptional in the nineteenth century, but commonplace by the early twentieth century. Photograph from the collections of the Texas/Dallas History and Archives Division, Dallas Public Library.

required a sales base of at least four thousand. Telephones came to Texas within two years after the demonstration by Alexander Graham Bell at the 1876 Centennial Exposition, but a population of six thousand was necessary for the telephone exchange systems that came ten years later. Although history presents irregularities, population size made a difference. It was a basic prerequisite, and these urban acquisitions were not available in the countryside.

The second major consideration involves the impact of the railroads on Texas. The railroad, accompanied by the clock and the telegraph, had the effect of a "rupture" of Texas society. That is, the penetration into Texas by railroads forever changed city life.[2] Time changed and access to information quickened. The event had a greater effect upon Texans than the economic bonanzas of cattle drives, yellow pine, and oil.

Railroads influenced city planning and architecture, investment, population numbers, and concepts about technology, labor, and business. Of course, there were continuities in Texas life, particularly in the countryside, such as with cotton cultivation, and in the cities with horses and wagons. The periodic monster locomotives rumbling down Main Street, however, demonstrated that conditions were not the same as before the trains. Life in the Texas city had become faster, more precise, more complex.

The great Texas historian Walter Prescott Webb explained the settlement of the West through the use of six-shooters, barbed wire, and windmills in *The Great Plains* (1931). This technology, of course, passed through the cities to the farmers and ranchers. At the same time the transformation of the Texas cities came through the technology of the railroad, the clock, and the telegraph.

★

PART THREE

The Amenities of City Life, 1900–1950

18

THE RURAL TO URBAN SHIFT

In the first half of the twentieth century the accelerating trend of Texas urban growth continued. In 1900 seven cities had twenty thousand or more residents. Dallas, Houston, and San Antonio had twice that number. In 1950 thirty-five cities had twenty thousand or more, while Dallas, Houston, and San Antonio each topped four hundred thousand. A viable town could double its size in a decade. During this extraordinary half-century Texas completed a hierarchy of urban places from small town to metropolis linked by improved transportation systems. Texas became an urban state and learned how to structure its cities for tolerable living. The amenities of urban life replaced those of the countryside and formed a new kind of Texan.

New urban residents came mainly from Texas farms and migration from other states. The nation experienced a widespread rural to urban population shift as farms became mechanized and cities became industrialized. It was in the 1930s, for instance, that efficient tractors replaced horses and mules on the farm. This released the land once used to grow fodder and also the people once used to tend the work animals. Crop reduction programs in the decade, furthermore, added to the shift; 60 percent of the tenants and sharecroppers left the land.

At the turn of the century, 81 percent of Texas blacks worked in rural

TABLE 18.1. Population of Texas, 1900-1950, Percent Urban

YEAR	NUMBER	PERCENT URBAN
1900	3,049,000	17
1910	3,897,000	24
1920	4,663,000	32
1930	5,825,000	41
1940	6,415,000	45
1950	7,711,000	60 (old def.)

Source: *Texas Almanac and State Industrial Guide, 1968-1969* (Dallas: A. H. Belo Corp., 1967), p. 168; Elizabeth Cruce Alvarez, ed., *Texas Almanac, 2010-2011* (Denton: Texas State Historical Association, 2010), p. 418.

agriculture, but they were slowly drawn off with jobs relating to railroads, docks, shipbuilding, lumbering, and oil fields. Black out-migration came only in the first decade. In 1950 blacks were counted as 60 percent urban, the same as the general population. They made up 20 percent of the total Texas population in 1900. By 1950, however, blacks had slipped to 13 percent of the increased total population although their actual numbers had gone up. Mexican Americans passed them at this point to become the largest minority group.[1]

LUBBOCK

The rural to urban shift can be illustrated in the explosive growth of Lubbock, from two thousand in 1910 to seventy-two thousand in 1950, the fastest in Texas. Demographer Winfred G. Steglich found that the newcomers came from open Texas country and small towns. The agricultural hinterland reflected a proportional decline as the city grew. Lubbock was an attractive magnet. It was the retail center of the South Plains, and its population was largely Anglo, male, and young. Fundamentalist Protestant religion was particularly strong, but it was tempered by Texas Technological College, which started in 1923, and by Reese Air Force Base in World War II.[2] During the Great Depression and Dust Bowl, therefore, Lubbock was a special type of boomtown.

It was this mixture, curiously, that nurtured the creativity of Buddy

Holly (1936–1959), who grew up there. While in junior high school he combined the gospel sound of Mahalia Jackson with the western style of Hank Williams, added hiccups and stretched words, and revolutionized the pop music of the mid-1950s.[3] Distant Lubbock possessed the access to materials, teachers, and communications to make that possible.

NEWCOMERS

Foreign immigration into Texas slowed in the late nineteenth century as the state ran out of inexpensive land. The Alien Land Law of 1892, moreover, prohibited ownership of land by foreigners past ten years' time. Migrants thus had to work for others and were forced into the towns. Xenophobia, war, and national immigration laws in the twentieth century, in addition, reduced the overseas flow into the nation. Small numbers of Italians, Greeks, and Russian Jews dribbled into Texas at the end of the nineteenth century. Chinese laborers arrived with the railroads and formed a colony in El Paso. During the abortive attempt to capture Pancho Villa in 1916, General John J. Pershing brought to San Antonio five hundred Chinese workers he had found abandoned in Mexico. Asians, like most other immigrant groups, generally amounted to only small numbers.

The Hispanic story was different. Their numbers sank to a low 4 percent of the population in 1887, but began an upward climb as a result of revolution in Mexico in 1910 to 1920. Upper-class Mexicans fled their home country and enriched San Antonio, Laredo, and El Paso society, while lower-class Mexicans sought safety in irrigated border farms and industry. Mexicans were exempt from the early immigration laws, and the population rebuilt to 13 percent of the Texas population by 1950. Seventy-eight percent of this ethnic group remained true to their Iberian heritage and became town dwellers. In Houston, for instance, the Southern Pacific railroad brought in Mexican laborers who gathered with refugees of the Mexican Revolution in Magnolia and El Segundo barrios east of downtown, near the ship channel industries. They developed into a viable community in the 1920s.[4]

In addition, outside winds of global dimensions far beyond Texas control influenced this urban growth. Technology and discovery in the eastern United States and Europe made petroleum valuable for lubrication and fuel. At first used to light lamps, it shortly became useful in locomotives and automobiles. When oil was discovered at Corsicana and then on the Gulf Coast, it started a bonanza that brought wealth and employment to the state for an indeterminate future. In addition, the raking gales of World War I, the Great Depression, and World War II swept over the state and forced a reaction from the cities and their inhabitants. Notably, this eruptive era began with two spectacular events.

19

THE GREAT GALVESTON STORM

Galveston, with a population of thirty-eight thousand in 1900, was the fourth largest city in Texas. It possessed the best port on the Texas coast, the state medical school, domination of the cotton trade, powerful banks, and a tropical ambiance that attracted tourists. It was vulnerable to hurricanes, however, with an elevation of only 8.7 feet above sea level. Escape to the mainland two miles distant was by boat, a wagon bridge, or a railroad bridge. Although the island had been struck before and people knew what had happened at Indianola, they nonetheless generally felt invulnerable to storms. They didn't think about it much. The tropical ambiance was soporific.

The United States Weather Service was in its infancy, and although Galveston had had a weather station since 1871, the prediction of hurricanes, their intensity, and their trajectory was largely guesswork. In September 1900 the service informed Isaac Cline, the resident climatologist, by telegraph that a hurricane had swept across Florida and was at sea somewhere between New Orleans and Galveston. He watched and noted slowly dropping barometric pressure, long waves breaking upon the beach, and a tide rising above normal.

Cline later wrote, "The storm swells were increasing in magnitude and frequency and were building up a storm tide which told me as plainly as though it was a written message that a great danger was approaching."[1] He advised people who lived along the beach to seek higher ground and sent the dreaded hurricane-warning flags—two large red flags with a black square in the center flying in tandem—up the flagpoles into the whipping wind to warn the populace.

Thus, there was a warning, but no one knew how bad it would be. The hurricane struck on Saturday evening, September 8, 1900, and even Clines' family in a fortified house was swept away in the swirling waters. The storm would be classified today as a level 3 or 4 hurricane. Measured wind speed reached 84 miles per hour before the anemometer blew down, and gusts probably reached 120 miles per hour. It created a storm tide of 14.5 feet that rolled into the town, tore to pieces 3,600 homes, and left a head-high, 30-block line of urban debris parallel to the gulf shore.

As the wind of the vortex shifted, the water of Galveston Bay flooded into the city from the mainland side, as happened again in 2008 with Hurricane Ike. The 1900 storm caused $30 million in damages and killed an estimated six thousand people, about one-sixth of the population. In terms of mortality from a natural disaster, the Galveston storm remains the largest in United States history.

During the emergency neighbors helped each other. Hysteria was largely absent and looting was minimal, contrary to media hyperbole. The next day Mayor Walter C. Jones established the Central Relief Committee, made up of civic leaders to take care of finances, burials, hospitals, relief work, correspondence, and cleanup. The Texas militia arrived to assume police work and manage the problem of convergence, where sightseers flock in and interfere with rescue work. Fortunately, Galveston was two miles off the mainland, so sightseer access was limited.

Men, black and white, were pressed into the service of cleanup, repair, and body disposal. Because of supersaturated soil, bodies could not be buried, so they were burned on piles of scrap lumber. Texas and the nation immediately responded with donations of money, food, and clothing.

Clara Barton and the national Red Cross appeared eleven days after the event and began to help with relief distribution. Her appearance, although late, confirmed the seriousness of the disaster to the nation and rallied the upper-class women of Galveston to take a role alongside the men in the distribution of clothing and food. This inspired women to take a greater role in health, politics, and urban preservation in the years to come.[2]

Cremation pyres burned into November, but the telegraph and water system were restored in the first week, the roads and alleys were cleared in the second week, and a train arrived over a repaired bridge at the beginning of the third week. Martial law then was lifted, assistance groups went home, saloons reopened, electric trolleys began to run, and freight began to move across the docks. On October 14, six weeks after the hurricane, a shipment of 30,300 bales of cotton cleared the port. By this time Galveston was back in operation, but a question of long-term survival remained.

As often happens in disasters like this, people are determined to defy nature and rebuild. In this instance this emotion was known as the "Galveston Spirit." For survival, leaders decided to build a seawall for protection against the force of hurricane waves, to raise the level of the island to decrease flooding, and to construct an all-weather escape bridge to the mainland. It was a bold technological response, and the city consulted leading national engineers for suggestions.

Using tax forgiveness by the state and money from county bonds, Galveston completed three miles of a 17-foot-high concrete wall in 1904. It was later extended to 10.4 miles with a magnificent marine drive on

Children at Galveston play in the slurry of sand and seawater from the bay, pumped under houses and buildings to raise the grade level. Photograph courtesy of the Rosenberg Library, Galveston, Texas.

The triumphal opening of an all-weather causeway to the mainland from Galveston Island, 1912. Photograph courtesy of the Rosenberg Library, Galveston, Texas.

top. To diminish flooding and to provide solid backing for the wall, the city sponsored raising the land elevation with bay sand from the top of the wall down in a gentle slope across the island to the harbor. This required lifting houses and buildings with jacks so that sand-slurry could be pumped underneath. The effort was not completed until 1911. The all-weather, arched, concrete causeway, financed by the railroads and the county, accommodated a 19-foot roadbed and three railroad lines. It opened in 1912.

It was a great urban accomplishment. Galveston was protected and survived, but there were unforeseen costs. The physics of wave action and seawalls, unknown at the time, resulted in washing away the beach right up to the wall. A century later Galveston, as well as other such places, required periodic renourishing of the beach with imported sand. It was essential for a tourist town.

In addition, sand barrier islands shift, as can be seen at Galveston, where sand accumulates at one end of the seawall and is lost at the other.

This brings into legal contention people who have had the moving beach disappear from under their houses. The state has claimed long-standing public ownership of the beach up to the vegetation line of the dunes. What do you do with houses left standing on posts in the water?

For Galveston, too, the timing of history was unfortunate. The hurricane struck with its well-published results shortly before the beginning of the oil bonanza on the Gulf Coast. What oil company would want to place its storage facilities, pipelines, and refinery at such a risky place? The oil companies, including those that attracted Galveston investors, located in safer places, and the Island City lost out while it spent its energy and treasure on survival.[3]

20

SPINDLETOP AND BEAUMONT

Four months after the Galveston hurricane, on the Spindletop salt dome south of Beaumont in eastern Jefferson County, Captain Anthony F. Lucas, an Austrian mining engineer, tapped into the most spectacular oil pool in Texas history. The Spindletop well erupted with so much force that it spit six tons of drilling pipe back through the top of the derrick. When it quieted, Allen W. Hamill, a farm boy from Corsicana turned oil driller, investigated:

> I walked over and looked down the hole there. I heard—sorta heard something kinda bubbling just a little bit and looked down there and here this frothy oil was starting up. But it was just breathing like, you know, coming up and sinking back with the gas pressure. And it kept coming up and over the rotary table and each flow a little higher. Finally it got—came up with such momentum that it just shot up clear through the top of the derrick.[1]

Imagine—a person walking across a shaking wooden drilling rig and looking down the drilling hole. The well sprayed a million barrels of oil over the countryside in nine days before it was stopped with a makeshift blowout diversion pipe. The next six gushers in the developing field produced more oil per day than the rest of the fields in the world added together.[2]

The Spindletop field was astounding. The state issued 491 oil company charters during the year, and the gushers brought such production that petroleum briefly sold for three cents per barrel in the field at Beaumont while drinking water sold for five cents per cup. The sensational discovery made newspaper headlines around the nation and altered the course of world history.

In Beaumont hundreds of speculators got off the special excursion trains from Houston, hired hacks for $10 to ride the rutted dirt road to the oil site, reserved cots or chairs in hotels for sleeping, and traded leases on the street or at the impromptu oil exchange of the Crosby House hotel. Restaurants, cafes, and saloons ran out of food and drink. Visitors, suffering with stomach troubles caused by drinking the public water, which came untreated from the Neches River, anxiously waited in line to use the downtown public toilets. Boys made money as professional line standers who would sell their places in line to the highest bidder.

The frenzy continued into the summer. Local hardware companies began to deal in oil field supplies, drillers hawked their services, homeowners offered boarding houses, brothels that endured until 1961 opened in the center of town, and new companies emerged from the chaos—Gulf, Texaco, Magnolia, and Humble Oil and Refining. The key to their successful growth was to hedge drilling bets with multiple investments. The Texas Company (Texaco), for example, had assets that included wells, refineries, storage tanks, pipelines, investors, and politicians.[3]

In that decade the city doubled in size to twenty-one thousand. Oil field work paid twice the going rate for inexperienced labor and as much as $15 per day for experienced drillers. Workmen poured into town.[4] The Magnolia Refinery (Mobil Oil Company in 1959) became the largest employer as oil replaced the prominence of the town's lumber mills.

After the Corps of Engineers channelized the Neches River in 1908 to Port Arthur, both the towns became seaports for refinery products. A turning basin with a 25-foot depth and a shipyard was added in 1916. During World War II these facilities became particularly significant for shipbuilding and oil refining.

Overcrowded housing in the segregated town, food shortages, Ku Klux Klan agitation (the KKK controlled the city in 1922-1924), Juneteenth celebration preparations, and rumors of two rapes of white women by black men combined to create a race riot between blacks and whites on June 15-16, 1943. Some two thousand white workers from the Pennsylvania shipyard marched on City Hall, broke into black stores, and burned terrorized black neighborhoods. Mayor George Gary called in the Texas National Guard, sealed off the highways, closed the parks and liquor stores, and arrested 206. Three people died, and twenty-nine were prosecuted for assault, unlawful assembly, and arson. Martial law lasted five days. Beaumont thus joined Detroit, New York, Philadelphia, and others on the list of bloody race riots of summertime 1943.

21

THE OIL TOWNS

A modest, shallow oil field had developed at Corsicana in 1894 after the town attempted to locate artesian water and discovered oil seeping into the wells. The find gave experience of oil field work to local farm boys, taught them rotary drilling techniques, and introduced them to the pollution difficulties of leaking storage tanks.

The Howard R. Hughes drilling bit of revolving cones, which could penetrate hard rock, James Abercrombie's blowout device, which could contain gushers, and the science of geophysics pioneered by Everett Lee DeGolyer, which reduced the chances of a dry hole by one-half, gradually improved the industry. Steel storage tanks, pipes, and derricks replaced wood as the oilmen penetrated into pools as deep as 4,000 feet in the 1930s. Welded, seamless, steel pipelines able to withstand heavy pressure evolved to allow the first long-distance gas transmission lines to Wichita Falls, Dallas, and Fort Worth from the Panhandle in 1926.

Petroleum was a far better energy source than coal. A test in 1913 to evaporate 1,000 pounds of water, for example, revealed that it took 30 cents worth of coal and only half as much for fuel oil. Petroleum, moreover, took less space to store. Texas coal use and production, consequently, began to decline.

The various ingredients of petroleum—natural gas, gasoline, kerosene, diesel oil, fuel oil, paraffin, wax, asphalt—boil at different temperatures, so by distillation refineries can separate and capture the components. Thermal cracking of hydrocarbon molecules to provide better gasoline, a technical breakthrough, started in 1913. Refineries to make high-grade gasoline and kerosene followed the bonanza. Joseph S. Cullinan (1860-1937) of Pennsylvania built the first Texas refinery in Corsicana in 1898.[1]

Refineries, connected by pipelines and railroads to the oil fields, generally gravitated to the seaports along the Gulf Coast. Transportation of products by ship was cheapest, and Texas possessed twenty-six refineries by 1917, mainly in the Beaumont and Port Arthur area. During World War II the "Little Inch" pipeline carried the products of these refineries overland to Linden, New Jersey, safely beyond the reach of German U-boats in the Gulf of Mexico.

As the oil patch replaced the cotton patch in the state, oil-fevered wildcat prospectors fanned out over Texas with visions of Spindletop and black gold burbling in their brains. Their rate of success was about one oil strike in ten attempts, but significant tips were sulphur springs, paraffin dirt, and oil traces in well water. When cattleman William T. Waggoner found oil in his new water wells in 1902, he recalled, "I wanted water, and they got me oil. I tell you, I was mad, mad clean through. We needed water to drink for ourselves and for our cattle to drink. I said damn the oil, I want water!"[2]

By the time the wildcatters were through, however, all but sixteen counties in Texas were known to produce petroleum, and the oil derrick had replaced the longhorn as the symbol of the state. In 1940 the value of oil and gas production exceeded the value of all crops raised in Texas.

Spindletop inspired Gulf Coast exploration of salt domes, often observed as broad bulges on the surface of the ground. In West Texas the major discoveries came in the Permian Basin, an area 300 miles long and 250 miles wide that bordered on New Mexico. The Big Lake discoveries in the southwest corner of Reagan County opened the field in 1923. Located on University of Texas scrublands, these wells enabled the institution to pay cash for professors, libraries, and buildings.

In East Texas Columbus, Marvin "Dad" Joiner, an impoverished independent driller, in 1930 brought in a successful well where experts had said there was no oil. The new field stretched across five counties and inspired 5,600 wells in two years around Kilgore and Longview. Joiner sold out to H. L. Hunt, who went on to become one of the richest men in the United States.

The oil bonanza generated boomtowns with similar growth patterns. First came a discovery well, followed by landsmen who bought leases on land around it. Then came derrick builders, drillers, roustabouts, and tank and pipeline assemblers. Next came a town for supplies, housing, and entertainment, with all the familiar characteristics of boomtowns—predominance of single young males to do the physical work, saloons, dance halls, brothels, poor living conditions, lawlessness, and a scarcity of old people, women, children, families, churches, and schools. The highest pay went to Anglo drillers, while the lowest pay went to blacks and Mexicans working on roads and pipelines, and women in food preparation and laundering.

County police enforced the law and itinerant county attorneys administered the courts. Dr. George Parker, who had gone to Spindletop to start his medical practice, observed at Saratoga a disliked attorney-judge who would arrive in town, round up the pimps and prostitutes, and profit from his usual charge of "vagrancy." He would ask the culprits if they had any visible means of support, and when they could not show any, down would come the gavel.

On one occasion he was surprised when a fifty-year-old, 200-pound prostitute replied that yes indeed she had visible means of support. "Very well, will you please show the court the means of your support, or pay a fine of twenty-five dollars." She did not hesitate; she reached down to catch the bottom of her skirt and began to straighten up.

The courtroom broke into an uproar as the attorney yelled, "Not guilty! Put down your dress. Not guilty!" When the means of her support appeared, the attorney-magistrate shouted, "Court adjourned!" The spectators roared with laughter, grabbed the flustered attorney, rushed him to a saloon, and made him buy drinks for everyone.[3]

The towns were roughhewn, temporary, unhealthy, rowdy, and dangerous. Fires, blowouts, poison gas, insects, snakes, bad water, accidents, and poor sanitation were common hazards. At times temporary "ragtowns," or tent villages, developed in the midst of the derricks, with wives trying to make their quarters as homelike as possible amid the oil smells and muck. House trailers did not arrive until the 1940s, when paved roads and trucks became common. As might be guessed, divorce rates were as high as twenty-four times normal.[4]

Oil boomtowns did not last long because of quickly dropping production, and the workers would move on to the next strike. Within a year the

Spindletop field had more than 440 wells and 138 gushers. The saltdome was punched full of holes, like a pincushion, and the pressure dropped. After yielding 47,000 barrels per day in 1902, it produced but 10,000 per day in 1904. Conservation was ignored because everyone from landowner to roughneck wanted to make as much money as possible in the shortest time. Having moved to other work, Captain Lucas revisited Spindletop in February 1904 and sadly noted the decline. "The cow was milked too hard," he said. "And moreover she was not milked intelligently."[5]

MIDLAND AND ODESSA

These oil towns, 20 miles apart, were at the center of the industry of the Permian Basin. Midland began as Midway Station, a section house of the Texas and Pacific Railway halfway between Dallas and El Paso. Sheep and cattle ranchers moved into the area, and in 1884 the name was changed to Midland in order to obtain a post office that did not conflict with other locations. It became the county seat, with the formation of Midland County in 1885. An Ohio real estate company organized a town site for one hundred families, and with the local newspaper advertising the "Queen City of the South Plains," Midland became a cattle shipping point for six hundred residents by 1890. In the early twentieth century the town had two banks, a stone courthouse, four Christian churches, an opera house, and an aldermanic government that lasted until 1940, when it was replaced by a mayor-council form.

It became known as the "Windmill Town" since almost every residence had a windmill in its yard as a source of water. After three major fires that burned through Midland between 1905 and 1909, however, the town leaders installed a water system and a fire department in 1910—barely in time to stop a fourth downtown fire. Midland had a population of 1,800 in 1920; the population had tripled by 1930 and reached 22,000 by 1950 under the influence of the Permian Basin oil discoveries.

It was a town that attracted oil executives with office and hotel space. Thirty-six oil companies established offices in the 1920s as the town improved with street lighting and street paving. A new four-story courthouse, the twelve-story Hogan office building, and an airport marked its importance in the early 1930s.

Depression relief came from the United States Army Air Corps, which set up a bombardier training school halfway between Midland

and Odessa at Midland Airport. With WPA funds and municipal moneys Midland purchased a private airfield in 1939, improved the runways, and installed landing lights. The city leased it to the United States government for $1 a year. The base hosted a peak population of 4,000 and trained 6,600 bombardier officers before it was deactivated and returned to Midland in 1947.

The Great Depression and the opening of the East Texas oil field forced a cutback, causing unemployment in the first part of the 1930s, but new oil discoveries in the basin, particularly after the war, brought expansion. Retail sales, building permits, and bank deposits jumped five times between 1945 and 1958. Humble Oil moved its district offices to town in 1935, and by the end of the 1950s about 650 oil companies had offices in Midland.[6] It was into this milieu that young George H. W. Bush plunged to seek his fortune after his service in World War II.

Nearby Odessa, to the southwest, like a younger brother, had a similar early history. It started as a water stop for the Texas and Pacific Railway, became the county seat of Ector County in 1891, shipped cattle, and boomed with the discovery of oil in the Permian Basin. Its history tracks the cycles of the oil industry as Odessa supplied the business with equipment and workers.

Its story illustrates the movement of rural people who migrated to the oil patch to perform industrial work in a rural setting. Local agriculture could not support a large population. It was so arid that wastewater quickly evaporated in the sun and garbage thrown out the back door dried rather than rotted. With a 1925 population of 750, Odessa expanded by four times into tents and shotgun houses in the 1930s, and three times more into government villages in the 1940s to reach 29,000 in 1950. Unlike conservative Midland, Odessa found cooperation with its county useful to carry out public health measures and expansion of its schools.[7]

During the postwar period drilling rigs were redesigned to fold like a jackknife so they could be trucked to a job. The town sold $338 million of supplies and pipe in 1948, and workers commuted from Odessa, where they maintained a more-or-less permanent residence. Reflecting the bias of the industry, the population in 1950 was 90 percent Anglo-American. Odessa had a gritty reputation. It developed the country's largest inland petrochemical center and fielded the toughest high school football teams in the state. Carl Weaver, a worker, commented: "Back during the war years you could go to a [night] football game in Odessa and from up in the stands you could see rig lights in a circle all around the town. Those rig lights and the gas flares, they just lit up the countryside."[8]

BORGER

In the Panhandle northeast of Amarillo a town promoter from Oklahoma, Asa P. "Ace" Borger, along with partner John R. Miller, bought a 240-acre town site in 1926 in oil country exploited by Phillips Petroleum. They advertised heavily and attracted forty-five thousand people to this new boomtown in ninety days. Within the year it had a railroad spur, post office, hotel, school district, jail, telephone service, electricity, and a hamburger stand that served the favorite meal of the oil patch. The mayor, a shady associate of Miller, ran a crime group that opened the door to bootleggers, prostitutes, and card sharks as well as to the roughnecks, fortune seekers, and oilmen. Borger became the most notorious of the oil boomtowns and inspired a folk tune:

> Let's sing a song of Borger,
> Famed for its graft and rot.
> It's just a wide place in the road,
> This town that God forgot.
> For this village boasts of deeper sin,
> Than Sodom ever knew,
> Come lend an ear, kind stranger,
> And I'll whisper them to you.[9]

Murder and robbery were commonplace in the dance halls, gambling dens, and brothels. Before it was over "Ace" Borger himself was shot down by Arthur Huey, the county treasurer. Both had been accused of financial irregularities, and Borger refused to help Huey. At the post office Huey accosted Borger and shot him five times with a Colt .45. He then grabbed Borger's gun and fired four more times. At the trial Huey argued self-defense; he said Ace was gunning for him. He was acquitted.

Texas Rangers, martial law, and state troops eventually tamed this town that God forgot, where the criminals were chained to a "trotline" for lawmen from around the state to inspect. One of the last of the famous Texas Rangers, Frank Hamer, worked at Borger. He was wounded seventeen times and left as dead four times. Described as "a giant of a man, moon-faced, always in boots, and as talkative as an oyster," he later successfully ambushed Bonnie Parker and Clyde Barrow, who had robbed banks and murdered people across North Texas.[10] The Great Depression, the Dust Bowl, and the decline of oil prices ended the boom. Borger was a small town of eighteen thousand in 1950.

KILGORE, LONGVIEW, AND DALLAS

In East Texas Kilgore began as a new town platted by the International–Great Northern Railroad in 1872. Named for the landowner, Constantine Buckley Kilgore, the town acquired a post office, gristmill, cotton gin, school district, and a population of 250 by 1885. It grew slowly, suffered from the Great Depression, and had but five hundred residents in the early 1930s, when the East Texas oil discoveries turned Kilgore into a boomtown.

It was in the geographic center of the new activity, and some twelve thousand contractors, roughnecks, and service operators flooded the town. For 50 cents they could rent sleeping space in a cot house for eight hours. The houses had no bathrooms; the men used public baths set up by the city. They drilled 1,100 wells within the city limits, and one downtown block, packed with forty-four derricks, was called "the World's Richest Acre."

Crowds from miles around would gather to see the excitement of blowing out a well fire with an explosion of nitroglycerin, which would deplete the oxygen. Lucille Glasscock, wife of a wildcatter, commented to one of her husband's friends, "I'd hate to live in a home with an oil well in the back yard." The oilman replied with a twinkle in his eye, "Mrs. Glasscock, that's my idea of plumb good landscaping."[11]

To deal with the overwhelming inundation of people, honky-tonks, shacks, tents, and hamburger stands, Kilgore incorporated in 1931. As large oil companies moved to town and gradually bought out the independent producers, the boom quieted, and the population leveled out to 9,600 in 1950. The independent school district in 1935, meanwhile, established Kilgore College, which offered associate of arts degrees and terminal vocational programs.

Notable for entertainment and publicity were the nationally famous Kilgore Rangerettes, a women's precision drill team begun in 1940.

Kilgore, Texas, in 1960. Photograph courtesy of the East Texas Photograph Collection, the Dolph Briscoe Center for American History, the University of Texas at Austin.

President B. E. Masters wanted to recruit more girls for the student body and also, incidentally, to discourage the boys from drinking under the football stands at halftime. He assigned physical education teacher Gussie Nell Davis to solve the problem, and she enlisted local oil millionaire Liggett Crim to pay initial costs.

The result was a strutting, well-trained, saucy, high-kicking line of creative student women wearing signature blouse, gauntlets, short circular skirt, white cowboy hat, and boots. It was the first collegiate women's precision drill team in the world (the New York City professional Music Hall Rockettes started in 1932), and has continued to the current time through succeeding generations of female students. The Kilgore Rangerettes have performed at presidential parades, world tours, and countless collegiate bowl games. When they perform on the field at halftime, the boys stay in their seats.

Longview, located several miles east of the oil field, escaped the boomtown stress of Kilgore. It was a cotton and lumbering town of five thousand when its parent, the Texas and Pacific Railway, moved its division offices to nearby Mineola in 1929. Longview had been quiet after a

THE OIL TOWNS 167

vicious race riot in 1919, sparked by a Chicago newspaper story about a black man in Longview in love with a white woman from Kilgore.

The East Texas oil discovery offered economic protection from the Great Depression, and Longview doubled its population in the 1930s. New business and Southern oil migrants brought in enough tax monies to build schools and a new county courthouse in 1932. During World War II the construction of the Big Inch pipeline began in Longview to carry East Texas crude oil eastward to allow uninterrupted supplies of oil and gas to the northeastern United States. This remarkable one-year effort (1942–1943) utilized a 24-inch welded steel pipe buried in a four-foot deep trench that crossed the Mississippi River and stretched 1,300 miles to New York and Philadelphia. It was sold as war surplus after the war to Texas Eastern Transmission Corporation of Houston for the transportation of natural gas.

Dallas was but 120 miles away and prepared to exploit the oil market. Dallas had been awarded a Federal Reserve System regional bank in 1914 through the lobbying efforts of local bankers and businessmen. Although it was a "bankers' bank," the FRS bank gave Dallas prestige and commercial backing for the industry. It made Dallas the financial center and leader of the southwest, an area encompassing New Mexico, Oklahoma, Texas, Louisiana, and Arkansas. Texas was no longer linked to Missouri and the Old South.

When the East Texas oil strike occurred, Industrial Dallas, Inc., a promotional organization, printed five thousand advertisements to portray Dallas as an oil headquarters and mailed them to the small, scattered oil companies in the region. Telephone and telegraph communications were set up in the small towns of the oil region, and the Dallas banks, particularly the First National, led by Nathan Adams, pioneered petroleum loans. He figured oil in the ground was like a warehouse filled with cotton. Magnolia and Sun Oil Companies set up Dallas headquarters, and oil magnates such as H. L. Hunt and Clint W. Murchison called the North Texas city "home." Dallas, thus, established itself as a financial and service center for the East Texas oil field.[12]

OIL CONSERVATION

The East Texas oil boom engendered a crisis of preservation and marketing. It was overwhelming. The East Texas field was 42 miles long and between 5 and 12 miles wide. It stretched across five counties, and 3,500-feet deep wells could tap a Woodbine oil sand that was high gravity and free of sulphur, just what the nearby coastal refineries preferred for gasoline.

Compelled by the "law of capture," people still drilled as fast as possible to prevent others from sucking the oil from underneath them. It was wasteful. Conservationists, landowners, the oil industry, and the Texas legislature splintered on courses of action. Through a protracted, involved struggle the Texas Railroad Commission (TRC), a trusted agency, eventually gained the authority to limit the rate of production of every well in order to stabilize prices and promote preservation. It was no easy task. Small producers resented government interference, and at a low point in 1931, oil sold at two cents per barrel. The situation was not resolved until the United States and Texas passed "hot oil" laws in 1935 to prevent the shipment of illegal oil.

HOUSTON, THE OIL CAPITAL

At the beginning of the oil bonanza in 1900, Houston had forty-five thousand residents, a radiating railroad network, a cotton economy, banks, and soaring ambition. Although larger by three thousand and dominant in the region, it was still in competition with pre-storm Galveston. Barges carrying cotton bales could thread through Buffalo Bayou, cross shallow Galveston Bay, and reach deepwater ships anchored in Bolivar Roads outside the obstructing sandbar of Galveston harbor. Houston merchants thus could avoid Galveston's dockage fees.

In 1896, however, the United States Army Corps of Engineers completed a 25-foot deep channel through an inhibiting sandbar to keep Galveston the leading harbor of Texas. Deep draft ships could now move directly to the docks. This event resuscitated an old Houston ambition to dredge Buffalo Bayou and Galveston Bay for a ship channel to the sea, and in the same year that Galveston opened its sandbar, Houston congressional representative Joseph C. Hutcheson introduced a bill to dig a 25-foot channel through Buffalo Bayou.

Delays, inspections, and political intransigence followed. Among other governmental demands, Houston had to quit using the bayou as a sewer. The city therefore approved a $300,000 bond issue to construct an advanced sewerage system designed by engineer Alexander Potter. It was a success soon neglected after permission for a channel had been gained.

In 1902, through the work of Congressman Thomas H. Ball (1859-1944), Houston received $1 million for the channel. The U.S. Army Corps of Engineers dredged an 18.5-foot deep watercourse in 1908 with a turning basin just above Harrisburg. Twenty-five foot depth, however, was necessary for ships at the time.

Mayor H. Baldwin Rice and Congressman Ball then devised a county navigation district to control the watercourse, sell bonds, and offer matching funds to the United States. At the insistence of banker Jesse H. Jones (1874-1956), Houston banks bought the unmarketable bonds in proportion to their capital. In 1914 the channel reached a 25-feet depth and oceangoing ships began to arrive. The ships bypassed Galveston, and, thus, Houston triumphed over its old rival.

Much more important was the role of the ship channel in the evolution of the oil industry. Oil field discoveries dotted the land around Houston, and just as refineries and oil facilities gravitated to ports at Beaumont and Port Arthur, so they came to the Houston Ship Channel. Access to deepwater shipping was the goal.

In 1905 petroleum from the Humble field a few miles north of Houston

The Houston Ship Channel in 1914, with a ship in the turning basin. The channel became the key facility for the success of the Bayou City. Photograph courtesy of the Houston Public Library, HMRC.

moved by rail and pipeline to Houston. Gulf Oil set up a mixing plant on the ship channel in 1915 with a pipeline to Port Arthur and the Goose Creek field. Galena-Signal built a refinery in 1916, Sinclair in 1918, Deep Water Refineries in 1919, Crown Oil and Refining in 1920, and Humble Oil and Refining in 1920. By 1930 eight refineries along the ship channel amounted to a $200 million investment.

Management also gravitated to Houston—the Texas Company in 1908, Gulf Oil in 1916, Humble Oil and Refining in 1917, and Shell Oil regional offices in 1933. They came to take advantage of banking and manufacturing opportunities.[13] Joseph Cullinan had prophesied the future leadership of Houston, and in 1908, when his Texas Company had outgrown its offices in Beaumont, he led the way to the Bayou City. He became president of the Houston Chamber of Commerce and from 1915 through 1919 vigorously worked to gain federal monies for construction and maintenance.[14] Other businesses found the ship channel an attractive site for manufacturing fertilizer, sulphuric acid, flour, and cement. More than fifty businesses had located along the waterway by 1935, and 40 percent of Texas petroleum moved out through the channel. Size and corporate affinity proved to be a magnet for the growth of Houston.

22

THE ELITE RULE OF THE CITIES

In the first half of the twentieth century, businesspeople in the towns and cities manipulated the development of their hometowns through a chamber of commerce. Elected officials were simply selected, influenced, nominated, and directed. In the larger places, where an open chamber of commerce was unwieldy, influential businessmen met informally to decide their town's fate.

The elite did not ignore the elected officials, who were often of their choosing. They were not unkind or vindictive, and were often philanthropic. Although oligarchic in nature, the elite were usually wealthy, intelligent, and beneficent toward their city. Generally, their attitude was that what was good for the city was good for them too.

Elite influence lasted into the 1960s, when the civil rights movement inspired competing political groups of blacks, Hispanics, gays, environmentalists, and women. Academics referred to such early business leaders as the "power elite," and in Texas their history begins in Galveston.[1]

GALVESTON

During the trauma of the 1900 hurricane, members of the Deep Water Committee (DWC), a loose organization of leading businessmen originally established to promote harbor improvements, secretly plotted to replace the aldermanic government of the city, which they had been unable to manipulate. They proposed a new commission form whereby the state governor would appoint commissioners for specific departments—finance and revenue, police and fire, water and sewage, streets and public improvements, along with a mayor. The DWC pointed to the success of the Central Relief Committee for hurricane recovery and presented their ideas to a convention in Fort Worth.

The scheme was patently undemocratic. No referendum on the idea was held at home; the DWC simply asked the legislature for a charter change, and elite control of the newspapers muted discussion. Heavy propaganda about the ineptitude of the old council flowed one way. The first edition of William B. Munro's textbook on city governments in 1912, for example, absorbed the criticism and condemned pre-storm Galveston as "one of the worst governed urban communities in the whole country." In the fourth edition (1926), after he had learned more, Munro moderated his opinion with, "The government of the city was no better, and perhaps no worse, than that of many other American communities of its size and type."[2]

With the approval of the Galveston state representatives, the legislature changed the charter, but required the election of two of the commissioners to maintain a semblance of democracy. This was done and in September 1901, one year after the storm, the commission government took over. Isaac H. Kempner, who had been treasurer under the old government, remained as the appointed commissioner of finance and revenue.

The new council could not prevent a default on city bonds—something unprecedented—which prevented further financing from New York. Kempner, however, negotiated a lower interest rate on the remaining bonds. He also gained approval of the sale of county bonds and relief from state taxes to support the local sale of city bonds. Thus, the city acquired the funding to support the reconstruction to protect Galveston from the ravages of the sea. It was the Galveston government that arranged the successful rebuilding, but it was a myth that a commission government form was necessary for success.[3]

In America the commission plan became popular before World War I with progressives and reformers, but then declined in favor of the city-manager structure after 1920. The commission plan possessed basic flaws; commissioners were individually elected with no obligation to cooperate with each other, and at-large elections diluted minority voting strength.

Seventy-five Texas cities, including Houston, Dallas, Fort Worth, San Antonio, and El Paso, nonetheless temporarily adopted an elective commission plan in the early twentieth century. Houston, Dallas, and Fort Worth gave up the plan after twenty years; Galveston, one of the last, finally changed in 1960.[4] Texas cities, meanwhile, reverted to some form of mayor-council arrangement, often with a professional city manager and at-large voting for council members.

Galveston never regained its upward movement, becoming instead a middle-sized city with a port, medical school, military posts, and growing tourism. Moderate military activity began in 1897 with the building of Fort Crockett, for coast artillery, and a thousand men camped on the beach for the Spanish-American War. Rebuilt after the hurricane, Fort Crockett became a mobilization point for the border difficulties with Mexico and for World War I. It was active in coastal defense during World War II, but most of the trainees were assigned to Camp Wallace, on the mainland near Hitchcock.

Military restrictions and pressure closed the infamous brothels of Galveston's Post Office Street during the two world wars. The red light district flourished openly in between times, and clandestinely at others. The prostitutes fed off the merchant seamen of the port, soldiers, medical students, local men, and tourists. It was world class in terms of numbers of prostitutes. Combined with open gambling and drinking during prohibition, prostitution created the "Free State of Galveston," as it was called, which defied all law enforcement.

Four influential, wealthy, dynastic, elite families ruled the city. The Moody, Sealy, and Kempner families ran the economy, set the standards of society, and directed politics. The Moody family was rooted in cotton, banking, and life insurance; the Sealy family made a fortune from railroads, banking, oil, and the port; and the Kempner family successfully invested in railroads, real estate, cotton, life insurance, and sugar refining. All possessed philanthropic instincts and interest in their hometown. The Moodys eventually established a Texas foundation dedicated to education; the Sealys donated to the welfare of the University of Texas Medical Branch; and the Kempners maintained an abiding interest in local politics.

A fourth family, the Maceos, was criminal, like a Mafia group. It controlled illegal gaming, served mixed drinks at nightclubs, and smuggled liquor during prohibition. Bawdy houses, incidentally, were owner

The remainder of the last brothel on Post Office Street in Galveston. The brothels closed in the 1950s. Photograph by author.

The Balinese Room, located at the end of a pier extending into the Gulf of Mexico, was the premier gambling casino of the Maceo operation in the 1950s. Its remnants were destroyed by Hurricane Ike in 2008. Photograph by author.

operated, and the Maceos were not known to be involved in any illicit drug trade except liquor.

Local police, judges, and the ruling families remained complacent about the Maceo operation, but in the 1950s the United States Internal Revenue Service and state attorney general began to apply pressure to shut them down. Court injunctions shuttered the bingo palaces and brothels, while Texas Rangers dumped confiscated slot machines into Galveston Bay. The threatening indictments scattered the criminal element to Hot Springs and Las Vegas. Meanwhile, Sam and Rosario Maceo, the patriarchs, died, and the Galveston organization fell apart. Thus ended the "Free State of Galveston." Councilwoman Ruth Levy Kempner later commented, "We'll obey the law. Galveston is not a place apart."[5] The Island City became a place for family recreation.

HOUSTON

The Houston power elite, ten or so, gathered regularly at George Brown's Lamar Hotel Suite 8F from 1930 to 1970 for informal talks. Leaders included Jesse H. Jones, Houston booster, real estate magnate, a principal fund-raiser for the building of the Houston Ship Channel, and head of the Reconstruction Finance Corporation during the Great Depression; George and Herman Brown, national large-scale construction contractors; James A. Elkins, Sr., banking lawyer; Gus Wortham, founder of American General Insurance Company; James Abercrombie, oil entrepreneur and founder of Cameron Iron Works; Leon Jaworski, lawyer in national politics; R. E. "Bob" Smith, oil and real estate owner; William Hobby, former governor; and Oveta Culp Hobby, the owner of the *Houston Post* newspaper and the only woman.[6] These were powerful, rich people, with extensive connections to diverse institutions. They interconnected on corporate boards and belonged to the same clubs.

No one took notes; no minutes exist. There are just fleeting references buried in personal papers and interviews about opinions and activities. Economic historian Joe R. Feagin claimed that members embraced a free enterprise, laissez-faire ideology that allowed for governmental help for infrastructure improvement that would aid business. They encouraged the Houston Chamber of Commerce to deal with particular problems; honored donation to the arts, education, and hospitals; reached out to local, state, and national political leaders; supported racial segregation and low taxes; and resisted unions, real estate regulations, and zoning. Gus Wortham, for example, did not particularly care for classical music, but he nonetheless supported the Houston symphony. While sitting for a portrait Wortham commented to the artist, "Young man, I don't profess to understand music. I'm not even sure I like it, but it's a damn fine thing for the community!"[7]

Largely, the elite worked behind the scenes and did not take an onstage role. For example, in the 1950s the group foresaw the need to build a larger international airport and bought land north of town. They held it until the city council came to the same conclusion and then sold it to the city at no profit. Gus Wortham raised money for the Fondren Library and for a new stadium at Rice University. The Brown brothers constructed the graceful stadium at cost.

An instructive exception to their quiet work came in the 1950s during a noisy controversy over control and funding of a new charity hospital. Baylor Medical School and the Harris County Medical Society squabbled over control of staffing and the location of the new hospital. Baylor won, but funding was a problem and the Harris County Medical Society resisted the establishment of a city-county taxing district. It was turned down four times by the electorate.

Meanwhile, a stubborn staphylococcus infection at the old charity hospital, Jefferson Davis, began to kill babies early in 1958. It was eventually controlled, but the hospital lost its accreditation. This was followed by a devastating portrayal of the hospital in 1964 by Jan de Hartog, a Quaker volunteer who wrote a book that described patients screaming in the night as cockroaches looking for blood tried to get under their bandages.[8]

At this point Leon Jaworski (1905-1982), a member of the Suite 8F group, gathered the signatures of sixty leading Houstonians and asked the city council to schedule yet another election for a hospital district. This time the Harris County Medical Society remained silent and the hospital district was approved in 1965.[9] At least for the moment, the charity hospital had adequate funding. In this case the elite ended a problem that was damaging the reputation of the city and also added to the growth of the Texas Medical Center, which ultimately became the largest employer of the city. It was an action that was beneficial both for the city and for business.

In the 1970s the group lost its influence because of the deaths and aging of key members. The expansion of the city, moreover, brought more executives and corporations from the outside that looked to the Houston Chamber of Commerce as the central organization for business.[10]

DALLAS

After working hard to coordinate the centennial celebration in Dallas, banker Robert L. "Bob" Thornton (1880-1964) said to a friend that what Dallas needed was an organization of bosses, "yes or no" men who would meet, work out solutions to city problems, commit their companies, and not have to return to their offices for permission. Instead of arguing policy in the newspapers, this group would settle problems in private and present the public with a single option. The emphasis would be on unity. It would be a "dydamic [sic] kind of organization," said the folksy Thornton, of people who could get things done.[11] Significantly, while he was mayor, 1953-1961, Thornton refused a desk at City Hall and operated from his office at the Mercantile Bank.

In November 1937, consequently, the state chartered the Citizens Council as a nonpolitical organization for civic and educational purposes. Membership was by invitation only and included prominent bankers, manufacturers, merchants, newspaper publishers, and insurance men. Professional people and labor leaders were more or less excluded; the Citizens Council did not intend to be representative. Its purpose was to promote Dallas as a whole while its surrogate, the Citizens Charter Association (CCA), took care of political matters and the chamber of commerce boosted business. It worked quietly and remained unnoticed until outside reporters probed the leadership of Dallas after the assassination of John F. Kennedy.

The Citizens Council was a formalized power elite with a state charter. It was run by an internal council of twenty-five that met monthly. The core leaders—Robert Thornton, who became mayor; Fred F. Florence of the Republic National Bank; Karl Hoblitzelle, chairman of the board at the Republic National Bank; and C. A. Tatum Jr. of Dallas Power and Light were all committed to the good of Dallas. The council supported slum clearance and federal low-cost housing for blacks after an exposure of dire living conditions by the local black newspaper, the *Dallas Express*, in 1938. The city then completed a series of low-rent housing developments in 1941-1942.

When Chance-Vought Aircraft needed a longer runway in order to move from Connecticut to Dallas, a phone call to D. A. Huley, the current president of the Citizens Council, solved the problem. In less than four hours the City Council voted to supply $256,000 to do the work. The Citizens Council mounted a massive advertising campaign to prepare for the inevitable integration of the public schools in 1960 and persuaded the media to downplay conflict and stress the benefits of peaceful desegregation.

During the 1970s, however, the Citizens Charter Association lost its political authority due to the interests in the city beyond the influence of business. New corporations, moreover, arrived and set up headquarters in the surrounding suburbs. Independent candidates challenged city council positions, and minorities demanded attention after the city council expanded from nine to eleven members.

Wes Wise, a popular independent radio and television newsman, was elected mayor in 1974 without CCA endorsement. In 1976 the CCA ceased making political recommendations, and although the Citizens Council of downtown business elites continued, it had lost its political arm and its power over the fate of Dallas.[12]

FORT WORTH

The Fort Worth Board of Trade, which had advocated the commission plan of Galveston at the turn of the century, became the chamber of commerce in 1912. Its energizing spirit and youngest president was Amon Carter (1879-1955), the owner of the *Star-Telegram* newspaper. He was *the* power elite of the town and Vice President John Nance Garner of Texas remarked, "That man wants the whole government of the United States to be run for the exclusive benefit of Fort Worth." Senator Tom Connally said, "The gates open when he comes to Washington and the Treasury Department puts on extra guards because they know he will take back some money for a civic improvement in West Texas."[13]

With his signature narrow-brimmed Stetson hat, Carter was known throughout the country. He was instrumental in bringing oil and aircraft companies to the city; he built radio and television stations; he championed Texas Christian and Texas Tech Universities; and at his death he donated a premier art museum for his collection of Russell and Remington paintings.

Carter was unforgettable and irrepressible. He referred to rival Dallas as "Big d." At the 1928 Democratic Convention in Houston he shot the Rice Hotel elevator with a pistol after becoming frustrated when the elevator passed him four times. He lost patience, grabbed a sheriff's .45-caliber pistol, and shot through the glass doors six times into the elevator shaft. No one was injured and the next time the elevator stopped.[14] Maybe the elevator would have stopped anyway, but this reckless event appealed to people caught in a similar situation.

A shadow group of businessmen known as the "Seventh Street Gang" followed Carter's lead. It was made up of H. B. Fuqua, chair of the Fort Worth National Bank; Sid Richardson, oilman; J. B. Thomas of the Texas Electric Company; W. P. Bomar, president of Bewley Mills; and Marvin Leonard and W. K. Stripling, both department store owners. It was informal, and like the Houston 8-F group, it met periodically to discuss the welfare of the city. These men were involved in the establishment of a regional airport, various philanthropic efforts, and the quiet integration of the city in the 1960s.[15]

CORPUS CHRISTI

In smaller places city promotion and leadership came from the chambers of commerce and mayor's offices rather than emanating from a shadowy power elite. An example is the history of Corpus Christi and its "boy mayor," Henry Pomeroy "Roy" Miller (1884-1946). He moved to Corpus Christi as an agent to sell railroad land to farmers for Robert Kleberg of the King Ranch. The large southwestern ranchers looked upon Corpus Christi as their town and built large mansions on the chalk bluff overlooking the business area. Miller, noted for his enthusiasm and outgoing personality, married a local woman from a prominent family, edited a newspaper, energized the Commercial Club (chamber of commerce), and became mayor at age twenty-seven, serving in that capacity for three consecutive terms starting in 1913.

Within a few years his administrations had paved 12 miles of asphalt streets, put in streetlights, installed a modern water and sewer system with sand filtration and chlorination, built an incinerator for garbage, organized a professional fire department, landscaped the bluff with a balustrade that still stands, constructed a new city hall, and sought means to make Corpus Christi a deepwater port. This was underscored when gas and oil was discovered at White Point across Nueces Bay in 1913. Basically, Miller led in modernizing his hometown.

In spite of these achievements he lost the election in 1919 after accusations that he had taken donations from businessmen for special civic favors. Gordon Boone, the new mayor, was a law partner of state representative Walter E. Pope, who owned extensive bayfront property. Pope was in cahoots with Archer Parr, the notorious political boss of neighboring Duval County. Governor William Hobby, Kleberg, and Miller had tried but failed to uproot Parr. Confronted with this convoluted political knot, all new work on the city halted, and the business community was left to grumble about their lost dream of becoming a port.

In September 1919, however, a powerful hurricane roared across the bay, destroyed the low-lying central business area, and killed between 350 and 400 people. Supposedly, a storm could not do that, but it did. As in Galveston, the residents faced a problem of recovery and of long-term protection from the ravages of the sea.

Interestingly, Mayor Boone appointed Roy Miller to lead the relief committee, which his rival did with his usual energy and effectiveness. Miller, along with seventeen committees led by local leaders, cleaned up the city in six months and took up once more the quest for a deepwater port. Working through the Commercial Club, Miller raised business donations and, surprisingly, was able to bring together the hostile elites Boone, Pope, Parr, and Kleberg for the project. Even the city of San Antonio, which had been tepid about the idea, gave its support.

Inspections by the Army Corps of Engineers took place and Miller traveled to Washington, DC, to lobby the government of President Warren G. Harding. The corps required a protected harbor, and following the Houston lead of a joint city-federal government venture, Miller successfully solicited the ad valorem taxes of seven surrounding counties to finance the project and set up a navigation district.

Corpus Christi thus was able to construct a breakwater—a jumble of granite blocks—and that was sufficient to start the dredging of a turning basin and deepwater channel in 1922. From Washington, Miller sent a laconic telegram that said, "We win." He was on the celebratory stage with Parr and Pope (Kleberg was ill with a stroke) at the opening of the port in 1926.[16]

Protection for the city below the bluff, however, was still incomplete. Two bond issues in 1938 raised $1.75 million, supported once again by the ad valorem taxes from surrounding counties. This bought a handsome stair-step seawall that was nearly four feet above the 1919 high-water mark to shelter the city and its people from the pounding of hurricane waves.

Miller resigned from the *Caller* newspaper in 1929, eventually became president of the Intracoastal Canal Association, and assisted in gaining the assignment of the Corpus Christi Naval Air Station during World War II. He kept houses in Houston, Washington, DC, and Corpus Christi, and when at home in Corpus the gregarious Miller flew Texas and American flags from his porch to announce that his door was open to visits from his friends.

SAN ANTONIO

San Antonio was sharply segregated into Anglo, black, and Mexican American politics and neighborhoods at the turn into the twentieth century. Nine-time mayor Bryan Callaghan, however, successfully ran a political machine based upon patronage to Germans and Mexicans, and withstood efforts by reformers to "oust Callaghan and keep him ousted" until he succumbed to Bright's disease in 1912.[17]

In 1914, San Antonio adopted a commission form of government. While the Anglos slowly lost dominance, another political machine, led by Mayor John R. Tobin and his successor, C. M. Chambers, formed an alliance with Charlie Bellinger, a black gambling boss, to control the city. This black-white accommodation lasted through the commission form to a council-city manager plan in 1951. Representatives were still elected at-large, which gave the Anglo vote a preponderance. A court order in the early 1970s forced election by district in both San Antonio and El Paso in order to allow an equitable representation of Mexican Americans on the city council. Meanwhile, in San Antonio the flow of money from three military bases and the gaiety of the brothels in the red light district (1890–1941) near the Alamo masked the poverty of the city.[18]

Beginning in the 1920s, pecan shelling was San Antonio's largest industry. Hand labor was so cheap that pecan companies such as the Southern Pecan Shelling Company, founded in 1926, set aside its mechanical shelling machinery. Southern used contract labor agreements whereby it supplied nuts for Mexican Americans to shell at home for six to eight cents per pound. With little overhead the company was enormously profitable.

A strike of twelve thousand workers—probably the largest in Texas history—led by the dynamic, twenty-two-year-old Emma Tenayuca, occurred in 1930. The workers sought higher wages, better working conditions, and a ban on child labor. The event featured police belligerence and social prejudice, and although it brought some temporary improvements, it achieved little lasting gain. The Fair Labor Standards Act shortly boosted wages, and the pecan companies reverted to mechanical shelling. Within a few months of the strike, the companies cut their workforce by 90 percent.[19]

Also drawing national attention to San Antonio was the adverse publicity given to the *corrales* of the Mexican American slums. *Corrales* were hovels formed in a U-shape around a common pit-toilet. No city in the nation had more deaths from tuberculosis, diarrhea, and enteritis.[20] In 1932 an outraged Jesuit priest from the west side slums, Carmelo Tranchese (1880–1956), began to lobby the Roosevelt administration for federal dollars to rehabilitate his parish. With the aid of Representative

Children playing stickball in the alley of corrales *in San Antonio in 1949. According to the photograph notes, the* corrales *were built in 1913 with six toilets and one shower to service one hundred people. Lee (Russell) Photograph Collection, e_rl_14646_0190, the Dolph Briscoe Center for American History, the University of Texas at Austin.*

Maury Maverick, Sr., and the San Antonio Board of Health he won enough money to clear thirty "corrales" for the first public housing project of the city, Alazan-Apache Courts. Each of its one thousand units had the rare amenity of a private bathroom. Other units were constructed for blacks and whites.

Tranchese also organized health clinics, distributed rations to striking pecan workers, and stuck like a cocklebur in the conscience of city politicians. "The city and state regulate stables for horses and cows; why not regulate human habitations too?" he asked.[21] He was known as the "Rumpled Angel of the Slums."[22]

In order to keep taxes low, public services—streets, curbs, sidewalks, sewers, and water—were left to subdivision developers or homeowners to finance. Major sewers, dependent on ten-year bond issues, were never sufficient to keep up with growth. If individuals could not afford such services, they were not built. At a board meeting in 1951, it was reported that six thousand residences lacked running water. A successful waterworks using well water, built by banker George C. Brackenridge in 1885, was finally bought by the city in 1925.

Available water encouraged the use of indoor toilets and baths. By keeping water prices cheap through a self-perpetuating four-member board, the city could argue that San Antonio was a good place to locate a business. It also meant, however, that the city provided poor services to its people, failed to look for future sources of surface water, and continued to rely on the finite Edwards Aquifer.[23] Even Brackenridge had noticed a diminished flow in the San Antonio River, fed by San Pedro Springs. It was a pending disaster.

EL PASO

El Paso had similar problems. As it moved into the twentieth century, El Paso was still a wide-open, frontier town. Reformers, in spite of using the same fraudulent tactics in elections, could not win against the conservatives, who were content with the gambling and prostitution. In 1904 a quiet, elite banker who preferred to work behind the scenes, Charles R. Moorhead, was elected mayor. He was subjected to pressure from the Citizens' Reform League and closed the red light district. The gamblers moved to Juárez and the prostitutes scattered.

Moorhead, however, was followed by "the Ring" politicians, led by city treasurer C. E. "Uncle Henry" Kelly and county judge Joseph U. Sweeney. These men took a more practical approach, and the purveyors of sin crept back into town. In 1913 it was reported that 367 women of the night worked on Utah Street. In 1915 reform lawyer Tom Lea was elected as mayor. He was able to banish the public displays of silken ladies in open carriages and move the district closer to the river, but he was never able to close it entirely.[24]

During the Mexican Revolution, Mexican refugees seeking safety and work poured across the river. An estimated 10 percent of the Mexican population, 1 million people, fled, and El Paso was a main exit point. The population of El Paso increased by nearly seven times from 1900 to 1930, declined during the depression, and then reached 130,500 in 1950.

Until 1940 most of the Mexican Americans of the city had been born in Mexico, and since 1920 El Paso has been the only large Texas city with a majority Mexican American population. The immigrants gathered in Chihuahuita, a "barrio," or slum, of one-story adobe houses that stretched from south of downtown to the river. It was a place of privation, crowding, and disease where the inhabitants dreamed of someday returning to Mexico.[25]

Water supply was a continual problem in a land of nine inches yearly rainfall and an erratic Rio Grande of flood and drought. Elephant Butte

Refugees cross the Rio Grande. Otis Aultman photograph A2868, courtesy of Border Heritage Center, El Paso Public Library. (Aultman was a photographer in El Paso at the time of the Mexican revolutions.)

Bhutanese architecture at the University of Texas at El Paso. Photograph by author.

Dam, 125 miles north of El Paso, created the largest man-made lake in the United States. Completed in 1916, it tamed the excesses of the Rio Grande and provided water for 160,000 acres of irrigated land in New Mexico, Texas, and Mexico. It stimulated the expansion of agriculture and the growth of El Paso. The city grew upward, with two hundred buildings designed by pioneer architect Henry C. Trost, and outward to the northeast, with housing developments toward Fort Bliss.

Water supply for the troops on the mesa was stretched thin in 1916, and this forced a relocation of the nearby Texas School of Mines and Metallurgy (1914) to a new campus donated by five citizens north of downtown. It was built with a unique Bhutanese style of architecture—deep-set windows, massive sloping walls, over-hanging tile roofs, spires, mosaic mandalas set in dark bands of brick—and became Texas Western College (1949), which in turn became the University of Texas at El Paso (1967). It was an architectural gem and a bursting educational center at the end of the twentieth century.

23

THE WORLD WAR I ERA

In 1916, border troubles with Pancho Villa prompted a mobilization of the Texas National Guard and a punitive expedition into northern Mexico led by General John J. Pershing of Fort Bliss. It proved fruitless, but gave Pershing and his officers experience in large command. President Woodrow Wilson's declaration of war came in April 1917. Almost 1 million Texans registered for the draft, and a total of 198,000 saw service, including 450 nurses. One nurse and 5,170 men died, one-third of them in the influenza pandemic of 1918.

Major army training camps sprang up: Camp MacArthur at Waco, Camp Logan at Houston, Camp Travis at San Antonio, and Camp Bowie at Fort Worth. Aviation schools appeared: Hicks Field in Fort Worth, Call Field at Wichita Falls, and Kelly Field at San Antonio. The nearby cities prospered as suppliers and builders for these installations. Military expenditures, besides those of Major Arnold in 1849, became important for Fort Worth for the first time. Texans contributed to Liberty Bonds and War Savings Stamps, and cooperated with food conservation—meatless Monday, wheatless Wednesday, and porkless Thursday. Schools suppressed German-language study.

On the Houston Ship Channel, Midland Bridge Company of Missouri and Universal Shipbuilding Company built oceangoing wooden transport vessels that were towed to Beaumont for the installation of engines. They completed about a dozen before the armistice of November 11, 1918. Seven other shipyards built wooden vessels, but it was a short war for the United States. Contracts were cancelled and most of the camps were quickly dismantled.[1]

RACIAL CONFLICTS

The war left behind an ugly residue. The brutality of fighting in the conflict not only unleashed the dogs of war, but also the passions of self-righteousness. Society was spaded over and left exposed and uncertain. In Houston, for instance, a black guard unit from Illinois was assigned to guard duty during the building of Fort Logan, west of town at the current site of Memorial Park. The black troopers were unused to segregation, the epithet "nigger," and the attitudes of local police. The town was uneasy with black men in uniform—the Civil War was still within easy memory. After a soldier was arrested in town for gambling and resisting arrest, the rumor spread in the camp that a policeman had killed a comrade. Fear that a white mob was en route prompted the soldiers to raid the ammunition tents and arm themselves.

Led by a black sergeant, seventy-five to a hundred men marched to Houston to punish the police. Shooting became random; sixteen whites and four blacks died in a two-hour melee. The town and police fought back, supported the following day by soldiers from Galveston and San Antonio. The scattered rebels returned to camp. In the largest court-martial in American military history the army hanged nineteen and sentenced sixty-three to life in prison. Later commutations set most of the prisoners free.

Other racial conflicts involving black soldiers occurred at Brownsville, San Antonio, and Del Rio. In the same summer, the infamous racial massacre at East St. Louis occurred, but the Houston riot was the only one in which more whites died. It demonstrated a rising black militancy, enhanced by World War I, that eventually ended the era of lynching in Texas.[2]

LYNCHING

The number of people executed by mob violence is a difficult statistic due to unreliable reporting. How big is a "mob," for example? The *New Handbook of Texas* (1996) reports 468 killed in 1885-1942. About three-fourths of the victims were black men, but victims from other races, as well as women and children, were also executed. It was often an urban crime.

The most gruesome example in Texas history occurred in Waco in 1916, when seventeen-year-old Jesse Washington, an illiterate black, was convicted of beating a white woman to death. He was grabbed by a mob howling "Get the Negro!," stabbed, hit with shovels and bricks, hoisted into a tree by a chain around the neck, and burned to death. The body was dragged through the streets until it fell apart; what was left was placed in a sack and hung on a telephone pole.[3]

Dallas and San Antonio newspapers, along with suffragettes, began to speak out against lynching, and it declined after 1922. Reformer Jesse Daniel Ames (1883-1972) of Georgetown looked upon lynching as bigoted, male aggression. It was not an action to protect female virtue, she thought; it was false chivalry. She founded the Association of Southern Women for the Prevention of Lynching in 1930 to convince women of that view.

Public opinion begin to shift, and blacks, trained and authorized to kill in World War I, began to fight back. In Paris, Texas, for example, an enraged white mob in 1920 threatened to tear apart the black part of town after a lynching, as they had done once before. Black veterans, however, refused to submit and advised their neighbors to barricade their homes and get out their shotguns. Mayor J. M. Crook and an anxious collection of leading citizens intervened with promises of fair treatment, a heavy police patrol, and dispersal of the white mob. The town made a choice for a nervous peace rather than a bloodbath. It was a choice increasingly made as lynching gradually decreased.[4]

KU KLUX KLAN

Mixed into this postwar bigotry was a brief appearance of the Ku Klux Klan (KKK). Like a flu virus spreading through American towns, the KKK in its second reincarnation (1915-1928) reached Texas in 1920 with parades in Houston and an initiation for two thousand in Bellaire, a suburb of Houston. By 1921, motivated by fears of crime and shifting morals, more than one hundred chapters spewed hatred about blacks, Jews, Roman Catholics, and immigrants.

With an elaborate secret ritual and robes, the organization of 150,000 men and women burned crosses on the hillsides, marched on city streets, and infiltrated the city councils, courts, and police forces. By August 1921 there had occurred fifty-two acts of hooded terrorism with no arrests or indictments. A retired Dallas dentist, Hiram W. Evans, rose through the ranks to become imperial wizard and attracted enough sympathetic votes to dominate the Texas legislature in 1922.

In Galveston spiritual leaders Rabbi Henry Cohen and Father James Kirwin stood shoulder to shoulder before the city commissioners to block a parade permit in 1922 so that the Klan never got a grip on the Island City. Joseph Cullinan and John Henry Kirby pushed a condemning resolution through the Texas Chamber of Commerce. Elsewhere, most people were intimidated.

At this point, however, Evans and the KKK overreached, entered into state politics, and tried to capture the governorship for the Klan. In a run-off campaign in 1924 Miriam Ferguson beat the Klan candidate, Felix D. Robertson, and became the first female governor of the state. Former governor "Pa" Ferguson campaigned for his wife and referred to Hiram Evans as the "Grand Gizzard." After the new legislature passed a law that outlawed wearing masks and disguises in public, the KKK declined rapidly. The stronghold chapters in Dallas and Fort Worth went bankrupt by 1926 as the virus, exposed to daylight, ran its course and died.[5]

WOMEN'S SUFFRAGE

Mixed into these urban disturbances of the early twentieth century was the leavening benefit of middle- and upper-class women's voluntary organizations, which variously agitated for prohibition, suppression of red light districts, establishment of libraries, city planning, urban health, protection of children, and the right to vote. The women spoke for the morality of the city and learned the art of politics.[6] They won the Married Women's Property Act in 1913, which gave wives control of their separate personal property and excluded their earnings from a husband's management.

The idea of women's franchise had been raised as early as the Texas Constitutional Convention of 1868; sputtering suffrage clubs kept the thought alive; and the Texas Woman Suffrage Association (1903-1905, 1913-1919) argued with the legislature that women were citizens, paid taxes, and should have the right to vote. When Lt. Governor William P. Hobby, who was sympathetic to the movement, replaced impeached Governor James E. Ferguson, women gained the right to participate in primary elections. In seventeen days 386,000 women registered for the Democratic primary and proved the potential of women's votes. In the next year, 1919, Texas ratified the Nineteenth Amendment to the Constitution, which granted women the franchise. Although it was a great victory and voluntary organizations continued, it took women another generation to establish political equity.[7]

24

THE ENTICEMENTS OF THE CITY

The spectacle of marching people dressed in sheets, burning wooden crosses, or housewives carrying suffrage placards was certainly exciting, since it was not the normal entertainment of the towns. The cities nonetheless offered high and low pleasures at all times that could not be found in the countryside. Much of it had to do with size, where a conglomeration of people could demand and pay for a variety of amenities.[1]

THE VICES

Gambling, prostitution, and drinking had been urban vices (low entertainment) since the beginning of villages. Whiskey came into the state from the Kentucky distilleries, and a saloon was easy to set up. All that was needed was a plank for a bar, some glasses, and a barrel of whiskey, which after 1893 had to be bottled-in-bond. That is, as a part of the pure food and drug movement, the whiskey could not be diluted.

By the twentieth century saloons had become more or less standardized, with a bar counter, a rail along the bottom, spittoons, and a back bar with bottles and a mirror or paintings. Beer came with the German immigrants, and the best was the lager beer of San Antonio, where about one-third of the population was of German descent. There were twenty-seven breweries in the state by 1870. The oldest continuing German establishment is Scholz Garten of Austin, which opened in 1866 and has endured as a place of entertainment for German residents, students, professors, and politicians.

Gambling was a part of saloon life until the progressive era of reform at the beginning of the twentieth century. In 1905 the legislature passed a law that allowed a local injunction to stop the use of any building for gaming purposes. This strengthened a little-used 1881 anti-gaming law and ended open casino gambling. The gamblers moved to Mexico. The final blow came in 1917, during the fever of war, with the passage of the Eighteenth Amendment of the Constitution, which prohibited the manufacture, sale, or transportation of intoxicating beverages.

The Texas legislature ratified the amendment in 1918 and Texas voters approved in 1919. Breweries shut down and saloons sold out lock, stock, and barrel. It was reported that one man, Zach White, bought the entire inventory of the Paso del Norte Hotel in El Paso for his personal use. In San Antonio, barroom owner Dan Breen simply placed the bottles on the bar and invited his patrons to drink it up. He joined in and dropped dead in the late afternoon of that final day. Texas thus began its longest drought.

In this period of self-righteousness the red light districts were forced to dim their lights. The Women's Christian Temperance Union (1874) joined hands with the Federation of Women's Clubs (1889) and finally with the American Social Hygiene Association (1913) to attack alcoholism and prostitution. Ministers and civic reformers fell in with the crusade to attack the red light districts, which existed in most of the major towns.

James T. Upchurch of the Berachah Rescue Society in Dallas, for instance, railed about the immorality, named brothel owners, and provided shelter for fallen women. The local churches and real estate owners closed the Dallas Frogtown reservation in 1913, which had been open only three years, with the result that prostitutes scattered throughout town. J. Frank Norris of the First Baptist Church of Fort Worth joined the movement and preached endlessly about the immorality of Hell's Half-Acre.

The legislature raised the age of consent for girls from ten in 1886 to twelve in 1893 to fifteen in 1895. By 1914 the red lights were out in Dallas, Austin, and Amarillo, and during World War I Secretary of War Newton Baker closed the remaining districts to protect young soldiers from venereal disease.

Of course, in spite of war, prohibition, and threats of immorality, drinking, gambling, and prostitution continued, albeit at a subdued level. Post Office Street in the "Free State of Galveston" revived after the war, the famous "Chicken Ranch" (1844-1973) of LaGrange survived, and the Dixie Hotel (1946-1961) of Beaumont flourished. A reporter from the *San Antonio Light* easily uncovered poker, blackjack, dice, and lottery games in the local hotels in 1929.

Deep Ellum, near downtown Dallas, became the "Broadway of the Black Belt" between the wars, where any vice could be found along with a nurturing cluster of nightclubs for jazz and blues. "Thunder Road," a three-and-a-half mile strip of the Jacksboro Highway north of Fort Worth, provided booze, sex, and gambling to soldiers and workers from West Texas in the 1940s and 1950s. The Hollywood Dinner Club and the Balinese Room of Galveston offered a high-class nightclub atmosphere with big-name bands for drinking and casino gambling from 1926 until 1957. Even though mixed drinks and gambling remained illegal, prohibition ended in 1933, to the relief of the nation and the Lone Star State.

PURE WATER AND HEALTH

Of all the luxuries of urban life, pure water pumped through a pipe to home and working place was the most important. The explorers and the early town builders sought clean water, and the quest has continued throughout Texas history. By the turn into the twentieth century most towns had established at least a rudimentary system of water supply—Houston, Galveston, San Antonio, Fort Worth, Dallas used water wells; Corpus Christi, Beaumont, Austin, El Paso, and others used river water.

The germ theory of disease was well known by the turn of the twentieth century. Anton van Leeuwenhoek, a Dutchman, first saw wee "animalcules" with a crude microscope in the mid-seventeenth century. Louis Pasteur in the mid-nineteenth century, with one of the great leaps of medicine, connected these microbes to human health. Shine Philips, a pharmacist in Big Spring, Texas, in the 1890s saw it this way:

> For a long time we didn't have any germs and then the germ theory got around. It scared most people to death. The first pictures we saw of germs painted them as fierce small animals that looked like a combination of a dog and an alligator, and I don't know if some of the doctors didn't get

the same idea. Our doctors didn't know much about germs but fifty years before they heard of them they boiled their instruments and washed their hands before any operation without knowing exactly why, but because they knew it was important to be clean.[2]

Experience with filtration in Germany in 1889-1890 was shown to stop cholera. Use of sand filters, chlorination, artesian water, and locating your source of drinking water above pollution points became standard to prevent water-borne diseases. Between 1890 and 1910 in the United States cholera epidemics ceased to occur, and typhoid deaths dropped from 58 per 100,000 to 21. In 1938, with other public health measures, such as pasteurization of milk, the typhoid death rate dropped to 0.67.[3]

Knowledge of this public health technology came to Texas through consulting engineers such as those who recommended hurricane protection for Galveston and sewage systems for Houston. A good example of this spread of information is the career of John B. Hawley (1866-1941). He worked his way through the University of Minnesota, majored in science and civil engineering, and graduated in 1887. He was kind, considerate, blunt in opinion, and favored strength in construction. It was said, "Hawley is not much for beauty, but he's heck for strong."

He worked as a hydraulic and sanitary engineer for a Chicago company, and traveled to Fort Worth as construction manager to build a pump house for the artesian water that the city found underneath it. Hawley remained behind in 1894, probably because he had met the Fort Worth woman he wished to marry, and became the first independent consulting engineer in Texas for water and sewer work. He taught chemistry at the Fort Worth Medical College, served as city engineer, founded the Texas Association of the American Society of Civil Engineers, and continued his private practice.

He consulted, for instance, with Dallas to build its first reservoir. For water the city used Browder's Springs, which was prone to going dry, and also the Trinity River, which was subject to upstream pollution from Fort Worth. No wonder that the drinking water tasted bad. Under threat of a drought, the City Council agreed with Hawley to construct a dam and build White Rock Lake, which promised better quality water. It was ready for use in 1914 and became the city's first chlorinated water supply.

At the same time he completed Lake Worth in his hometown, which used a new sand filtration plant and reduced the bacteria count from an average of 582 per milliliter to 59. Previously, with raw water from the Trinity River, the count had been 19,000, which went down to 200 after filtration.[4] His results were a strong endorsement of the urban use of upstream reservoirs and filtration.

This became essential knowledge, particularly in dry regions. Abilene was among the first when it scooped out Lake Lytle (1897), Lake Abilene (1919), Lake Kirby (1927), and Lake Phantom Hill (1937). Odessa, another example, voted for ground water and sewer bonds in 1927, but population growth and summertime shortages required a change in the 1940s. Water consumption and population trebled between 1938 and 1948. To prevent the town from drying up, the city council voted to join Big Spring and Snyder in the Colorado River Municipal Water District Project (CRMWD) in 1950.

The state authorized in 1949 the impounding of storm and floodwater, and the use of unappropriated water from the Colorado River and its tributaries. By 1981 thirty-one other towns had joined the Odessa group. At first water well fields were utilized in the summertime, and in the winter the aquifer was artificially recharged with water taken from Lake J. B. Thomas.

Located on the border of Scurry and Borden Counties, this dam on the Colorado River, designed by Freese and Nichols, who were corporate descendents of Hawley, created this lake in 1952. It had to be deep to minimize surface evaporation, but it was on top of a producing oil field. Unique were the islands in the lake to raise the oil wellheads above the water. The CRMWD issued bonds to build pipelines, pumping stations, reservoirs, and rights-of-way to service its customers. The organization functioned without the use of governmental funds—a source of pride for the independent-minded West Texas participants.

Both Juárez and El Paso drew drinking water from the Rio Grande and filtered it with mashed prickly pear leaves, but El Paso turned to water wells in the Hueco Valley aquifer at the start of the century. The water was plentiful, pure, and required little treatment. By the end of the twentieth century, however, the water table had dropped 60 to 80 feet, and saline incursions into this water source fomented an urban crisis that involved stubborn farmers in New Mexico, Colorado, and Mexico; large populations in El Paso and Juárez; the U.S. Army at Fort Bliss; and court control of waterways with no new sources of water. The problem has been only partially solved with conservation, recharging the aquifer with wastewater, and juggling the amounts drawn from the river and the aquifer.

Houston began to tap the water flow of the San Jacinto River during World War II for the ship channel industry and built a reservoir, Lake Houston, in 1953. After agreement with the Trinity River Authority, reached after a long battle, Houston also began to draw from the Trinity River. This resulted in Lake Livingston in 1969. For the first time the Bayou City installed filtration plants.

Upstream, Dallas had built reservoirs, but they did not withstand the 1950s drought, and as its reservoirs neared depletion, Dallas had to pipe salty water from Lake Texoma on the Red River for three years. Fort Worth, also threatened, planned to take water from the Brazos River, but spring rains in 1957 made this unnecessary. By the end of the century the Trinity River, with twenty-two reservoirs, was just about tapped out. To their peril, El Paso and San Antonio continued their dependence upon well water. The quest for pure water thus continued as the cities grew.

SEWAGE

The other side of this search for clean water was what to do with the wastewater, the dirty water, of the cities. It was a part of urban metabolism, a metaphor that is sometimes used to apply to the history of water, air, and land pollution. The usual urban sequence of events according to environmental historian Joel A. Tarr was that once a city obtained running water, people wanted water closets, and this led to overflowing cesspools. Then, city dwellers demanded sewer systems, and this raised the question of sewerage disposal. Most places simply dumped it into the closest watercourse and hoped dilution would clean it up.[5]

The Texas legislature in 1913, however, directed that all cities of over fifty thousand residents stop dumping untreated sewage into streams. A response took time, and when Fort Worth completed its first disposal plant in 1923 it was still dumping raw sewage along with packinghouse offal directly into the West Fork of the Trinity River. The swill flowed downstream to where Dallas drew out its domestic water. Reflecting an old animosity, in the washroom of a Fort Worth office building at the time a posted sign on the toilet water closet read, "Pull the chain. Dallas needs the water."[6]

Houston had pioneered sewage treatment in order to obtain federal approval of the ship channel. Once installed, the system was largely neglected, and in 1916 the mayor estimated that 70 to 80 percent of the sewage went directly into Buffalo Bayou. In 1917 and 1918, however, under the direction of city engineer Edward E. Sands, the Bayou City constructed two innovative activated sludge plants, one of them the largest in the nation. Instead of simply trickling water through collected sewer materials, the activated sludge system used forced aeration and agitation to hasten the disintegration process. Such sludge, less malodorous, could be turned into lagoons to decompose and dry. San Marcos, San Antonio, San Angelo, Sherman, and Paris, Texas, also adopted this system.

Cleaned effluent could be returned to a watercourse, but water pollution remained a constant problem for urban Texas. Sewage treatment did not keep up with the need, and at mid-century Houston's Buffalo Bayou, the watercourse of the ship channel, was still 80 percent polluted—fouled with grease, oil, chemicals, blood, manure, and raw sewage.[7]

It cannot be assumed, incidentally, that within cities there was a uniform benefit from sanitary engineering. Environmentalists David R. Johnson, Derral Cheatwood, and Benjamin Bradshaw studied the maldistribution in San Antonio in the 1930s due to political and social cleavages. The overcrowded west side of San Antonio had evolved as an impotent Mexican ghetto with a poor black neighborhood on the east side. Middle-class and upper-class whites lived north and south of downtown.

To maintain power, the Anglo politicians, representing 47 percent of the population, courted the east-side blacks rather than the disorganized Mexicans, with the result that the black and Anglo neighborhoods were rewarded with good light, sewer, and water connections. Inappropriate sewage disposal and water supply thus was not a problem for the east, north, and south sides. On the teeming west side as many as thirty families shared a single water faucet and used pit toilets unconnected to the sewer system. In 1935, when 126 Mexican infants died of diarrhea on the west side, only 2 black infants died on the east side.[8]

In Houston a study from 1969 of the northeastern Settegast area of 1,500 black homes revealed open sewage ditches, unpaved streets, rat infestation, no city water, and 25 percent use of privies. At mid-century El Paso lacked equitable distribution in South El Paso and Smeltertown, where Mexican people lived in adobe houses with dirt floors, few bathtubs, and high infant mortality. The slums of West Dallas had three thousand people with no piped water and eight thousand homes with no bathtub or shower. In the world of segregation the poor and minority did not share equally in the amenities of city life.

GARBAGE

Garbage disposal in the slums was also spotty, and for the larger cities it was discovered that open burning added to air pollution while incineration was too expensive. Most cities, including Houston, stopped burning in the 1960s. Mainly, cities just dumped the garbage, and after World War II the choice method became a sanitary landfill—burying garbage under layers of dirt. The common difficulty, of course, was where to put the dump. As Mayor Louie Welch of Houston once commented, "You know, when it comes to garbage, people want us to pick it up, but they don't want us to put it down again, especially if it is near their house."[9]

In the late nineteenth century and early part of the twentieth century urban health improved with the establishment of the state medical school in Galveston and various private hospitals and clinics, such as Spohn Sanitarium in Corpus Christi. In Houston in 1942 the M. D. Anderson Foundation established the Texas Medical Center, which featured a state cancer hospital run by the University of Texas. The center shortly began to attract other hospital and medical teaching facilities such as Baylor Medical School, which eventually led to medical eminence in Texas and the world.

Cities thus became healthier. In 1950, the public menace of yellow fever, cholera, and typhoid had been banished; still, tuberculosis, poliomyelitis, gonorrhea, and syphilis remained to stalk Texas streets.

MOVIES

The cities, meanwhile, provided higher levels of recreation and entertainment. They literally provided the bright lights. Electric power for the cities had been demonstrated by Thomas Edison and others, and most of the larger Texas cities had electric power plants and wiring by the end of the century to supply arc lighting and electric trolley cars. Residents already had experience with telephones and telegraphs. Lighting and electric appliances soon entered into the home and factory, and by 1920 electricity had become the most important power source for American cities.

Elm Street in downtown Dallas in the 1920s. This photograph demonstrates the attractions of the city in that era, with its cars, trolleys, pavement, electricity, and entertainment. The Garrick Theater, on the right, is featuring Richard Dix in the silent 1923 movie To the Last Man. *Photograph from the collection of the Texas/ Dallas History and Archives Division, Dallas Public Library.*

The inventive Edison made a primitive movie projector called a "vitascope" and demonstrated it in New York City in 1896. Ten months later it was in use at the Dallas Opera House, while variety theaters statewide scrambled to add a movie to their acts. Cheap storefront theaters called nickelodeons swept the nation, followed by multi-reel movies that demanded venues with comfortable seating and restrooms. Movie palaces with cushioned seats, lobbies, nurseries, decorative plasterwork, chandeliers, stages, and orchestra pits appeared in the second decade of the century, such as the Isis in Fort Worth, the Alhambra in El Paso, and the Queen in Houston.[10]

The best were built and operated by Karl St. John Hoblitzelle (1879-1967) of Dallas. He ran a clean, family vaudeville circuit for Dallas, Fort Worth, Waco, Houston, and San Antonio, and built theaters that he always named "Majestic." He operated a Majestic in Dallas that had the largest marquee in the South—five stories of flashing lights with a bird on a revolving ball. It had mirrored doors, a Roman garden motif, a fountain in the lobby, two balconies, a section for blacks with a separate entrance, ceiling fans, and a play area for kids in the basement. In 1973 the Hoblitzelle Foundation gave this French Renaissance building to the city as a center for the Dallas Ballet.

Hoblitzelle built another Majestic in Houston in 1923 that was the first air-conditioned theater in Texas. The Majestic in San Antonio, constructed in 1929, had 3,700 seats. Hoblitzelle sold his assets to RKO in 1929, just before the stock market crash, retired, and then bought them all back in 1933 to salvage the Texas movie industry. Having sold high and bought low, Hoblitzelle made a fortune, which he graciously shared with his hometown and state.[11]

Movies provided cheap entertainment—10 cents to a dollar—and a chance to cool off (home air-conditioning did not arrive until after World War II). Unlike live theater, the movie could produce close-ups, panoramas, and exotic scenes. In 1927 the movies learned to talk, and in 1932 to use technicolor. They followed their customers to the suburbs and catered to automobiles with drive-in theaters in the 1930s. Exclusively black theaters in Dallas, Fort Worth, Corpus Christi, and El Paso acquired films with black stars from the Dallas distribution center, and Hispanics imported films from Mexico to show in tent theaters in South Texas.

Almost every town of consequence had a movie house by 1950, and it is estimated that every Texan saw at least one movie per week. From the beginning Texas inspired thrilling themes of cowboys and Indians, pioneers, gunfighters, cattle, and oil as offerings to the industry. The movies provided an enormous communal experience and helped to homogenize American and Texas culture.

RADIO

In addition to movies, radio provided easy entertainment. Stations in Pittsburgh (1919) and Detroit (1920) began to broadcast, and with a crystal detector, headphones, and a coil wrapped around a cereal box, people could snatch invisible voices from the air. WRR in Dallas became the first Texas station in 1921. It was owned by the city and used for fire dispatch, with the spare time taken up by weather reports, jokes, sports, and music. When the city decided to close it in 1925, five thousand people protested. WRR continued, and the city changed frequencies for the fire and police departments.

Amon Carter launched station WBAP in Fort Worth in 1922 because he had heard that radio might compete with his newspaper. By 1927, when the Federal Radio Commission began to impose order on the chaotic and overlapping airwaves, there were thirty-two commercial stations in Texas.

Radio provided entertainment night and day to an unseen audience free of charge in exchange for listening to advertisements aimed mainly at an expanding urban audience. It offered immediate information and intimacy for its listeners. Sears Roebuck began to sell radios through its catalogue in 1923, and after World War I almost every household came to own a set. It became a part of the living room furniture. Radio required only hearing and imagination for programs such as *Amos 'n' Andy*, the most popular series of the 1920s. It meant nothing that Amos and Andy were actually white men imitating blacks. In San Antonio the film operators at the Majestic would stop the movie for thirty minutes so that the audience could listen to the program in the lobby.

In Dallas in the late 1940s, Gordon McClendon simulated baseball games that came to him by teletype. Major League games were not broadcast nationally at the time. He would provide artificial sounds of baseball hits, crowd noise, and the national anthem. When there was a delay in the teletype McClendon would make up fights in the stands, dogs on the field, and foul balls. People listened even though they knew it was a simulation. Fans liked the "Old Scotchman," who humorously identified himself as "eighty-three years old this very day."[12]

THEATER

Neither radio nor motion pictures completely killed off legitimate theater, which continued to thrive with local actors and professionals. Community theater was as perennial as grass and had always been entwined in the history of Texas cities. The Little Theater movement of amateurs spread across the United States in 1915, even though two-thirds of the live theaters outside of New York died between 1915 and 1930. More of them perished during the Great Depression.

Small amounts of federal money trickled down during the hard times, however, and gave opportunity to people like Margo Jones (1911-1955), an innovative young woman from Livingston, Texas, who started an amateur group for the Houston Recreation Department. Nine people showed up for her first meeting in 1936 of the Houston Community Players, which flourished with no rules, dues, or officers—just Margo. They presented sixty plays in five years and ended up with six hundred members.

Jones possessed enormous energy, smoked incessantly, read new plays daily, called everyone "Baby," "Honey," or "Darling," and talked unceasingly about the theater. She thought that viewers could experience other lives through the actors and thus enrich their own lives. "With more great theatre, great art, great music throughout the world, life is bound to be better," she said.[13] It was her formula for human improvement.

She badgered the Houston City Council to obtain money to rent the air-conditioned ballroom of the Lamar Hotel to present plays in an arena setting with the audience on all sides. "Honey," she said to the assembled men, "I don't care what it costs, you got the money. Houston's got the money. Give me the grand ballroom in the Lamar Hotel. What the hell's a ballroom when you haven't got a damn ball? When you can have *theatah*, when you can have plays. Wonderful, magical plays. Honey, we got to have some magic, some wonder. Give me that ballroom!"[14] They did, and Jones put on summertime plays at the Lamar Hotel. After World War II she pioneered the concept of theater-in-the-round in Dallas.

SPORTS

A different sort of performing art pleasurable for both participants and audience was sports. Various city sports blossomed in the first half of the twentieth century—swimming, diving, tennis, basketball, softball, baseball, football, golf, track and field. The two biggest were baseball and football. Northern soldiers assigned to Texas after the Civil War played baseball on a field in Galveston and taught the game to local boys. Men on the island formed amateur squads and challenged others. "Honest John" McCoskey (1862-1940) toured the state with a professional team in 1888 and inspired the formation of the Texas League, which brought minor league baseball to Austin, Dallas, Galveston, Houston, and San Antonio.

Teams came and went, built small stadiums, and reminded people of the supposedly idyllic, slow-paced rural life that they had left behind. A parallel black league formed in the 1920s that used the stadiums during off times. The best place was Buff Stadium of the Houston Buffaloes, with fourteen thousand seats and a persistent breeze blowing toward home plate. It encouraged pitchers and discouraged hitters. The stadium was noted for high humidity, rain, mosquitoes, and the beginning of "Dizzy" Dean's pitching career. Perhaps most important, this minor league effort nurtured a desire for Major League baseball in Texas.

Developed by eastern colleges, football arrived on Galveston Island when the YMCA, high school, and local clubs began to play one another in 1890. It spread from there and appealed to the mythic Texas frontier personality—rough, gritty, male, and combative. The University of Texas began to play a four-team, home-and-home schedule in 1893 and a traditional end-of-the-season game with Texas A&M University in 1900. Baylor, Rice, and Texas Christian fielded teams and together they formed the Southwest Conference (1914–1995).

The first president of Rice Institute, Edgar Odell Lovett, deliberately introduced football to his campus in 1912. "I've never regretted it," he said later, "although I believe I have spent more time on football problems than anything else. The mischief is that you have to win."[15]

To promote their state fair, Dallas invited football teams to play inside of a horse-track oval in 1902, and then built a fifteen-thousand-seat wooden stadium without locker rooms in 1921. Starting in 1929 a game between the University of Texas and the University of Oklahoma, the "Red River Shootout," became a regular feature.

In 1930 workmen replaced the wooden stands with Fair Park Stadium, a forty-six-thousand-seat oval with a playing surface excavated 24 feet below the surface, the dirt piled up around it, a wooden deck, and redwood benches. It was the largest in the South and became known as the "Cotton Bowl" after 1937 when the Cotton Bowl Classic began to be played there on New Year's Day.

In the postwar years, 1947–1949, Doak Walker of Southern Methodist University won All-American and All-Southwest Conference honors as well as the Heisman Trophy in 1948. The state fair sold $1.28 million in bonds, reconstructed the bowl in concrete, and added an upper deck on the west side as SMU switched its games to the bowl to meet fan interest. In 1986 Fair Park officials posted a plaque at the main entrance that simply stated: "The Cotton Bowl, the House that Doak Built."[16] But it was more: the stadium was also a monument to an important part of Texas culture.

ZOOS

Zoos were another major recreation amenity of Texas urban life. Zoos in cities had long been a symbol of urban sophistication, a place of education and a source of family entertainment. The earliest in Texas were Fort Worth (1909), Dallas (1912), Houston (1923), El Paso (1925), and San Antonio (1928). Later, zoos appeared in Austin, Tyler, Waco, Gainesville, Abilene, Lufkin, Amarillo, Victoria, and Brownsville. These were places that parents took their young children, and the joy of watching the animals was long cherished. Woe to the politician who wanted to cut a zoo budget.

The key to success for the Fort Worth Zoo was a local zoological society, formed in 1939 to attract donations. In time, the society came to manage the facility while the city retained ownership of land and buildings—a private-public arrangement. In San Antonio in 1928-1929 the local zoological society built a dramatic facility at an abandoned city-owned stone quarry that exhibited the animals in a dramatic open environment without bars, separated from viewers only by a moat. Dallas placed its zoo south of the Trinity River at Marsalis Park and maintained a separate aquarium (a zoo for marine life), the best at the time, at Fair Park.

Dallas used the services of Frank "Bring 'Em Back Alive" Buck (1884-1950) to stock its cages with animals from around the world. Buck, who grew up in Dallas, was among the last of the big game hunters, and zoos after his tenure traded stock with each other. Houston located its zoo at Hermann Park, near the center of the city, and acquired its first elephant, a zoo prerequisite, in 1923 from a passing circus.

Currently, zoos are criticized for taking freedom from animals. The counterargument is that zoo animals live comfortable lives free of predators and serve to educate and humble the human species. More people—175 million—visit zoos and aquariums annually in the United States than attend all the professional sports games combined.

LIBRARIES

Another quiet urban amenity important for education and entertainment was the public library. The idea of tax-supported public libraries springs from the impulse that democracy needs informed voters and reaches back to Benjamin Franklin. Boston opened the nation's first public library in 1854, but the oldest functioning one in Texas is the Rosenberg Library of Galveston. It resulted from the bequest of merchant Henry Rosenberg, who left money for the construction and support of a public library "as a source of pleasure and profit to the people and their children and their children's children through many generations."[17]

The state granted a charter and the Rosenberg Library opened in 1904. The first librarian, Frank Chauncy Patten (1855-1934), was one of the first students of library science from Columbia University, and he not only expanded the book collection but also built an archive. This was unusual for a public library. Patten, however, recognized the historical

The Jefferson Carnegie Library at Jefferson, Texas. Photograph by author.

significance of Galveston and packed the attic with discarded boxes of business letters, ledgers, and personal mail. Considered unnecessary in his time, Patten's hoarding efforts resulted in a premier source of archival information about early Texas history. Used mainly by scholars and genealogists, today Patten's archive is irreplaceable.

The state library is older than the Rosenberg, but it has a checkered history of inactivity, poor management, abandonment, and fire. In 1897, however, a conference of eighteen women's literary clubs met in Waco and started a federation that in turn began the Texas Library Association (TLA) in 1902. The TLA successfully lobbied for the establishment of library schools in state colleges, a historical commission, and a county library system. It was the educated women of the literary clubs who agitated and led the movement for libraries. Fortunately for the time, the distant Carnegie Foundation provided funds of opportunity.

Carnegie, the richest man of his time, spent much of his fortune to build public libraries so that people could educate themselves by borrowing books. His plan was to have towns provide the land, books, and management while he gave the money for a building. The structures were built to formula with books and library services on the main floor and meeting rooms and art galleries on the second floor. Between 1886 and 1917 he funded 1,700 libraries in the United States, including grants and construction money for thirty of the fifty-one public libraries in Texas. The state had a poor reputation for meeting Carnegie's standards, but Dallas, Houston, Fort Worth, Gainesville, and other towns benefited from Carnegie generosity.

Book collections can have a subtle influence. Eight-year-old Dan Rather, who later gained television fame as a news anchor, for example, was a poor newsboy in North Houston when "Miss Rose," a social worker, said to him, "You know, your only way out is to read." She personally escorted him on a streetcar to the downtown Carnegie Library of 165,000 books and he just gawked. He began to read. It became "a defining adventure of my life," he later commented.[18]

NEWSPAPERS

If a public library serves as a memory for a city, then the local newspaper functions as a diary. Major newspapers in English, Spanish, and German appeared in the cities and became important historical documents. The

Telegraph and Texas Register (1835-1877) of San Felipe and Houston, for example, tracked the progress of the Texas Revolution and later the Civil War. Almost every town of consequence supported a newspaper, such as the *San Antonio Express-News* (1865-), the *Dallas Morning News* (1885-), the *Houston Post* (1880-1995), the *Houston Chronicle* (1901-), the *Fort Worth Star-Telegram* (1906-), and the *Corpus Christi Caller-Times* (1929-). In 1950 Texas had 115 daily and 562 weekly newspapers, including those for the Hispanic and black populations.[19] They served their communities with information about local, state, and national affairs as well as entertainment with cartoons, comic strips, photographs, advertisements, sports, and news opinions.

TROLLEYS

The internal public transportation of Texas towns was first transformed by rail cars pulled by mules and then by electric trolleys. The mules traveled no faster than a person could walk, but they kept riders out of the heat and mud. Trolleys moved faster and farther. They appeared in Dallas, Fort Worth, and Laredo in 1889; in San Antonio in 1890; and in Galveston, Houston, Waco, and Sherman in 1891. In El Paso the McGinty Band, of course, gave a musical escort and ride to the last mule of the city's system in 1902.

Thirty-three cities supported an electric streetcar system, and streetcars dominated public transportation until World War II. With their extended range—a person could travel three times farther in the same amount of time that it would take to walk—the trolleys encouraged the building of "streetcar suburbs" that helped to determine the growth patterns of the cities. Businessmen could now live in subdivisions such as Highland Park in Dallas or Houston Heights in Houston and easily reach their downtown offices. The segregated "Jim Crow" trolleys, moreover, could carry servants and workmen into most parts of town.

A natural outgrowth of the trolleys was the electric interurban system (1901-1948) in Texas, which particularly flourished in the early part of the century. Electric lines interconnected places poorly served by the railroads with light-rail passenger service. About 70 percent were concentrated in the Dallas-Fort Worth area and the rest in the Houston-Galveston-Port Arthur territory. They were convenient for day trips—for example, from the Rice Hotel in Houston to the beach in Galveston.

Automobiles and improved highways eventually made the interurbans obsolete, and only two remained in operation in 1941.[20]

MOTOR VEHICLES

Automobiles and trucks began to make an impression in Texas during the early twentieth century at the height of interurban and trolley popularity. French and German engineers invented and refined lightweight four-cycle, gasoline, internal combustion engines during the last years of the nineteenth century. American inventors perked up to automotive possibilities with the Chicago World's Fair in 1893 and a well-publicized but sputtering race in 1895. Fifty inventors planned to enter, eleven registered, five showed up, and two completed 50 miles on snowy suburban Chicago roads. Still, at the turn of the century some thirty American companies were producing cars. By 1904 the United States was the world's largest manufacturer, and Henry Ford began mass-producing his remarkable Model T in 1908.[21]

No great investment was needed to build small numbers of cars since they were assembled from various parts manufactured by others,

The popularity of the automobile soon gave rise to motels such as this one on Galveston beach, pictured in 1927. Photograph courtesy of the Rosenberg Library, Galveston, Texas.

customers paid cash in advance, and the cars were shipped by railroad. Henry Ford began with fluid capital of only $28,000. What was necessary was a supply of skilled mechanics to piece the vehicles together. They were found in the larger diverse cities with a history of bicycle or wagon making, tool shops, and tire manufacture, such as Detroit.

The automobile provided unfettered freedom for the owner and family. People could go where they wished, and when they wished. It was an inspiration for tourism, for state parks, and for tourist camps in the cities to replace the old wagon yards. In Amarillo businessmen constructed a tourist camp on the old courthouse square in 1924, while Galveston opened auto camping places along the beach. The machines as well as the popular bicycle ran better over smooth streets. Consequently, in the cities large enough to support automotive invention and service there occurred an additional desire for better streets.

STREET PAVEMENT AND ROADS

In 1900 half the streets in the major American cities were still dirt, but this declined to 15 percent within twenty-five years. The dirt was covered over with macadam (crushed stone), gravel, granite, cobblestone, shell, wooden blocks, concrete, brick, or asphalt. Wooden blocks were best for horses' hooves, and they also muffled the sound. Granite was slippery when wet; macadam was subject to wheel ruts; cobblestones were hard to clean; and concrete would crumble under the repeated pounding of iron horseshoes and heavy wheels.

Fort Worth and Dallas tried macadam; Houston and Galveston used crushed shell. Galveston experimented with wooden blocks, but they floated away in the storm of 1900. Asphalt became the material of choice on 40 percent of American streets by 1925. In Texas it was a by-product of the refineries and could be mixed with gravel or laid as a cover for concrete and brick. Asphalt might soften in warm sunshine, but it provided a smooth surface that was easy to clean and repair.[22]

Outside the cities the roads in Texas were the responsibility of the counties. The counties would sporadically survey, remove brush and trees, and flatten the surface of roadways with passing wagons, livestock, horses, oxen, and pedestrians. Road obligations gradually transferred to professionals paid by tax revenues. The famous Texas construction company Brown and Root (it became Halliburton in 1962), for instance, got its start as a county road contractor in 1919. The national Good Roads Association (1880–1920) and the American Automobile Association (1902–), as well as bicycle enthusiasts, farmers, and railroads, agitated for better highways. A problem of uniformity and quality of roads prompted the state to take over the county obligation in 1932.

The greatest boost to improve intercity roads of the time was the Federal Aid Road Act of 1916, which provided assistance for improving rural post roads (those that carried the U.S. mail). Seizing the opportunity, Texas in 1917 set up the State Highway Department (now the Texas Department of Transportation). It was supported by auto registration fees along with matching funds from the federal government.

The department initially registered 195,000 cars and designated a post highway system. World War I engendered additional federal funds and brought attention to the requirements of heavy military trucks in highway transportation.[23] In 1923 the legislature authorized a one-cent-per-gallon gasoline tax. Three-fourths of this money was allocated for highways. In 1929 the state began to place state and federal route signs on major roadways, and during the Great Depression highway crews worked to shorten routes, eliminate blind spots, provide roadside parks, and improve aesthetics. All of this set up a perpetual cycle—better roads attracted more cars that resulted in more gasoline sales that raised more money to improve the roads that attracted more cars.[24]

After World War II Dallas, Fort Worth, San Antonio, and Houston experimented with limited-access expressways. They were inspired by the Federal Highway Act of 1944, which proposed a modern interstate highway system of 41,000 miles to interconnect cities with over three hundred thousand population. The federal government, moreover, offered a 50 percent match and funds for urban expressways. In search of cheap access, the highway engineers often mashed through older neighborhoods to the harm of the voiceless poor. Deep Ellum, a mixed-race entertainment area near downtown Dallas, for example, was forever ruined when a portion of the evolving freeway system bisected the neighborhood.

Houston opened an expressway through town in 1948, and then straight down a 50-mile abandoned, interurban right-of-way to Galveston. Houston thus completed the four-lane Gulf Freeway in 1952; the federal and state governments paid 86 percent of the price. The freeway cut travel time between Houston and Galveston in half.

In Dallas in 1949 the mayor's wife christened the new Central Expressway, which ran from the central business district northward to SMU along the old right-of-way of the Houston and Texas Central Railroad, with a bottle of cologne. Cologne! That could happen only in fashion-sensitive Dallas, but it illustrated the Texan love of automobiles. In 1950 Texas had 2.7 million licensed drivers for 3.1 million vehicles. Considering the size of the adult population, this meant that every other adult was driving a truck or car somewhere.

CARS ON THE STREETS

Edward Howland Robinson "Ned" Green (1868–1936) is usually credited with owning the first car in Texas. He was the son of the notorious Hetty Green, a flint-eyed financier of Wall Street. Ned was six feet four inches tall, weighed 300 pounds, and had a wooden leg. He moved to Texas in 1892 to manage his mother's Texas-Midland Railroad; placed his headquarters in Terrell, Texas; married a former prostitute; and became an enthusiastic transplanted Texan with linkage to New York.

In 1899, along with a driver, he traveled the 35 miles of wagon roads from Terrell to Dallas in five hours to prove it could be done. He also organized the Dallas Automobile Club in 1904 and promoted the use of asphalt streets. By mid-1913, Dallas had registered 4,500 cars and supported thirty car dealers on Commerce Street.[25]

As might be expected, horses thoroughly disapproved of the cars on the roads. In Amarillo, for example, Sue Beverley Bivins recalled meeting a horse and buggy in her car. The horse rolled its eyes, whirled around and around, broke the buggy shafts, tried to climb into a house window, and bolted down the street to the Polk Street Methodist Church, where it tried to get through the large double front doors before it was finally calmed.[26]

Regulations for the protection of life, limb, and property quickly came forward. In New York at the turn of the century, laws called for speed limits of 12 miles per hour, lights, right-lane driving, rights-of-way, license plates, and no drivers under the age of sixteen. The laws in Houston of 1907 were much the same, but set a speed limit downtown of eight miles per hour and a minimum driver's age of eighteen years. The *Saturday Evening Post* introduced the phrase "traffic jam" in 1910, and Detroit policeman William Potts invented the traditional green-yellow-red traffic light in 1920. Houston lagged by seven years and installed its first electronic signals in 1927.[27] Children had to be taught to stay out of the streets, and drivers had to agree to follow the new rules of the road. Policemen took on the duty of directing traffic at busy city intersections and later rode motorcycles to enforce the law.

As more people obtained cars, suburbs could be extended farther out and the middle class, mainly Anglos who could afford the vehicles, abandoned the crowded, dirty, noisy, and uncomfortable trolleys. For wealthy people automobiles were a symbol of prestige, and for much of the population they became a necessity of life. Although cars were a more expensive mode of transportation, many places were better reached with a car. Horses and wagons, along with the livery to support them, largely disappeared from the city streets in the 1920s. The roadways became cleaner, but just as crowded.

It was during this interval of 1923-1924 that Will Hogg, Mike Hogg, and Hugh Potter planned River Oaks as an automotive, residential suburb for the elite in west central Houston. It was designed by Kansas City landscape architects Hare and Hare around the River Oaks Country Club, with rigid building codes, large lots, buried utility lines, and curved streets. Architect John F. Staub built elegant homes of quiet wealth for oil millionaires. Deed restrictions and unwritten sales agreements excluded Jews, blacks, and other minorities. The development company operated independently for three years before it was annexed by the city. Today, River Oaks is located in the geographic center of the city and is the exemplar of wealthy living in Texas.[28]

For most of Houston the 51 miles of trolley track in 1910 transported the urban population, but in order to compete with the growing number of jitneys and private motorcars the Stone-Webster Company added buses in 1923. In 1927, with 224 trolleys and 90 miles of track, the company carried 152,000 passengers per day, 80 percent of the people who traveled downtown. But, it was the high point of a losing war, and a turnabout came quickly.

A survey in 1939 indicated that 80 percent of the vehicles entering downtown were automobiles and that they carried 85 percent of the commuters. The decline of public transportation was precipitous, and in 1941 the trolleys ceased to operate. This left public transportation to the despairing buses. The bus system struggled on to receivership in 1966 and then to a takeover by the city in 1978. Houston, regardless of the

Great Depression, for better and worse had become a quintessentially automotive city.[29]

AIRPLANES AND AIRPORTS

A legend maintains that Jacob F. Brodbeck, a German inventor and school supervisor, built a windup airplane powered by coiled springs that flew 12 feet high and 100 feet forward before becoming unwound and crashing. The flight took place at Luckenbach or possibly San Antonio in 1865 or 1868. Reports are sketchy, Brodbeck was unable to persuade investors, and no drawings exist. So, the story remains unproven, a Texas legend.

Following the successful flight of the Wright brothers in 1903, demonstrations took place in Texas cities starting with Louis Paulhan, a dapper Frenchman complete with a curled mustache, in Houston in 1910. Texans built their own experimental aircraft, and Katherine Stinson, of the famous Stinson flying family of San Antonio, became a noted stunt pilot. She set a long-distance record by flying from San Diego to San Francisco, toured Japan and China, and was the first woman commissioned as a mail pilot. She was rejected for World War I because of her sex, but she served as a volunteer ambulance driver in Europe. She caught tuberculosis and retired to Santa Fe, where she died at age eighty-six, a tough lady.

With its good weather and flat terrain, Texas attracted flying schools during the world wars, such as Randolph Field in San Antonio, which became known as the "West Point of the Air." Love Field in Dallas started in 1914 as an army training base named for a killed cadet from California. It was bought by the city in 1927. The following year limited passenger service began to San Antonio and Houston. National Air Transport used the field to fly the first airmail to Chicago.

Thomas E. Braniff (1883–1954) made Dallas the center of his regional air service in 1934, and American Airlines began to route through Dallas. The airport became a training base again for World War II. This so expanded its facilities that it became the largest passenger terminal in the Southwest in the postwar years. This brought it into heated competition with Meacham Field of Fort Worth, which had followed a similar development. The clash resulted in a spectacular airport rebalancing in the 1970s that transformed the entire urban configuration of North Texas.

Pan American World Airways linked Texas with Mexico City and Central America through Brownsville International Airport, which opened in 1929. Pan Am set up a maintenance and training station in Brownsville that pioneered the aviation industry in Latin America with Fort Tri-Motor aircraft.[30] Texas had 142 municipal landing facilities by 1932; the age of air passenger service had begun.[31]

THE CITY BEAUTIFUL AND CITY PLANNING

The "White City" of Chicago's Columbian Exposition in 1893, which was harmoniously designed for function and beauty, awakened visitors to the possibilities of urban planning. They returned home with thoughts about civic design, and soon the nationwide City Beautiful movement took root. Although Texas cities already had some plazas and public parks, such as Browder's Springs in Dallas, San Pedro Park in San Antonio, and Hermann Park in Houston, there had been little consideration given to overall planning for the comfort and aesthetic inspiration of the community. It was time to remove the trains from city streets and to plant trees. Texas cities such as Dallas (1905), Fort Worth (1909), and Houston (1910) now appointed park commissions that recognized for the first time the value of open space and planning.

Dallas, Sherman, Fort Worth, Wichita Falls, and El Paso hired George E. Kessler (1862-1923), a landscape architect from Kansas City, to design parks and thoroughfares to guide their growth. Although born in Germany, Kessler grew up in Dallas and then returned to study civic design in Germany, France, and Russia. He worked in Kansas City, St. Louis, and Dallas, where he drew up a famous "Kessler Plan" in 1909 to save the city from dangerous railroad crossings, Trinity River lowlands, and narrow downtown streets. He was noted for using the banks of watercourses for urban parks, but as in the case of Dallas, it took a long time to work out his suggestions. San Antonio hired Harland Bartholomew of St. Louis for a civic plan in 1929, but because of the Great Depression, his ideas remained on the shelf.

William C. Hogg (1875-1930), one of the developers of River Oaks, worked out a comprehensive plan for Houston in 1929. Following a family motto, "A beautiful city makes better citizens," and with Kessler as a consultant, he advocated acquiring parklands and building a civic center. In those ambitions he was successful. His overall plan for Houston, however, was rejected in a bitter fight about the zoning implied in the scheme.[32]

It is a curiosity that Houston voters have steadfastly rejected the concept of zoning, which is a common tool of urban planning. Other places, such as Dallas, have embraced it, but conservatives and real estate developers in Houston have viewed zoning as an unnecessary police power of government. Houston, consequently, is the largest unzoned city of the United States. It relies upon deed restrictions, real estate sales discretion, the laws of its incorporated suburbs, and a certain common sense that dictates against trying to place a refinery in the middle of River Oaks.

THE FINE ARTS

Will Hogg and his sister Ima (1882-1975) planted the seeds of development of the fine arts in Houston. They believed that a great city needed to display examples of human creativity and worked with others to establish an art museum in 1924-1926. Will bullied his rich friends for funds and donated his collection of Frederick Remington artworks.[33] Ima eventually donated her home, Bayou Bend, which was filled with art, to the museum, but she is best known for her long advocacy and support of a resident Houston symphony.

Starting in 1913 "Miss Ima," as she was affectionately known, according to Southern custom, provided money, enthusiasm, prodding, and a place to live for visiting conductors. A municipal orchestra was accomplished in 1931 and began a halting maturation, with Miss Ima as an unflagging inspiration for musical excellence that stabilized with Ernst Hoffman as conductor (1935-1947). Hoffman had to tolerate a cigar-smoking tympanist and a bassoonist who played with his shoes off. Oilman Hugh Roy Cullen (1881-1957) and insurance leader Gus Wortham (1891-1976) took turns funding the organization and brought it near to national prominence by 1950 in spite of a poor venue.[34]

RETAIL SHOPPING

Perhaps the greatest amenity of the city was the consumer goods offered to the public—the larger the city, the greater the variety. At the time women, spending 85 percent of the income, were the purchasing agents of the family, and they paid attention to quality and convenience. They embraced the City Beautiful movement as civic housekeeping and looked upon themselves as moral guardians of their towns. Stores in the

1920s began to study white female shopping behavior as retailers began to recognize the economic impact of women. In a survey of Texas shoppers in 1929, William Reilly discovered that rural women were also drawn into a big-city shopping habit.[35]

In the large cities middle-class housewives, children in tow, periodically boarded a streetcar and shopped their way through the downtown area. In Dallas, for example, they had a choice of venerable stores: E. M. Kahn (1872), Sanger Brothers (1872), A. Harris (1887), Titche-Goettinger (1902), and Volk Brothers shoe store (1889).[36] The bellwether of all Texas department stores, however, was Neiman-Marcus.

Herbert Marcus, his sister, Carrie Marcus Neiman, and her husband, Al Neiman, opened the store in 1907 to sell superior and fashionable merchandise to upper-class customers. They nurtured a clientele from North Texas, profited from the East Texas oil millionaires, imported fashions from New York, and weathered the Great Depression with little difficulty. Stanley Marcus (1905–2002) brought the store to prominence with

Sears Roebuck store on South Main, Houston, 1936. Bailey (Bob) Studios Photographic Archive, e_bb_3846, the Dolph Briscoe Center for American History, the University of Texas at Austin.

national advertising, a stunning seasonal Christmas catalogue, fashion shows, and superior customer service. He opened the first branch store in 1951 in Dallas and another in Houston in 1955.

Stanley Marcus became a liberal force in conservative Dallas and a legend in the history of merchandising. One Christmas Eve, for example, he observed a wealthy, neglectful man desperate for a last-minute present for his wife. Marcus asked her sizes and told the man to wait ten minutes. The merchant then took a giant brandy snifter that had been used for a display and filled it with colored layers of cashmere sweaters. On top he placed a white angora sweater to suggest whipped cream and a ten-karat ruby ring to serve as a cherry. The cost was $25,350. The customer when he saw it exclaimed, "That's exactly what I was looking for! I'll take it!"[37]

Department stores began to abandon downtown for suburban shopping centers in the 1940s, and variety stores such as Woolworth and W. T. Grant began to die off. Sears Roebuck, however, pioneered outlying department stores. In 1939 the company built a three-story art deco store on South Main Street in Houston with lighted parking for six hundred cars, air-conditioning, and escalators. Located thirty blocks from downtown, it was a first.[38]

In segregated Texas, unfortunately, most businessmen ignored the potential of the black communities ringing the downtowns. The self-concepts of women, moreover, had begun to shift after women began to own cars and experience the self-confidence of wartime jobs. Shopping, although still interesting, was no longer the prime directive of the housewife. There were other things to do, and the movement for women's liberation was just over the horizon.

25

THE GREAT DEPRESSION

Texas prosperity, like that in the rest of the nation, evaporated on "Black Tuesday," October 29, 1929, with the collapse of the New York stock market. In spite of brave talk, denial, and President Herbert Hoover's trickle-down aid to banks and big business, the depression continued and deepened. Cotton and oil prices fell, workers were laid off, and churches found themselves unable to meet the demands for charity. The general assessment is that the Great Depression struck industrial states harder than Texas, but it was bad enough.

To make matters worse, drought in West Texas contributed a dust bowl of "black blizzards" that had the power to dust the desks of Congress in Washington, DC. A particular storm in April 1935, as an example, was 1,000 feet high and 200 miles wide. It traveled 60 miles per hour from the northern plains. The rolling dirt blotted out the sun, drove ducks and birds in front of it, and caused barbed wire tips to glow with St. Elmo's fire. It was in Dodge City, Kansas, at 2:49 p.m.; at Lamar, Colorado, at 4:15 p.m.; Boise City, Oklahoma, at 6:00 p.m.; and Dalhart, Texas, at 6:20 p.m. "I thought the end of the world was coming" was the common expression.[1]

In Lubbock—a city of churches where one-quarter of the population went to pray every Sunday, where some preachers blamed the depression on sin, and where most religious groups gave food to the hungry—three children nonetheless starved to death in fall 1930. City officials turned city hall square into a turnip patch the following summer to help feed the poor.[2]

Churches everywhere did their duty, as Hoover expected, but the problem was overwhelming. Extended families clung together as working members supported the unemployed and marriages were postponed. With the new administration of Franklin Delano Roosevelt, Texans took a political chance to set aside conservative attitudes and accept help. The New Deal eventually spent $1.46 billion in Texas.

John Nance "Cactus Jack" Garner of Uvalde was vice president, and seven other Texans held prominent chairs in house committees. That helped. The most important Texan in Washington, DC, however, was Houston banker Jesse H. Jones (1874-1956), who had been recruited by President Hoover to hand out the money of the Reconstruction Finance Corporation (RFC). President Roosevelt held him over, and by 1938 he had disbursed $10 billion in loans to banks, railroads, agriculture, and public works. At a time when a few cents could buy a cup of coffee, these were enormous sums of money. Jones was once overheard to say in a telephone negotiation, "I'll not give a nickel more than two billion dollars for it!"[3]

As the New Deal progressed, the cities depended upon the relief programs of the Federal Emergency Relief Administration, the Public Works Administration, and the Works Progress Administration, all of which spent federal money on relief, hospitals, libraries, roads, schools, and athletic facilities. The Federal Writer's Project hired historians to write city histories and index newspapers; the Federal Theater Project employed impecunious actors to present plays; and the Federal Art Project put poor artists to work decorating public buildings with murals.

About one-third of the money went to laborers on the roads, and by the end of the period one-fourth of the Texas highway system had been given "high type" surfaces, and another half had been improved over simple earthen conditions.[4]

The general thrust was to improve infrastructure where possible but, most importantly, to provide employment for working people. It was a question of survival and pride. A WPA recipient in Houston said, "You know, it's been a year since I've taken home a paycheck. That's a long time to tell your kids there's no money for ice cream."[5]

President Franklin D. Roosevelt and Jesse H. Jones in the latter 1930s. Photograph courtesy of the Dolph Briscoe Center for American History, the University of Texas at Austin.

The New Deal produced no great transformation of urban form or custom. Dallas, for example, suffered severe declines in the construction, wholesaling, and merchandising segments of the economy, but the city government remained defiantly solvent by reducing municipal salaries 5 to 20 percent, laying off city workers, halting paving and sewer contracts, and supplying its welfare cases with groceries instead of cash. Attempts to unionize the Dallas Ford factory and textile companies found no support from the city or courts.

It was common in Dallas and other cities to discharge married women under the assumption that the husband would bring home money, and there was little objection to this assumption except from poor women trying to support a family. Segregation went unchallenged, and black businesses faced extinction as city services shrank. Welfare depended mainly upon federal funding. In 1935-1936 federal moneys amounted to 81 percent of the total for welfare in Dallas and 80 percent in Houston.[6]

Yet, federal dollars resulted in concrete, visible changes. The Texas state park system still utilizes Civilian Conservation Corps improve-

The contemporary River Walk of San Antonio, an urban gem for tourism. Photograph by author.

ments; trees were replanted in East Texas; and Austin was given a reprieve from future floods by the dams of the Lower Colorado River Authority. The Paseo del Rio, or Riverwalk, in San Antonio was created in the 1930s with a combination of a WPA grant and local bonds.

The Riverwalk had been the dream of architect Robert H. H. Hugman and others to use the downtown bend of the San Antonio River as an urban park with restaurants, shops, benches, stairways, landscaping, and a walkway instead of following a business suggestion from 1911 to encase it in concrete and use it as a sewer. Hugman gave speeches, agitated, and argued for the commercial and aesthetic possibilities, and the idea finally won civic approval. It was completed in 1941—twenty-one blocks and 8,500 feet of riverbank—but did not reach its full potential until the celebration of Hemisfair '68. Since then the downtown Riverwalk has been a major tourist attraction and a delight to the city.

THE TEXAS CENTENNIAL

Federal and state funds helped make possible the Texas Centennial in 1936. Various sites benefited, but significant was the erection of the San Jacinto Monument and Museum in Houston on the grounds of the decisive battle of the Texas Revolution. The octagonal shaft of reinforced concrete faced with Texas limestone soared 570 feet, 4.5 inches above ground level.

This made it higher than the Washington Monument—a point of contention—but Jesse Jones, who was complicit in its conception, told his Washington friends that it was 5 inches shorter, which was true if

The San Jacinto Monument, near Houston, shortly after completion, 1939. Photograph courtesy of the Houston Public Library, HMRC.

Big Tex welcomed visitors to the fair for years, but burned in 2012. He has since been reconstructed. This is the old "Tex." Photograph by author.

measured from the peak of its star at the top to the platform on which it rested. The monument and its museum put an exclamation point on the battleground, which had been a place of casual visitation since before 1883, when it became a state property.

Dallas won the greatest prize with its $8 million cash commitment to host the Texas Centennial celebration at its fairgrounds. The state and Congress each contributed $3 million more for the permanent, air-conditioned art deco buildings illustrating Texas history and progress.

They included the Hall of State, the Hall of Negro Life (the first of its kind), various exhibition buildings, and an aquarium.

The celebration opened June 6, 1939, and over the following two years attracted 6.4 million visitors. Next door in Fort Worth a competing celebration with fleshy stage shows welcomed 986,000 tourists. Eleven thousand billboards scattered in surrounding states proclaimed, "Go Elsewhere for Education, Come to Fort Worth for Entertainment."

Spending involved eight thousand workers, and the tourism of the centennial eased the depression in both cities. Afterward, Dallas continued to host a state fair, which gave it a separate identity from the rest of the state. The widespread publicity and effort to promote visitation, moreover, marks a milestone in the tourist industry of the state. The first color highway map was produced and distributed at thirteen tourist stations along major roadway junctions. In the words of historian Kenneth B. Ragsdale, 1936 was "the year America discovered Texas."[7]

26

WORLD WAR II

As it did elsewhere in the United States, the massive governmental spending to fight World War II brought the Great Depression to an abrupt halt. Everyone could find a job. Men, and some women, entered into the armed services, and women filled male places in the offices, factories, and fields. A 10 percent increase of women in the workforce occurred. Families supported the war effort by saving stamps; buying war bonds; planting victory gardens; rationing gasoline, tires, sugar, shoes, and coffee; and sacrificing their young men.

About 750,000 Texans served in uniform, 19,000 died, and 33 of them won a Congressional Medal of Honor. The federal government constructed in Texas thirty-five airfields, twelve army training camps, five naval air stations, and eight hospitals—more than in any other state. Manufacturing increased fourfold during the war years, and a half-million people left the farms, poured into the Lone Star State to work in the factories and shipyards, and remained afterward rather than return to farm labor. The war was the great catalyst for growth in Austin, Dallas, Fort Worth, San Antonio, and Houston. These cities increased in population by about 50 percent. When the decade was over, Texas was no longer a rural state—a line crossed by the northeastern states a century earlier.

FORT WORTH

In Fort Worth the chamber of commerce offered a deed for 1,450 acres near Lake Worth, and the city agreed to clear land and build roads in order to receive a new B-24 bomber plant in 1941. Voters approved a bond issue for sewers, drainage, streetlights, and traffic signals; contractors worked around the clock to complete the facility in nine months; and Consolidated Aircraft Corporation, using assembly-line techniques, produced its first four-engine B-24 Liberator by April 1942. In 1943, with 30,600 employees, it was producing two hundred airplanes per month. A pilot and crew training post (later Carswell Air Force Base) shortly opened next door, as Fort Worth added to its military facilities with a hospital, a quartermaster depot, and a seaplane docking station.[1]

The population jumped by 58 percent and the city ran out of buses. People with pickup trucks pulled trailers with sideboards for workers to ride to the plant where "Rosie the Riveter" women made up one-third of the workforce. The war broke down gender discrimination as the Technical High School began to train civilians for factory work in riveting and machine tool operation.

Housing in one- and two-bedroom apartments was quickly built with federal funding at Liberator Village, which gave preference to Consolidated workers. Liberator Village became a suburb of White Settlement, and for those who migrated from rural places, the apartments—equipped with electricity, running water, and indoor bathrooms—were astonishing. Although telephone service was unavailable, there were paved streets, a shopping center with movies, and an elementary school. Other housing suburbs, River Oaks and Westworth, developed in much the same manner.[2]

After a century of sleep, Fort Worth, with a dozen new military installations, had become a military town once again. Following World War II, when a contraction might be predicted, orders to produce the B-36 sustained employment, and Fort Worth became a permanent part of the modern military-industrial complex. Fort Worth was a segment of the "gunbelt," a major economic phenomenon of the postwar United States, with Texas usually among the top ten states to receive prime war contracts.[3]

SAN ANTONIO

As might be expected from its long military tradition and bases, San

Antonio boomed during the war. Its population expanded by 61 percent during the decade of the 1940s. Fort Sam Houston in 1940 was the largest army post in the United States and in 1949 had 1,500 buildings. It was headquarters of the Fourth United States Army. Kelly Air Force Base (1917-2001), established for flight training and aircraft maintenance, was used mainly for maintenance in World War II. Lackland Air Force Base took over preflight training for almost all personnel from Kelly in 1942 and has continued to the present time. Randolph Air Force Base was designated for pilot training in 1930, as was Brooks Air Force Base. Brooks trained paratroopers in World War II and turned to medical research, including aerospace, in 1959-1960.

This military complex employed about one-third of the population and remained the main driver of the San Antonio economy. Because of the many marriages between soldiers and civilians, San Antonio became known as the "mother-in-law" of the army.[4] San Antonio's effort to attract war industry failed, however, because the city refused to provide free land for business location and it became instead a great military reservation.[5]

AUSTIN AND DALLAS

Austin grew during the war decade from the normal expansion of state government and the University of Texas, as it had before, but also from Bergstrom Air Force Base (1942-1993). Dallas advanced slightly less than the others, but hosted German prisoners of war, employed 38,500 workers at the nearby Grand Prairie North American Aviation factory to make P-51 Mustang fighter aircraft, squabbled with Fort Worth about a joint airport, and watched the local Ford assembly plant put together ninety-four thousand jeeps.

Failing to annex the wealthy Park Cities suburb in 1945, the city absorbed the land surrounding Park Cities and enjoyed an immediate postwar boom by adding thirteen new manufacturing plants every month. In fifteen years, 1945-1960, the square miles of Dallas leaped from 50 to 283.[6] Grand Prairie suffered when North American Aviation abruptly shut its factory in 1945 and returned to California. Fortunately, United Aircraft Corporation moved into the old aircraft plant, and Grand Prairie developed additional economic assets in tourism and the manufacturing of furniture, boats, and mobile homes.

HOUSTON

With nearby large, essential deposits of natural gas, oil, salt, and sulphur, a petrochemical complex came forth from the necessity of World War II. The federal government and business invested $600 million during the fighting and another $300 million afterward. Under government contract, Humble Oil and Shell Oil made toluene, an ingredient in high explosives; Humble Oil and Shell Oil also produced aviation fuel; the Defense Plant Corporation mixed butadiene from Humble Oil and ethylene from Monsanto Chemical at Texas City to make Buna-S synthetic rubber, which was used to make tires, lifeboats, and balloons in Akron, Ohio.

Through interconnecting pipelines, the output of one refinery became the input of another. Butylene, hydrogen, ethylene, butadiene, acetylene, acetone, chlorine, and ammonia flowed through the pipes. The major corporations of the chemical industry—Shell, DuPont, Monsanto, Union Carbide, Dow, Celanese, Diamond Alkali, and others—joined in the petrochemical complex that formed a "golden triangle" stretching from Houston to Freeport to Port Arthur.

This evolved further after the war and made Texas the nation's second-largest producer of chemicals, behind New Jersey. *Houston* magazine commented in 1957, "If an air-to-ground X-ray were made of Harris County, these interlaced pipelines would show up like a nerve system around the backbone—the Houston Ship Channel—of an industrial giant."[7] From 1942 to 1952 the Port of Houston cleared more tonnage than any other port in the nation except New York. Thereafter, it fell into closer competition with New Orleans and Philadelphia. Sam Houston's namesake city had become an oil and petrochemical center, an energy capital.

One of the most dramatic coastal war industries was shipbuilding. The U.S. Maritime Commission contracted with Todd Shipyards to assemble Liberty Ships, transport vessels, on the Houston Ship Channel. Within four months in 1942 Todd expanded from six thousand to twenty thousand employees, where only 3 percent had knowledge of shipbuilding. Using assembly-line techniques, Todd reduced the construction time from 254 days to 53 and turned out 222 ships during the war. Using the same process, Brown Shipbuilding Company built three hundred subchasers, destroyer escorts, and landing craft on nearby Green's Bayou. Brown launched its vessels broadside with a great splash into the water.

The Houston Ship Channel in 1952. The expansion in the area and the growing problem of industrial air pollution can be seen in this picture. Rare east or northeast winds sweeping up the channel concentrated the pollution to such an extent that it could change lead-based paint to black in color. Bailey (Bob) Studios Photographic Archive, e_bb_2988, the Dolph Briscoe Center for American History, the University of Texas at Austin.

The shipbuilding industry employed forty thousand and paid a $2 million weekly payroll.

During the war forty-five Houston companies held prime contracts, and in 1945–1948 Harris County led the nation in industrial construction. The migrants from the countryside did not go home. They remained to become urban cowboys, and the population of Houston increased by 55 percent in the 1940s. The South Houston suburban towns of Deer Park, Jacinto City, Galena Park, and Pasadena expanded to house the workers. In 1948 Houston was ranked as the fastest-growing city in the country.

27

THE IMMEDIATE POSTWAR YEARS

The military-industrial boost of the war continued as the country became involved in the Korean War, the Cold War, the Vietnam War, the War on Terror, and other military adventures. There were lulls, of course, but military appropriations did not cease. The Truman Doctrine, developed to protect democratic nations, resulted in a permanent war economy after the Korean War, whereby defense spending amounted to roughly 5 percent of the gross national product of the nation. The contracts, pensions, and permanent war installations thus became an income stream for the larger cities. Ancillary companies bloomed as Texas became an industrialized state. It took Texas this long to shake off the remnants of a rural frontier and redirect its human capital and resources to building a city-based society.

At home and abroad Texas had achieved a magnificent war record, but there were rumbles of unrest. Wherever government contracts were canceled, women were the first to be laid off. The women pilots of the Women Airfare Service Pilots (WASP), who had trained at Sweetwater, Texas, and flown almost every type of aircraft to its site of operation, for example, found themselves summarily dismissed without recognition. There was an attitude that women worked during the war to allow men to go fight. When the men came home it was expected that the women would stand aside to permit the men to retake their old jobs and authority. This created gender tension and misunderstanding.

In addition, the state was still rigidly segregated in schools and neighborhoods. The State Constitution of 1876 divided the schools; state legislators segregated railroad cars in 1891; and in 1909 the lawmakers required separate waiting rooms in railroad stations. Blacks rode at the back of the buses, drank from separate drinking fountains, sat in the balconies at movie houses, did not expect service at white restaurants or department stores, stepped off the sidewalks to allow whites to pass, and experienced the worst of the public schools.

A race riot occurred at the shipyard in Beaumont in 1943 about a presumed rape of a white woman; the Dallas police department delayed the hiring of black police officers, while black homes were dynamited and segregation was built into the new plans for city expansion; photographs of black brides were not published in Fort Worth newspapers; and deed restrictions in Houston prevented blacks from moving away from traditionally black neighborhoods.

Mexicans, even though counted as white by the census, were not expected to commingle with Anglos even in San Antonio, El Paso, or along the border. In death honorable Mexican American veterans had to be buried in separate cemeteries. Women could vote, but could not serve on juries and hardly counted in politics. Unions were without respect; right-to-work was the revered standard. Almost everyone, however, had served dutifully during the war to defeat a great menace to democracy and now, as could be sensed, social fairness was out of balance. This all pointed to future problems for Texas, which had grown by 20 percent during the war. Every fifth person was a newcomer—someone from the outside who might not "understand" the traditional culture.

★

PART FOUR

Great Texas Cities, 1950–2012

28

POPULATION AND URBAN EXPANSION

During the next sixty years, with a completed central place network of small, medium, and large cities, the larger urban places expanded at an extraordinary rate, dominated the state, and revealed flashes of excellence. In the midst of the historical noise and confusion, such flashes provide meaning for the irreversible headlong urban rush that would place 88 percent of the people in an urban environment. They also reveal insights into Texas civilization.

Peter Hall, who surveyed major world cities during their "golden years" of accomplishment, found commonalities of large size, trade, elements of capitalism, wealth, cosmopolitan population, and a certain amount of disorder.[1] Charles Murray, a scholar who tracked the lives of noteworthy people in the arts and sciences, 1400–1950, made a case for the significance of "elite cities" such as Rome during the Renaissance, or London during the Industrial Revolution, that attracted people of ambition, talent, and creativity.[2] These were places where innovative people gathered and pushed civilization to a higher plane.

A contemporary urban economist, Richard Florida, has sharpened the point by emphasizing the home choices of contemporary creative people. He discovered that they prefer places of diversity, tolerance of cultural differences, and openness to new thoughts. "Creative cities," as he called them, often contain high-tech industries and elite universities that embrace talent, technology, and tolerance. They attract highly mobile knowledge workers that included engineers, professors, software designers, architects, scientists, writers, musicians, poets, and actors.[3]

In a search for greatness in Texas, it would seem reasonable to pay attention to the central cities. They are the largest, richest, and most diverse. They have sheltered creative people. The quest in this section is to find excellence in Texas urban life as an expression of the civilization and for a historical explanation of how it was achieved.[4] Such accomplishment is a measure of greatness for Texas cities and a reason for their existence.

Size of population and its growth in Texas continued to be a dominating theme for the remainder of the twentieth century and into the next. The census of 2010 named three cities with over a million people—Houston, San Antonio, and Dallas. Houston was the fourth largest in the United States. Another three cities—Austin, Fort Worth, and El Paso—had over a half-million residents, and nineteen other places posted over one hundred thousand. More than 4,100 other towns remained under that number, many in places of less than 1,000.[5] The numbers generally support the pyramidal central place and hierarchy of cities hypothesis about a few large cities servicing intermediate and smaller places.

In 1949 the Census Bureau began to designate metropolitan statistical areas (MSAs), which counted dominant cities and their dependent

TABLE 28.1. Population of Texas, 1950-2010, Percent Urban

YEAR	NUMBER	PERCENT URBAN
1950	7,711,000	63 (new def.)
1960	9,580,000	75
1970	11,197,000	80
1980	14,229,000	80
1990	16,987,000	80
2000	20,852,000	82
2010	25,146,000	88

Source: *Texas Almanac and State Industrial Guide, 1968-1969* (Dallas: A. H. Belo Corp., 1967), p. 168; Elizabeth Cruce Alvarez, ed., *Texas Almanac, 2010-2011* (Denton: Texas State Historical Association, 2010), p. 418.

counties. Used mainly for statistical analysis, the MSAs indicated the economic and political power of a city and region. Twenty-five Texas MSAs existed in 2010. The largest ones were the Dallas–Fort Worth–Arlington region, with a population of 6,372,000; Houston–Baytown–Sugar Land with 5,963,000; San Antonio with 2,143,000; and Austin–Round Rock with 1,759,000. Dallas–Fort Worth was fourth largest, and Houston–Baytown–Sugar Land was sixth largest (fifth in 2012) in the nation.

The leading MSAs possessed the fastest-growing cities. The state's population increased at a rate of 20 percent for each decade except the 1960s and outpaced the nation in every decade. While the birth rate was twice that of the death rate, in-migration from other states and nations made up half the advances. People still found opportunity in Texas.

DIVERSITY

Large numbers of people are prerequisite for a diversity of people, and diversity is needed for creativity.[6] The most dramatic demographic change is the 42 percent increase in the Hispanic population during the past several decades. The state stands currently at 45 percent Anglo, 38 percent Hispanic, 11 percent black, and 6 percent "other." Dallas County (Dallas) is 40 percent Hispanic and 34 percent Anglo; Harris County (Houston) is 42 percent Hispanic and 32 percent Anglo; Bexar County (San Antonio) is 58 percent Hispanic and 31 percent Anglo.

In two decades Houston shifted from a biracial black-white city to one of remarkable diversity, with 37 percent Hispanic, 31 percent white, 25 percent black, and 7 percent Asian. Following the fall of Saigon in 1975, Indo-Chinese refugees (Vietnamese, Cambodians, Laotians, and Thais) streamed into California and Texas. Just ten blocks from downtown Houston a neighborhood of Indo-Chinese shops and restaurants infuses the locale with Asian smells, sounds, and movement.

It is no wonder that the ruling white conservative politicians became increasingly nervous. These massive demographic moves portended possible trouble. Demographers knew the cities were changing and the political ground was trembling. For the presidential election of 2008 all the large cities except Fort Worth voted for the liberal Obama irrespective of the firm conservative Republican grasp on the state. The same happened in 2012, with conservative Romney Republicans winning in the surrounding counties of the metropolitan areas while losing the cities.

CITY LIMITS

Another aspect of size has been the extension of city limits—a spatial expansion that has complicated politics, civic services, urban planning, and transportation. The Municipal Annexation Act of 1963 permitted cities of population over 1,500 to assume a ring of extraterritorial jurisdiction reaching one-half to five miles beyond their city limits. In a home-rule city a vote of the city council could annex up to 10 percent of its land area and accumulate amounts up to 30 percent. Residents of the area to be annexed had no choice in the matter unless they were independently incorporated, and any developers in the extraterritorial ring had to comply with existing city ordinances. The expanding central city had to provide its normal city services within three years.

This law enabled a municipality to keep up with its tax base—people who worked in the city but avoided paying taxes by living in suburbs. In Texas annexation had the effect of keeping a white majority in power even though it had joined in a white flight from the central city. It also allowed the parent city to avoid being surrounded by small incorporated towns that blocked growth. The law was supposed to facilitate gradual expansion, but confirmed an already aggressive annexation war going on among the cities.

When the affluent Highland Park and University Park, for example, refused to merge with Dallas in 1945, the miffed Dallas City Council dismissed Park City representatives from their committees and annexed all the land around them. The city expanded from 50 to 90 square miles, but by 1976 Dallas itself was encircled and escaped only by persuading the town of Renner to become a part of Dallas. Then, it had a breech from which to outflank the outliers that strangled it and move into unincorporated land in bordering Collin and Denton Counties.[7]

Houston swallowed Bellaire, Galena Park, Jacinto City, South Side Place, Pasadena, and West University Place in 1948-1949. The towns of Pasadena, LaPorte, Lomax, and Deer Park to the southeast then conspired to stop Houston and take a quarter of Harris County. Houston answered with a first council reading to annex all unincorporated land in Harris County. "Annexing the entire county is preposterous," exclaimed flabbergasted Mayor Lewis W. Cutrer. That would have expanded Houston to 1,560 square miles, but it stopped the local war because the first reading gave Houston a priority claim that it did not have to act upon.[8]

San Antonio annexed a strip of land 116 feet wide and five miles long in order to extend its extraterritorial jurisdiction. Upholding the action, the Texas Supreme Court said that annexed land required no specific length, width, shape, or size. Fort Worth, experiencing the same problem, annexed a strip around its southwestern edge. During the 1970s, at the height of the craze, Texas cities annexed 1,472 square miles containing 456,000 people. As French journalist Pierre Voisin exclaimed in 1962, "There is no plan. I am horrified. Everyone is doing just as he pleases, building here and building there . . . Houston is spreading just like a spilled bucket of water."[9] By 2010 the Houston city limits covered 656 square miles; San Antonio, 412; Dallas, 386; Fort Worth, 299; Austin, 272; and El Paso, 250.

In general, it was expensive to annex. City services—water, police, fire, sewerage, paving, lighting—had to be extended eventually, sometimes across empty land. If a subdivision was taken in, the central city had to absorb the utilities already in place along with the original bonds sold to install them. Seventy-four individual water districts, for instance, existed on Houston's perimeter in 1967.

For San Antonio, water supply became a nightmare. The city had stubbornly refused any water development beyond drilling of the Edwards Aquifer, but city growth to the north over the recharge zone in the 1970s brought the problem to the forefront. The wooded, hilly, quiet terrain was attractive to builders compared to the flat, noisy land near the air force bases to the south.

Starting in 1972, local environmentalists aligned in a coalition that included Congressman Henry B. González to block federal Housing and Urban Development support for construction of a new town called San Antonio Ranch. Eruption of protest came once more to stop the building of a large regional shopping mall in 1975. In 1977 the San Antonio City Council tried to enforce a moratorium on building in the recharge zone, but it was forced to modify it under legal threat and court ruling.[10] The problem of urban water supply remained.

Henry Cisneros, the city's first Hispanic mayor, recommended conservation, recycling, and the building of a surface reservoir. The reservoir idea was twice defeated by water activists who disliked the expense and who ignored the new regional Edwards Aquifer Authority, which was beginning to limit pumping rights. The Mayor's Citizens Committee met for six months in 1996–1997 with little agreement about water management versus water quantity. In 2014 the trustees of the water system contracted to construct a massive desalination plant to process brackish South Bexar groundwater.[11] In San Antonio, consequently, the age-old question of urban water supply continued.

There were few geographical limits to inhibit the spread of Texas cities, and it was easy to annex land. It meant, however, less density of population per square mile in the cities—Houston in 2010 was 3,500; San Antonio 2,900; Dallas 3,500; Fort Worth 2,200; Austin 2,700; El Paso 2,500. For comparison, the density of New York City was 28,000 and Los Angeles was 7,500 per square mile. People had to travel farther for the amenities of the city. The contrasting urban model was to build upward rather than outward. Texans chose to sprawl outward; there was a lot of available land.[12]

29

SUBURBS AND SUBDIVISIONS

Cleanliness, quietude, safety, spaciousness, home ownership, better schools, and similar neighbors have always drawn people to reside on the outskirts of cities whenever their money and circumstances would permit. Transport by mule cars, trolleys, buggies, buses, and automobiles have all had an impact by allowing people to reach farther into the expanding ring of the city. Among the rich suburbs have been River Oaks in Houston, Highland Park in Dallas, and Alamo Heights in San Antonio; middle-class places have been rooted in such places as Bellaire and West University Place in Houston, Oak Cliff in Dallas, and Terrell Hills in San Antonio. Lower-class housing remained behind in the old city neighborhoods near the downtowns, and in low-rent housing projects.[1]

In 1950 the Fifth Ward of Houston, to the northeast of downtown, was the city's largest black neighborhood, but the penetration of the I-10 and U.S. 59 expressways divided the ward and cut off the residents from its business core. As a result the Third Ward, to the south of downtown, became the center of black cultural and business life. Spillover into the adjoining wealthy MacGregor neighborhood made these streets the "richest black neighborhood in Texas." The ward grew by 39 percent in the 1970s, and Houston came to have the largest black community in the South. Blacks, as usual in Houston, historically bore the burden of unemployment in bad times, and the location of solid waste dumps at all times.[2]

San Antonio, Dallas, and Houston built low-cost housing under New Deal legislation. With federal funds Houston built two projects for whites and two for blacks in the 1940s. Through the generosity of philanthropists Will and Susan V. Clayton, the city put up 348 units mainly for Hispanics in 1952. Houston was hindered in future efforts by the lack of a general zoning plan, which is required for federal funding. Clovis Heimsath, of the Governor's Committee on Mental Health Planning, commented, "Houston has a very difficult problem with itself."[3]

In response to the Housing Act of 1937, the Dallas City Council created the Dallas Housing Authority (DHA), which undertook a public housing program between 1939 and 1942. It erected more than 1,500 units for whites, blacks, and Hispanics as a part of a slum clearance and low-income housing program. Shifting political ideology, however, brought attacks on urban renewal by Dallas Republican Congressman Bruce Alger and his conservative followers in the 1950s that eventually led to an end of the effort.[4]

Sympathy for low-cost housing projects faded away until the sensational urban riots of the mid-1960s brought national attention once again to urban problems. The federal government established the Department of Housing and Urban Development as part of President Lyndon Johnson's Great Society in 1965 and initiated block grants to states to improve city infrastructure. Federal interest in urban revitalization, however, faded again with succeeding administrations to the point of becoming a "romantic memory," in the words of urban historian Roger Biles.[5]

SHARPSTOWN

Retail housing developers in Houston, as elsewhere in the nation, responded to pent-up postwar demand. Frank W. Sharp in 1954 launched Sharpstown, a $400 million, 6,500 acre, 15,000-unit, middle-class community in southwest Houston that became a model for the nation. It had planned space for schools, an air-conditioned mall, recreation, and automobiles. Sharp donated 10 miles of land for the construction of the Southwest Freeway to downtown Houston. The well-built, three-bedroom bungalows and traditional houses on large lots were meant for Anglos, but later attracted black, Hispanic, and Asian homebuyers to the neighborhood as Houston changed complexion.[6] The recession of the 1980s influenced the shift by lowering housing prices by 14 percent.

Reporter Jan Jarboe found a divided Sharpstown in 1993. "There is impenetrable segregation of all kinds: by race, class, ability, and aspiration," she wrote. "The Asians stick to their own and don't like the blacks, who don't like the encroachment of the Hispanics. As for the whites, many feel they've been left high, dry, and lonesome." Sharpstown High School was 32 percent black, 28 percent Hispanic, 24 percent white, and 16 percent Asian. It was racially integrated, but still separated as everyone tried to be different and equal at the same time.[7]

Research by Rice University's Kinder Institute nonetheless uncovered an increase of diversity and a decline in racial segregation for Houston housing over the past twenty years.[8] Perhaps an important cultural shift toward tolerance has taken place; perhaps not.

WOODLANDS

City expansion inspired other subdivisions, and among the most interesting was the Woodlands, 27 miles north of downtown Houston near the town of Conroe. It was the dream of Galveston oilman George Mitchell to build a "new town" within metropolitan Houston that would present a planned variety of housing with superior cultural, educational, and recreational facilities. It would be a harmonious, healthy, pleasant place to escape the inner-city problems of pollution, blight, and traffic. The Urban Growth and New Community Development Act of 1970 provided guaranteed federal backing of bonds and notes for the project, and Mitchell broke ground in September 1972.

The plans called at first for forty-nine thousand residential units of mixed single-family, patio, townhouse, and condominium homes, with 15 percent reserved for low-income buyers. It was arranged in six villages designed by Scots landscape architect Ian McHarg, each with recreation and school areas nestled respectfully in a wooded landscape. The integrated planning was reminiscent of Columbia, Maryland, and Reston, Virginia. With forethought, Mitchell and his staff asked the City of Houston to extend extraterritorial jurisdiction. This helped them to fight off annexation two years later by an opportunistic group from Conroe.

In 2007 the Woodlands incorporated on its own with the permission of Houston. Championship-level golf, tennis, and swimming facilities were built, and Mitchell completed a home office for his Mitchell Energy and Development Corporation in an office park in 1980. This was followed in the next two decades with other corporate campuses. One-third of office construction in metropolitan Houston was at the Woodlands in 2000.

Mitchell's dream failed to produce a communal religious arrangement or a branch campus of the University of Houston, and the relationship with the Department of Housing and Urban Development ended when the department gave up new community development in 1983. Still, by this time the Woodlands had a population of sixteen thousand, with 9 percent minority representation. Of fifteen new towns begun under the Great Society, the Woodlands was the only success, due in large measure to George Mitchell's attention and wealth. The population grew to ninety-four thousand in 2010 as the Woodlands became the choice upscale residential and business office location of the Houston metropolitan region.[9]

The Woodlands, with its 90 percent white population, demonstrated an urban phenomenon tracked by journalist Bill Bishop and sociologist Robert G. Cushing in *The Big Sort* (2008). Some 4 to 5 percent of the U.S. population moves every year, and since the mid-1960s people have been microscopically sorting themselves into neighborhoods of similar political, economic, religious, educational, and social interests.

The sort has not been based on race. It is a function of increased wealth and mobility, and it has resulted in an income segregation, or segmentation, of society. Bishop and Cushing have proven the folklore wisdom of "birds of a feather flock together" and support the observations of Richard Florida about creative people. The danger, according to the authors, is a fragmentation of society into homogeneous geographic groups untrusting of others. "White flight" really meant high-income people, mainly Anglo, moving to counties that became strongly conservative. The authors found that schools, interestingly, have begun to resegregate; at least they are less integrated than they were in the 1970s. The exchange of ideas, the cross-fertilization needed for creativity, is thus diminished.[10]

30

SEGREGATION AND INTEGRATION

Although income stratification in contemporary American society is entrenched as a measurement of success, racial segregation in schools, housing, and civic society has been largely suppressed. It was an important step for cities along a path toward greatness because talent does not come gender- or color-coded. In 1950, nevertheless, the separation of races in Texas was sharply defined in law and society. During the following two decades, however, due to federal laws, the pressure of black groups, court decisions, business attitudes, and a certain amount of good sense, racial segregation broke down. In Texas cities, to their credit, violence was largely avoided, and confrontation was settled between groups with compromise and accommodation.[1]

The National Association for the Advancement of Colored People (NAACP), a major actor, established itself in Texas in 1915-1918, and retreated before the Ku Klux Klan onslaught in the 1920s. Juanita Craft of Dallas and Lulu White of Houston reestablished the organization in the 1930s. White commented, "I may be called dumb, but I cannot see equality in segregation. I hope that I die just that dumb."[2]

In 1944 the NAACP won a Supreme Court decision that struck down the Texas white primary, wherein only white people chose political candidates. This opened a door to greater political participation for both blacks and Hispanics. Over the next decade the NAACP hammered the courts with cases to end segregated and unequal education.

SCHOOL INTEGRATION

Most important, the NAACP backed Heman Marion Sweatt's (1912-1982) successful attempt in 1946-1950 to gain admission to the all-white University of Texas law school in Austin. Sweatt, a black Houston teacher and substitute mailman, argued that there was no law school of equal quality for blacks in Texas. This undermined the long-standing defense of segregation of "separate but equal" facilities.

The state resisted, and as the sensational case wound through the court system, the state created Texas Southern University with a law school for blacks in Houston. The case nonetheless reached the Supreme Court, which agreed with Sweatt. Although he cracked open the doors of a segregated law school, his marriage fell apart, he did poorly in classes, and after two years he dropped out, suffering poor health.[3] He ended his career working for the National Urban League in Atlanta, Georgia.

Integration in education, meanwhile, continued apace elsewhere in Texas. Integration in undergraduate classes for all races began in 1952 at Del Mar College in Corpus Christi, followed by Southern Methodist University and Texas Western College (now the University of Texas in El Paso) in 1955, and North Texas State College (now the University of North Texas) and Lamar State College in 1956. Other major Texas universities integrated in the 1960s include Rice University, which went to court to break the racist will of its founder in 1963. Lest it be thought that everything changed overnight, the women's dormitories at the University of Texas did not integrate until 1964.

The famous case of *Brown v. Board of Education of Topeka* in 1954 started the integration of grade schools. The NAACP pushed hard and met resistance. In 1954 Allen Shivers, who was opposed to integration, won reelection as governor. The Texas Rangers were used to hinder the efforts of black students to attend school in Texarkana and Mansfield, while the state attorney general harassed the NAACP to a point of ineffectiveness. Enforcement of the law, however, came from the federal government and the state government retreated into passivity.

By 1957 over 120 school districts, including those in Austin, San Antonio, San Angelo, El Paso, and Corpus Christi, had initiated integration of their classes and faculty, often starting in the primary grades. Court orders issued in 1960-1961 forced the large school districts in Houston and Dallas to begin integration. Contrived delays put off completion of the task in the big systems until the 1980s, and Dallas remained under court oversight until 2003. Even in places of peaceful integration, black students were simply ignored. Alice Darden Davis, a black student, recalled about Reagan High School in Austin during the 1960s, "I was there, but it was as if you weren't there."[4]

A concurrent long-term result was a white flight of students from the large city schools into suburban and private schools. The Houston Independent School District in 1968, for instance, was 71 percent white (Hispanics were counted as white until 1970) and 29 percent black. It lost sixteen thousand students in 1970-1971. In 1974 the system was 42 percent black, 39 percent white, and 19 percent Hispanic. In 1980 it was 45 percent black, 28 percent Hispanic, and 25 percent white. By 2001 it had lost 85 percent of its white students. In 2009 it was 62 percent Hispanic, 27 percent black, 9 percent white, and 3 percent Asian.

Only one high school had a majority white population—one of the magnet schools set up to encourage integration—and sadly, three thousand Houston students were homeless. The Houston district, which covered much of the metropolitan area in 2012, taught 203,000 students. It was the largest in Texas, seventh biggest in the nation, and reflected the changing demographics of the city.

The same pattern occurred in the Dallas Independent School District, where the white students fled and Hispanic students gained a majority. In 1961 the Dallas School Board began a stair-step integration plan that involved only one grade at a time. There occurred little hostility, but also limited progress. Only 131 black students out of 9,400 appeared in desegregated classrooms in three years.[5]

It was too slow. Various busing schemes for integration were tried in 1971-1996, with poor results exacerbated by the rapid decline in the number of white students in the system. In 1980 the Dallas system was 45 percent black, 28 percent Hispanic, and 25 percent white. By 2006 the system was 64 percent Hispanic, 30 percent black, and 5 percent white. Test data indicated that smaller classes, better teachers, and improved facilities were more effective than bus rides across town.[6]

The current folklore states that the students are Hispanic, teachers are black, and the taxpayers are white. The folklore is obviously a stretch, but it raises a question of accomplishment about the historic struggle of school integration. On the 2011 Scholastic Aptitude Test (SAT), Texas students trailed 30 points behind the national average, with blacks and Hispanics dragging down the scores. Only 15 percent of the graduates from the Houston system attain a BA or BS college degree; 23 percent is the national average. Despite the hesitancy of a current conservative state government to finance public education, however, no one questions the basic fairness of integration.

CITY INTEGRATION

The breakdown of segregation occurred in multiple ways. In 1951 the Austin City Council decided it was cheaper to allow blacks to use the public library than to build an equivalent one for blacks in East Austin. Dallas opened its library to blacks when it built a new facility in 1955. The 1964 Twenty-Fourth Amendment to the U.S. Constitution banned poll taxes.

Sports provided a breakthrough. Don Haskins, the basketball coach at Texas Western College (now the University of Texas at El Paso), used an all-black lineup to defeat the venerable Adolph Rupp and his all-white University of Kentucky team at the 1966 championships. When asked if he was trying to make history, Haskins simply replied, "I played the best players who could help us win."[7] At the same time black professionals played for the Dallas Cowboys in football and the Houston Astros in baseball.

Jerry LeVias in 1965–1968 cracked open the all-white Southwest Conference when he played football for Southern Methodist University. He endured being shunned in class, having to wait for showers to empty so he could bathe, being spat upon, and receiving death threats to shoot "that dirty nigger LeVias." He replied with sensational punt returns in the Cotton Bowl and won All-Southwest Conference honors in 1966, 1967, and 1968. He helped the Ponies to win a conference championship in 1966. Most importantly, he won the admiration of his teammates and demonstrated to the coaches a source of talent that they had blindly ignored.[8]

In 1950–1954, five black men in Houston sued to gain the use of municipal golf courses for which they had paid taxes. They won their case when the U.S. Supreme Court refused appeal and the city gave up. In 1955 six black golfers in Beaumont won a federal lawsuit for the right to use a city golf course—the reasoning was that segregation was unconstitutional.[9]

Jerry LeVias playing for SMU against TCU in the 1960s. Photograph courtesy of Fort Worth Star-Telegram Collection, Special Collections, the University of Texas at Arlington Library, Arlington, Texas.

GALVESTON

In Galveston, after a runaround for five years, a group of blacks in 1958 simply went to the golf course and began to play. The greenskeeper came out, collected the fee, and that was it. At the Galveston beach a section had been set aside in the 1920s for a black bathhouse—the only black access to a public beach in Texas—and black students in 1960 tried without success to gain access to white Stewart Beach, the main municipal beach. The frustrated students then struck with a series of sit-ins at Galveston stores and downtown lunch counters.

The crisis was settled with common decency. At one of the business meetings about segregation, George Clampett, a co-owner with Grady Dickinson of the downtown Star Drugstore, stood up and said, "You know, Grady and I got together and discussed this business about losing business, causing trouble, and we finally got around to the ultimate question—what is right?" They concluded that trade should be total, not just toothpaste and Kleenex, but also hamburgers and Cokes. They were persuasive. The leader of the students, Kelton Sams, restrained his followers; the media maintained silence; and the lunch counters reopened with no restrictions.[10] The board of governors of Stewart Beach announced at the start of the season in May 1962 that the park was open to all regardless of "race, creed, or political affiliation."[11] Segregation in Galveston was gone.

HOUSTON

In Houston Hattie White became the first black female elected in Texas when she won an at-large election to the Houston Independent School District board in 1958. Two years later restless black students from Texas Southern University began the first lunch-counter sit-ins in Texas in March 1960 to force equal service. They hit Weingarten's grocery, Woolworth's, Grant's, and the City Hall cafeteria. Weingarten's removed the stool seats.

Max Levine and Bob Dundas of Foley's, an upscale department store, however, talked to other storeowners, asked the press to keep quiet, offered to transfer employees, and requested plainclothes policemen. The black groups agreed to infiltrate quietly with well-groomed individuals, and integration was accomplished with no trouble or fanfare in downtown.

In 1961 the Houston City Hall cafeteria began to serve both races; in 1962 the major hotels desegregated; and in 1963 the city swimming pools and movie theaters opened to everyone. In a search for better housing blacks burst the bonds of the Third Ward and began to spread southward into posh Riverside Terrace and across Brays Bayou, while panic-stricken whites tried to maintain their real estate values.[12] It gave blacks access to higher-quality housing.

In a remarkable micro study of integration in the Houston Police Department, historian Dwight D. Watson tracked the changes from a "Jim Crow" department in 1939 until the 1990s. The police clashed with black activists on the campus at Texas Southern University in 1967 and later killed Carl Bernard Hampton, a local Black Panther leader, in a forty-five minute shootout. Charges of police brutality, particularly in the case of José Campos Torres, who in 1977 ended up dead in Buffalo Bayou, roiled community relationships until Mayor Kathy Whitmire withstood the taunts of police unions in 1982 and appointed the first black chief of police, Lee Patrick Brown, a former public safety commissioner from Atlanta. He became the model of a professional police manager who set a high standard for future community police work. For the Houston Police Department, Watson concluded, "Eventually, change did come in its attitudes toward the races and its racial composition."[13]

DALLAS

Housing was a major factor in Dallas integration. Despite overcrowded and substandard housing for blacks, the city council refused to sanction building more public housing units in 1950. Between 1945 and 1949 the building industry put up more than thirty thousand new homes, but fewer than a thousand for blacks in spite of an increase of thirty thousand in the black population in the 1940s. A. Maceo Smith, the black racial relations advisor to the Federal Housing Administration, commented, "It is harder to find homes for Negroes in Dallas than in any other city in the South."[14]

In South Dallas, where black families had begun to move to be close to the black Lincoln High School (1939), sticks of dynamite were tossed onto the porches and roofs of eleven black homes. The city council promised protection and appointed an interracial committee. Ten persons were arrested and indicted, but no one was convicted. The bombings did inspire the construction of residential homes for middle-class blacks at Hamilton Park, financed by wealthy members of the Dallas Citizens Council.[15]

At the mayor's request the Dallas Citizens Council also undertook an effort for peaceful integration in 1960. C. A. Tatum, Jr., the council president, headed a public relations committee to emphasize the benefits of peaceful integration and to suppress disturbing news stories. It was not easy. Black attendance at the Texas State Fair had been restricted to "Negro Achievement Day," but this would no longer do. In May 1953 the directors opened the fair to all races, including all midway rides except two where there might be physical contact between the races.

In 1955 the Youth Council of the NAACP, led by firebrand Juanita Craft, arranged pickets and signs—"Don't Sell Your Pride for a Segregated Ride"—at the entrance gates to force open all concessions and to encourage black rejection of achievement day. The black parade and marching bands refused to cross the picket line, profits were threatened, the city caved in, and all rides opened.

In January 1961 a black theology student and thirty white companions staged a sit-in at the University Drug Store across from the SMU campus. The owner retaliated by fumigating his store and thoroughly spraying the students, who covered their faces with handkerchiefs. The event was picked up by the wire news services; the story was covered in Fort Worth, but not in Dallas.

Through the spring and into the summer the NAACP, led by its youth council, staged demonstrations at downtown theaters and organized a boycott of downtown stores by turning in credit cards and refusing to buy Easter clothes. Under national pressure, hotel chains integrated all at once and the restaurants fell into line. By the end of the summer businesses were taking down discriminatory signs and extending services to all customers regardless of race.[16]

Neiman-Marcus held training sessions with its employees to be certain that everyone was treated politely. When the moment of integration occurred, all went well, even though they lost a few accounts, closed by women who protested not only sales to blacks but also the use of black sales personnel. Under the leadership of Stanley Marcus, however, the leading department store in Texas embraced both integration and affirmative action.[17]

FORT WORTH

In Fort Worth the owner of Leonard Brothers department store, which had a long history of sympathy toward blacks, simply sent out a notice of change in 1956 that everyone was to be served at the lunch counters and all discriminatory signs at restrooms, drinking fountains, and fitting rooms were to be removed.[18] Apparently, Fort Worth integrated easily in the early 1960s. According to journalist Oliver Knight, by the time the first black civil rights activists arrived to convert the lunch counters in 1963, the task had been already accomplished.

A busload of Freedom Riders entered the downtown Worth Hotel coffee shop and defiantly occupied the counter seats. Minnie and Alma, two longtime white waitresses, served them coffee and announced as they did to all the regulars, "If you want sweet potato pie, order it now. There probably will be none left when you finish your meal." The Freedom Riders ate their lunch unchallenged, paid their bill, got back on the bus, and left town.[19] That was that.

WACO

Waco followed the lead of Dallas, seeking to avoid violence. The white chamber of commerce asked black leaders to engage in discussion in order to end wildcat boycotts and to form an interracial committee. Widespread integration was agreed upon. On "I" [Integration] Day (July 10, 1963), Baylor's conservative Baptist president Abner McCall (1915–1995), along with other white Waco leaders, simply took a black person to lunch. This community gesture of integration was accepted by motels, hotels, and theaters. The chamber of commerce persuaded Louisana-based Piccadilly Cafeterias to end segregation, and public facilities were thus integrated.[20]

31

THE HISPANIC IDENTITY

In the cities with large Hispanic populations and traditions, the issue of segregation had not cut as deep into the social fabric. Hispanics, for example, had never been enslaved during their history in Texas and there was no constitutional provision of "separate but equal" for Hispanics. Yet there existed long-running prejudice and the drive for civil rights and respect was as urgent for Hispanics as for blacks.

Urban Hispanics, although often poor and jammed into barrios, escaped the deep bigotry that generally characterized the countryside and small towns. Hispanics in Houston, for example, were moving into the suburbs in the 1950s, where an expanding middle class found little systematic segregation in real estate or jobs. Houston hired its first Hispanic policeman in 1950, and strong political organizations such as the League of United Latin American Citizens (LULAC) and the American G.I. Forum spread from Corpus Christi to provide a political presence. It was Reverend Herbert Meza, the Hispanic vice president of the Houston Ministerial Association, for instance, who invited presidential candidate John F. Kennedy in 1960 to reconcile his Roman Catholic religion with his prospective duties as president.[1] It was an event that permitted a Kennedy victory and changed history.

The most important touchstone for Hispanic urban history was elementary school education. Houstonian Felix Tijerina, while president of LULAC in 1956, for instance, initiated the "Little School of the 400" to teach Spanish-speaking preschool children four hundred basic English words so that they could be successful in the first grade.

Hispanic education, furthermore, became entangled with the problem of school integration in a formative manner. Before integration Hispanics were counted in the census and school records as white. There might be social advantages—not being black at that time—but the integration fight brought a new identification. Hispanics found themselves being used to substitute for Anglos in balancing white-black quotas at a time of white flight from the schools. At the same time the rise of militant Hispanics engendered a pride in Hispanic culture.

Chicano activists questioned the idea of joining mainstream American society, rejected "whiteness," and argued in favor of preserving *la raza*, a unique cultural personality. The Mexican American Youth Organization (MAYO) of Chicanos started in San Antonio in 1967 and took root in the barrios. It alerted residents to Mexican American issues, railed against police disrespect, and prodded their elders to action.[2]

In Houston MAYO brought national attention to insensitive teachers, poor facilities, and lack of participation in the federal free lunch program. The situation boiled up into a school boycott in fall 1970 over a court integration plan to pair black and white students, who would be exchanged through busing. The plan focused on northeast Houston in twenty-five elementary schools where Mexican Americans served as white surrogates in the exchange. The boycott involved 3,500 students who stayed home, a rally of 5,000, pickets, and disruption of school board meetings.

The boycott lasted three weeks, and an amalgamated group calling itself the Mexican American Education Council (MAEC) monitored the protest. The boycott renewed in February 1971 and a federal judge ruled against MAEC attorneys. The bemused judge stated, "Content to be 'White' for these many years, now, when the shoe begins to pinch, the would be interveners wish to be treated not as whites but as an 'identifiable minority group.'"[3] Indeed.

In 1973 the U.S. Supreme Court stopped the pairing scheme with a Denver case and recognized Mexican American legal identity. The Houston school district by 1972 accepted Hispanics as an ethnic minority and deliberately hired Hispanic teachers. The U.S. Census Bureau, moreover, began to regularly count the Hispanic population starting in 1970.

EL PASO AND SAN ANTONIO

In El Paso Hispanics were not a minority, but along with blacks suffered poverty, poor housing, and lack of political representation. Through notable persistence—a fight that started in 1924 and eventually ended at the U.S. Supreme Court in 1944—Dr. Lawrence A. Nixon, a black supported by the El Paso NAACP, broke the back of the white primary. Following this victory in politics, discrimination for seating on public transportation and in the public schools ended. The El Paso schools were the first to end segregation unconditionally. In addition, a 1955 court case opened the door at Texas Western College for a black woman student, Thelma White.

In 1957, when Raymond Telles became the first Mexican American elected mayor of the city, it was a shock to the white business community. "How can we hold our heads up in the State of Texas when we have a Mexican mayor," wailed one of them. It was a victory for the "Juan Smiths" of the city; a "revolution, not an election," according to attorney George Rodriguez. In the 1960s the city council, still dominated by Anglos, passed nondiscrimination ordinances for the renting and buying of homes.[4] Segregation had come to an end in El Paso.

San Antonio passed a desegregation ordinance for city facilities in the mid-1950s and elected a Hispanic mayor in 1981, the first since Juan Seguín of the revolutionary period. The Good Government League (GGL), run by Anglo businessmen, dominated the at-large elections from 1952 to 1976, and only one quarter of the city council members had Spanish surnames at a time of expanding Mexican American population (a majority by 1975). Only 13 of 117 council members of the period lived on the Mexican American west side of town. Texas, moreover, required residency of one year and annual registration for voting.

The leader of the GGL, W. W. McAllister, who had been mayor for a decade, retired in 1971 and the GGL, which saw itself as a civic organization of elites, had disbanded by the end of 1976. In 1979, a city election gave majority council votes to the candidates from six lower-income areas, and in 1981 Henry Cisneros, a Harvard-educated Hispanic, became mayor. San Antonio thus became the largest American city with a Mexican American mayor.[5]

In a military town like San Antonio the thrust for equality received a shove when President Harry S. Truman racially integrated the armed services in 1948. Within the ranks there was greater equality. María Jiménez of San Antonio, for instance, chose to join the army because she did not like the discrimination in the private sector. She said, "Here in the military, I'm a female, I do this job, I have a counterpart, same rate, same time and service as I am, he's male. We get paid the same."[6] This was an example, widespread and not forgotten, of equality in race, gender, and work that was necessary not only in the armed services, but also in society at large for exceptional people to excel.

32

JOHN F. KENNEDY AND DALLAS

Several tragedies have occurred in Texas cities that have stained their history. On November 22, 1963, President John F. Kennedy was assassinated on the streets of Dallas. This was the worst. The spotlight of the country and the world focused upon the city and its culture, searching for explanation. Much has been written.[1] Dallas' rabid conservatives were accused, but how can an entire city be blamed for their actions? Care, moreover, must be taken about assigning anthropomorphic qualities to a civic entity. Nonetheless, a short time before the event Adlai Stevenson, there for a speech, had been spat upon and whacked with a placard. Also, Vice President Lyndon Johnson and his wife had been assaulted by demonstrators while crossing a downtown street. The conservative, red-baiting *Dallas Morning News* published a full-page anti-Kennedy advertisement on the morning of the president's arrival.[2]

The assassination stunned the Dallas leadership. The reaction was, "It was not our fault. It could have happened anywhere. Dallas is a great city."[3] True enough, but Dallas was condemned, nonetheless, by the American public. It was a relief to find out that the murderer, Lee Harvey Oswald, was a white Marxist who acted alone. The later entertainment success of the Dallas Cowboys football team and the television series *Dallas* (1978-1991) helped to salve the memory.[4]

Designed by architect Philip Johnson in 1970, the Kennedy Memorial stands in downtown Dallas next to the old City Hall. Photograph by author.

In 1970 Dallas citizens erected a John F. Kennedy Memorial downtown at Dealey Plaza. In 1989, twenty-six years later, Dallas County opened the Sixth Floor Museum at the Texas School Book Depository where the assassin had hidden. The city thus acknowledged the event. Texan Lyndon B. Johnson, of course, went on to achieve most of his predecessor's civil rights agenda.

33

THE VOTING RIGHTS ACT AND THE CITIES

In the turbulence of the civil rights legislation of the mid-1960s, which provided federal protection for race, religion, and gender in housing and politics, the Voting Rights Act had the greatest impact on urban politics. It passed in 1965 to block discrimination against blacks in voting, outlawed the use of literacy tests, and appointed examiners where black registration had been low. Changes in local election procedures of suspected states had to have approval of the U.S. Justice Department. The poll tax had already been removed by the Twenty-Fourth Amendment to the Constitution, and the Supreme Court case of *Reynolds v. Sims* in 1964 established the concept of "one man, one vote" in apportionment cases. In 1975 the voting act was expanded to cover places of large Spanish-, Indian-, or Asian-language minorities.

In Texas the difficulty often focused upon at-large versus district elections for a city council. At-large elections favored Anglo majorities, well-known incumbents, and those who could afford citywide campaign expenses. Conservative business groups usually won at-large elections to the exclusion of blacks, Hispanics, labor unions, women, liberals, gays, environmentalists, and even suburban Republicans.

Annexations that diluted black or brown (Hispanic) voting strength in at-large governments were disapproved by the U.S. Justice Department.

Houston, which ignored the Voting Rights Act, found itself besieged by a coalition of disparate groups that blocked annexation attempts in 1978. In agreement, the U.S. Justice Department halted city elections.

Houston had been using at-large voting—only one black, no women, and no Hispanic had ever been elected to the city council. The city and the U.S. Justice Department agreed to a plan for a council of nine members elected from single-member districts plus five elected at large. As a result, in 1979 three blacks, two women, and one Hispanic were elected.

San Antonio ran into the same difficulty with annexations, and after facing the prospect of de-annexing, the voters accepted a plan for ten single-member districts. As a result five Hispanics and one black joined a council that represented areas frequently ignored in the past. In Dallas the council in 1975 was reworked to include eight single-member districts and three at-large seats. The U.S. Justice Department made certain that there were two predominantly black districts and one Hispanic district.[1] In 1995 Dallas elected Ron Kirk, the first black to head up a major Texas city.

The result was that the rule of business groups was broken in Texas cities. The Citizens' Charter Group of Dallas, for example, had won a majority in twenty-one of twenty-three city councils between 1930 and 1975.[2] The Good Government League of San Antonio had won eighty-five of ninety-nine races between 1954 and 1976. No longer. White male supremacy was broken as blacks, Hispanics, women, and others began to share political power. Big city politics became a game of compromise and accommodation, and sometimes of push and shove.

WOMEN IN POLITICS

Barbara Jordan is an example of a politician who benefited from the Voting Rights Act. She was born in the black Fifth Ward of Houston, earned a law degree at Boston University, and twice ran unsuccessfully for the Texas House of Representatives. The Voting Rights Act forced a redrawing of districts to enforce "one man, one vote." In 1966 and 1968, consequently, she won a seat in the Texas Senate—the first black woman ever and the first black person since 1883. Her good sense, hard work, and stentorian voice won her selection to the U.S. House of Representatives in 1972, where she became famous as a member of the House Judiciary Committee during the investigation of the Watergate scandal.

Although women possessed the right to vote and participate in

This bronze statue of Barbara Jordan, 2009, by artist Bruce Wolfe, is at the University of Texas at Austin. She is one of the few women so honored on campus. Photograph by author.

politics, they rarely did. Female leaders in Texas were unexpected and unusual despite the examples of Ma Ferguson, Oveta Culp Hobby, Ima Hogg, and Babe Didrikson. In Houston, politician Poppy Northcutt described the situation as a parfait: "White males float like whipped cream at the top. Underneath are minority males. They are followed by white females, and at the very bottom are minority females."[3]

Urbanization, the responsibilities of World War II, and the feminist movement changed the parfait paradigm. Hermine Tobolowsky, a Dallas lawyer, and the Texas Federation of Business and Professional Women's Clubs won a fourteen-year struggle to attain legal recognition that equality under the law could not be denied because of gender. Texas voters approved her Equal Legal Rights Amendment for the Texas Constitution in 1972 by a four-to-one margin, and the Texas legislature approved the national Equal Rights Amendment the following year. Houston hosted the National Women's Conference in 1977, the first since the Seneca Falls, New York, meeting in 1848. The conference, a grand gesture, however, fractured over various unresolved issues such as antifeminism and abortion, and achieved little.

Women nonetheless became much more active in Texas politics. According to political scientists Wendell Bedichek and Neal Tannahill, the number of women on city councils increased from 121 in 1968 to 525 in 1978.[4] Francis Farenthold ran for governor in 1972; Lila Cockrell became the first female mayor of a large city when she took over San Antonio in 1976; Carole Keeton McClellan served as mayor of Austin in 1977; Kathy Whitmire became mayor of Houston in 1982 and Annise Parker in 2009; Ann Richards became the first woman in fifty years elected to state office when she became state treasurer in 1982 and governor in 1991; Myra McDaniel became the first black to hold an appointive cabinet position in 1984; and Annette Strauss became mayor of Dallas in 1987.

On the night of her election triumph Strauss' husband described her as "the loveliest, strongest, brightest and toughest steel butterfly I have ever met in my life."[5] As journalist Molly Ivins observed: "But now all of a sudden Texas women are running whole cities with multibillion-dollar budgets. Straight from 'Hey Honey' and 'Yew cute li'l thang,' to 'Madam Mayor' and 'Yes, Mayor, right away.'"[6]

The wrenching removal of segregation was liberating for Texas society. It was first intended for blacks, but as the civil rights movement broadened it also gave relief to Hispanics and opened opportunity for other suppressed groups, including women. Prejudice and constricting custom did not disappear all of a sudden, of course. The 1998 racial attack of three whites against James Byrd, an innocent black in Jasper, Texas, who was dragged to death behind a speeding pickup truck on a dark country road was a reminder that the grapes of wrath can still produce bitter vintage.

Yet, the enduring laws and efforts of integration have released creative energies of tolerance for the benefit of a society on an upward climb to a better life. Theodore Youngblood, a dignified longtime well-liked black porter at the Driskill Hotel in Austin, summarized the new attitude when asked about integration: "I'm not saying—after all, I've got kinfolks on both sides."[7]

34

LAND TRANSPORTATION

Together with the suburbs, the automobile forced the construction of major streets and expressways into a wheel-like, or spoke and hub, pattern. Attempts to build public transit systems with buses and light rail in Dallas and Houston had only sputtering success because of cost and access as well as a public preference for cars. The central business district remained important in the large cities as places for bankers, politicians, government workers, and lawyers. In spite of improved communications a desire, or need, for personal interaction remained. Grocery stores, department stores, doctors, travel agents, movies, and restaurants all followed their customers to the suburbs. The twice-daily pulsebeat of a rush hour along the spokes to the center continued, but about twice as many people commuted to work between suburbs.

This resulted in the construction of expressway loops, joined to the interstate system, to circumnavigate the central business districts. Construction began in the 1960s and ten Texas cities eventually built loop configurations. Dallas, San Antonio, and Houston have two loops positioned roughly like concentric rings. Unlike the roads carrying traffic to the central business districts, which suffer with rush hour surges, the loop traffic moves in both directions in equal amounts most of the time. Expressways and loops have a bad trait of filling to capacity almost at the

The spokes of the suburban wheel. Underneath MoPac and Highway 183 in Austin, Texas. Photograph by author.

moment of completion, and there is constant pressure to improve speed and accommodation.

As a stunt for charity in 1985, car dealer and race car driver A. J. Foyt, Jr., drove the 38-mile circuit of Loop 610 in Houston at 7:00 a.m. It took him 1 hour, 43 minutes, and 54 seconds (22 miles per hour), and he had to get off the freeway at one point to go around a wreck. He concluded that Houston drivers were among the worst in the country. "People are always trying to block you and then making hand gestures," he said. This event, however, was the origin of an urban myth and every commuter's sometime fantasy that Foyt once drove the Houston freeways at 200 miles per hour.[1]

Most Texas cities gladly accepted the interstate system even though it was a defeat for mass transit. In 1959 the City of Olmos Park, however, forced San Antonio to keep its expressways on home turf. This encircled incorporated suburb rejected the request of San Antonio to nip off a corner for a freeway and demonstrated the power of small places within larger domains. In addition, the San Antonio Conservation Society opposed construction through historic neighborhoods and eventually caused the city and state to build its North Freeway without federal funds.

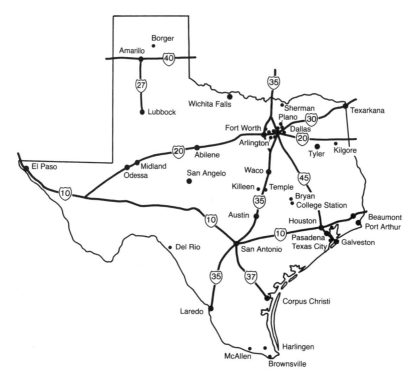

The interstate highways of Texas. Map by author.

Meanwhile, San Antonio promoted HemisFair, a world's fair in 1968 that required 1,600 people to move aside for large-scale projects. As an offset San Antonio acquired the first two historic districts in the state, King William and La Villita, with the aid of urban renewal moneys.[2] Although the fair lost $6 million, the 6 million visitors were charmed by the efforts to mix the traditional restored buildings with new architecture on the 147-acre site.

Austin chose to put an elevated roadway for I-35 on top of its obsolete Interregional Highway in 1971–1975 and constructed an expressway bifurcation that left the poorer section of the city on the eastern side. It was the completion of a black-white separation that had started in the 1920s.

The superhighway changed everything it touched, and even places it did not. Coordination with existing highways and streets was often ignored. Off ramps could mean life or death to filling stations and diners. The iconic Old Stage Coach Inn at Salado, Texas, for example, was left with no exit ramp and business declined to a dribble. The owner, Dion VanBibber, wrote to his senator, Lyndon Johnson; Johnson contacted the Texas Bureau of Public Roads; and the Old Stage Coach Inn shortly received a life-saving "point of access."[3]

As I-35 reached Laredo the roadway cut through a supposed blighted area that had been platted in 1767 and included one of the original plazas. An elementary school had to be closed and 390 residents evicted. With four bridges crossing the Rio Grande to Mexico the bits and pieces of I-35 came together finally in 1992. This north-south interstate, which coursed north to Duluth, Minnesota, became the largest international trade corridor in the United States. About half of the traffic between Texas and Mexico now comes through this point, especially after the implementation of the North American Free Trade Agreement in 1993, which removed trade barriers between Mexico, Canada, and the United States. Laredo became a boomtown with 250,000 people in its metropolitan area, and Nuevo Laredo across the river added some 400,000 more to the region.

The 2,900 miles of the interstate system in Texas, which linked the major cities and made driving easy on the wide expanses of West Texas, was a triumph for interurban transportation. It unfortunately inspired the 2003 idea of the Trans-Texas Corridor, a 1,200-foot-wide, 4,000-mile toll road for trains, trucks, and automobiles from Brownsville and Laredo northeastward to Houston and Texarkana. The Texas Department of Transportation gathered commentary and held forty-seven public meetings only to discover that most Texans did not want a quarter-mile-wide megahighway cutting through their farms and historic properties. Enough was enough, and after six years the legislature dropped the project.

THE INTERSTATE AND THE CITY

The interstate system, freeways, loops, frontage roads, and access ramps, however, transfigured the large cities. They drained the central city of its energy and people and flung them to the periphery. Bernard Sakowitz of Houston surprised his competitors in 1959 by building a branch of his clothing store at Westheimer Road and Post Oak, a major intersection on the western edge five miles from town. He closed his downtown store in 1985 and the newer store became his flagship as the Galleria built up around him.

The ice skating rink inside the Galleria, the largest mall in Texas. Photograph by author.

Located at the intersection with Loop 610, the Galleria (1969–1986) amounted to 45 acres of a mixed-use combination of hotels, offices, and shopping center that developer Gerald Hines characterized as a new downtown. It had over eleven thousand parking spaces and an indoor ice skating rink that impresses overheated Houstonians to this very day. It became the largest mall in Texas and attracted other offices and hotels. The most significant architectural symbol of the area, however, was the sixty-four-story Transco Tower (1983), the third tallest building in the city. It was a severe, straight shaft with art deco setbacks near the top and reflective glass. It was designed by architect Philip Johnson to stand slightly apart from the other buildings of the Galleria area as an exclamation point for the entire cluster.

This same kind of mixed-use expansion along a loop also occurred in North Dallas along the Lyndon Johnson Freeway (Loop 635), where Hines put together another Galleria in 1982. Farther out, the older communities of Richardson and Plano became satellite towns, and to the west the master-planned suburb of Las Colinas in Irving emerged like the Woodlands of Houston. Las Colinas attracted corporate executives who needed access to both Dallas and the Dallas-Fort Worth International Airport.

It was a part of the wedge-like growth of metropolitan Dallas from the central business district to the north and northwest, magnetically stretching toward an important transportation hub. The towns between Dallas and Fort Worth—Irving, Grand Prairie, Arlington—had to assert their territorial rights in the late 1940s to prevent being gobbled by Fort Worth in the west and Dallas in the east.

SATELLITE CITIES

The explosive growth of the large peripheral cities in Texas and elsewhere has puzzled urban scholars. Just what were these office nodes on the loops? New towns? Satellite cities? Suburbs? How does this affect the central business district? Are Dallas and Houston now multi-nucleated? The galleria areas contain at least one-third the amount of office space as their central cities. But that is not all. There are other built-up outlying areas like the gallerias (edge cities), six each in Houston and Dallas, as well as low-density buildings scattered throughout the metropolitan areas without particular boundaries (edgeless). In 1999 Houston possessed 38 million square feet of office space downtown, and 64 million in the edgeless areas. Metropolitan Dallas had 37 million square feet of office space in the downtown, and 52 million scattered in edgeless places.

In the scramble to the cheap land of the suburbs, the central business districts slowed down, losing shoppers and department stores. This raised a question about the vitality of the old centers; the best answer came from New York architectural critic Jane Jacobs and her book *The Death and Life of Great American Cities* (1961). The key to safe and enduring neighborhoods, she thought, was density of residents, mixed economic uses that brought people out at different times, short blocks, and a mingling of old and new buildings.[4] In essence, cities required variety and density. As urbanologist Edward Glaeser has warned, "Connecting in cyberspace will never be the same as sharing a meal or a smile or a kiss."[5]

Dallas and Houston built downtowns for the benefit of corporate offices, banks, and politics. At five o'clock the buildings empty out, the restaurants close, and the parking lots clear. An unwary visitor is left afoot, alone in darkening concrete canyons. It is a chilling, dangerous experience.

FORT WORTH AND VICTOR GRUEN

The Federal Housing Act of 1956 provided funding for commercial redevelopment, and mayors began to dream of revitalizing their central business districts. J. B. Thomas, president of Texas Electric Company, hired Victor Gruen (1903–1980) of Los Angeles to draw up a plan for Fort Worth and present it to the upscale Fort Worth Club in 1956. Thomas was a member of the "Seventh Street Gang" of informal Fort Worth leaders who looked to the welfare of the city.

Gruen, an emigré from Austria, was well known as an innovative designer of suburban malls, and he offered a plan to make downtown Fort Worth a mall with a ring highway, parking garages on the perimeter, streets converted to pedestrian walkways, and underground truck tunnels for store deliveries. Arcades, flags, kiosks, outdoor cafes, bandstands, street entertainment, flowerbeds, special lighting, exhibits, and modernized stores promised the suburban housewife a pleasurable shopping experience.

The press applauded, the politicians voiced enthusiasm, and businessmen pledged support. The Gruen plan, however, remained a $150 million dream. The Texas legislature refused authority for Fort Worth to condemn buildings, sell off property, operate parking garages, or direct development. The highway department declined to fund the ring highway. A Fort Worth bank president who had invested heavily in two private downtown parking garages argued persuasively that public-owned garages would lead to socialism.[6] Thus, the Gruen plan and city planning failed, and Fort Worth missed a future that would have made it shine. Fort Worth also became entangled with its old rival to the east about a regional airport.

35

AIRLINES AND AIRPORTS

Following World War II the demand for airline passenger service, with its speed, novelty, and glamour, increased dramatically. There were 1 million Texas passengers in 1950, 3 million in 1960, 10 million in 1970, and 26 million in 1980. It was a time when people dressed up to board an airplane and attractive stewardesses treated travelers as guests. Eastern, Trans-Texas, KLM, Braniff, Mid-Continent, and National airlines jockeyed for counter space.

The Airline Deregulation Act of 1978, however, left it to the airlines to sort out routes and schedules, and flying became less pleasant. In 1980 planes were about 60 percent full, in 2011 they were 80 percent; but the cost was 40 percent lower.[1] The situation gave opportunity to the no-frills, low-cost, open seating Southwest Airlines in 1971 to fly between Dallas, San Antonio, and Houston.

Jet aircraft, which required longer runways, replaced piston-driven planes in the 1960s, and Houston Intercontinental Airport, later renamed for President George H. W. Bush, opened in 1969. Of radical design, it featured a cube-like central terminal with fingers that radiated to passenger loading areas. It utilized escalators, elevators, and an automated series of railcars to minimize the need for passengers to walk long distances.

As might be expected with the growth of the airlines and the interstate system, railroad passenger traffic declined precipitously. The number of Southern Pacific Railway passengers declined every year after 1946 except during the Korean War. The Union Station in Houston, which had serviced thirty-three passenger trains, declined to three trains in the 1960s and closed in 1974. The last passenger train left Dallas in May 1969. Amtrak took over in 1971, maintaining at least a semblance of continued intercity railroad passenger service.

DALLAS VERSUS FORT WORTH

During World War II Love Field in Dallas served as the headquarters of the United States Air Transport Command, which so expanded the facilities that Love Field became the largest such facility in the Southwest. The problem was that Love Field had reached its limits for safety. Meacham Field in Fort Worth had the same difficulty; the logical solution was to build a regional facility to serve both cities, located just 30 miles apart.

It was not a new idea; discussions had started in 1940. Fort Worth, Dallas, and Arlington, along with Braniff and American Airlines, agreed in 1941 to the construction of Midway Airport, with the Civil Aeronautics Administration (CAA) to fund the landing area and the airlines to erect hangars and buildings. It was to be directed by a joint board consisting of one member from each city and two from each airline. Dallas, however, withdrew from the project when it was revealed that the terminal would be located on the Fort Worth side. Arlington and Fort Worth proceeded with the plan, World War II intervened, and Dallas expanded Love Field.

In 1947 Fort Worth purchased Midway from Arlington for one dollar, christened it Greater Fort Worth International Airport, expanded it the next year, named the terminal in honor of Amon G. Carter, and opened it in 1953. The Federal Aviation Administration withheld funds for further Love Field expansion in 1960 amidst concerns for safety about flights over an urban area and homeowner law suits about jet noise.

The Civil Aeronautics Board (CAB), which oversees air route assignments, held meetings in 1962–1964 to investigate once more the idea of a single regional airport. Its decision was that neither Love Field nor Greater Fort Worth was adequate and that there should be a single facility. Furthermore, the CAB stated that the two cities should designate a site within six months or the CAB would select a space for them.

This meant that Dallas and Fort Worth had to negotiate in good faith in a true partnership. It also meant an end to the petty, long-standing jealousy between the cities, left over from the nineteenth century. To this end it was helpful that the two most relentless boosters, Bob Thornton of Dallas and Amon Carter of Fort Worth, were now gone. Thornton died in 1964 and Carter in 1955. When the city councils signed a letter of understanding in 1965, Mayor J. Erik Jonsson of Dallas called it a "historic milestone in cooperation."[2] The feud was over.

The new airport was controlled by an eleven-member board with seven representatives from Dallas and four from Fort Worth, a ratio based upon the comparative population sizes of the cities. Construction started in 1969 and ended in 1973 with the symbolic landing of a supersonic British Concord jet aircraft. Commercial operations commenced in 1974, led by Braniff, American, and Delta Airlines. The Dallas-Fort Worth International Airport (DFW) covered 17,500 acres and featured four (now five) semicircular terminals connected with a tramway that later had to be replaced because of slowness. Passengers were missing connecting flights at other terminals.

DFW, the Dallas/Fort Worth International Airport. Photograph from the collections of the Texas/Dallas History and Archives Division, Dallas Public Library.

DFW, which cost $1.6 billion, however, was an immediate success. It captured 55 percent of the Texas air passengers in 1975. Houston was next with 22 percent. The DFW dominance continued and in 2009 DFW transported 41 percent and Houston 29 percent. DFW was the point where transfers took place, and where travelers were held if bad weather existed along the flight paths. As Texas comedian Kinky Friedman commented, "Whether your destination is heaven or hell, you always have to change planes in Dallas."[3]

THE METROPLEX

A lot of people and companies did not change planes. They got off and stayed in the Dallas-Fort Worth metropolitan area. It was midway in the continent, easy to access, a convenient place for business meetings, the weather was usually good, and Texas had no state income taxes.

Among the important companies was Texas Instruments (TI), founded by J. Erik Jonsson and others in 1951 from an electronics company that worked on seismic oil exploration. In 1958 Jack St. Clair Kilby (1923-2005), a newly hired electronic engineer, invented the first integrated circuit, or microchip, in the TI laboratories. This invention broke through a "tyranny of numbers" for transistor circuitry by placing multiple circuits on a single piece of semiconductor material. It allowed the miniaturization of electronic devices, which in turn led to other instruments, including handheld calculators, invented by Kilby in 1966. He won the Nobel Prize for physics in 1969, and the millions of cell phone users today using his technology can thank Jack Kilby.

Dallas boomed. It built 29 million square feet of new office space in 1983-1984. The metro area ranked third behind New York and Chicago for headquarters in the number of companies with over $1 million in assets. The space between the two former rival cities became a mecca for entertainment, with the stadiums of the Dallas Cowboys football team (in Irving, 1971; in Arlington, 2009), Texas Rangers baseball team (in Arlington, 1972), and Six Flags over Texas amusement park (in Arlington in 1961). The name adopted for this regional growth phenomenon was "The Metroplex," which came from the promotional materials in 1971 for DFW.[4]

Relaxed banking regulations opened the door to the formation of bank holding companies and ignited a ten-year banking acquisition frenzy. The problem with the boom was that Dallas became the epicenter of a savings and loan bust. Unrestrained real estate developers defaulted on huge loans, and oil prices dropped at the same time in the 1980s.

Overextended banks consequently fell like dominos and the Federal Deposit Insurance Corporation had to perform extensive salvage operations. In 1988 Texas lost 113 banks, including the prestigious RepublicBank of Dallas. The Texas banks were sold or merged with more powerful institutions outside the state, and Texas thus lost its opportunity to become a major financial center in the United States.[5] Only Comerica, which moved from Detroit, a failed city, to Dallas in 2007 ranks among the top fifty banks that have a headquarters in Texas. About one-third of the office space in the Dallas downtown was vacant in 1993. The city barely recovered before facing the Bush recession of 2008.

36

URBAN EXCELLENCE IN TEXAS

The Dallas–Fort Worth Metroplex became the fourth largest metropolitan area of the United States, and its sheer size supported places of achievement. According to Richard Florida, creative cities need museums and institutions of higher education. Texas Christian University in Fort Worth ranked 92nd and Southern Methodist University in Dallas placed 58th in the 2013 survey by *U.S. News and World Report* of the best two hundred national universities.[1] Both were expensive private schools with religious affiliation, places for a majority white student body, and schools that emphasized undergraduate teaching.

SMU maintained a theology school and law school of note, however, and recently acquired the George W. Bush Presidential Library. Presidential libraries such as the Nixon and Kennedy Libraries are of little use for education or research, whereas the LBJ Presidential Library at the University of Texas has enlivened the campus with speakers, conferences, and research materials. It remains to be seen whether or not the Bush library at SMU will contribute to scholarly assessments of politics or merely be a sounding board for local conservative political dogma.

FORT WORTH

"Cowtown" was able to sand down the rough edges of its reputation with

Designed by Philip Johnson, the graceful Amon Carter Museum led the way for art in "Cowtown." Photograph by author.

a museum complex. The city bought the land of Casa Mañana, the Fort Worth answer to the Dallas Centennial Fair Park of 1936, and it became a site for museums. Amon Carter had wanted a repository for his seven hundred paintings and sculptures of western art, and at his death his daughter, Ruth Cater Stevenson, selected a hilltop location. Architect Philip Johnson designed a graceful building with a two-story glass façade with a vista of downtown Fort Worth. It opened in 1961, and later curators added space to extend the collection for American art and photographs.

The second-floor art gallery of the old Carnegie Public Library, meanwhile, inspired businessman Kay Kimbell (1886–1964) and his wife Velma to begin collecting art in 1931. The Kimbells amassed a fortune from food processing and oil, and at their death they donated their art and fortune to the Kimbell Art Foundation. The directors, led by Richard Fargo Brown, contracted with genius Philadelphia architect Louis Kahn (1901–1974) to design a museum that was also a work of art.

It opened in 1972 and consisted of a series of circular vaults with acrylic skylights. It was such an acclaimed architectural triumph that when a later director suggested an addition, the idea was shouted down by architects and admirers from around the country who wanted the building left untouched. The Kimbell Art Museum acquired the best of old world masters for display, and although the original museum structure is still considered one of the finest in the world, a concrete and glass annex designed by architect Renzo Piano is scheduled to open in 2013.

Fort Worth donors built another facility of enduring excellence—a zoo, of all things. Zoological parks have often been overlooked as urban accomplishments and attacked as cruel prisons for captured animals. Yet, as an institution of education about life in the world, a zoo is unmatched; it is important for demonstrating the human place in the animal kingdom. A zoo, moreover, is an inexpensive place of entertainment for young families and a refuge for animals. Consider, for example, the foreseeable plight of polar bears in a warming world. Their only place of salvation may be a zoo.

The Fort Worth Zoo is ranked the fifth best in the nation according to *USA Travel Guide, Family Life, USA Today, and the Los Angeles Times.* It won an exhibit award from the Association of Zoos and Aquariums in 2011. It began with the menagerie of a broken-down circus in 1909—a lion, two bears, an alligator, a coyote, a peacock, and a few rabbits. The city and a local zoological society developed the facility over the years into a theme park. It is the most visited zoo in Texas and the most important tourist attraction of the city, worth an estimated $100 million per year.

DALLAS

On the other side of the Dallas–Fort Worth Metroplex, the Dallas Zoo has never been able to match the popularity or excellence of the Fort Worth Zoo, but Dallas has achieved excellence with its architecture. The downtown skyline is stunning, Fair Park offers one of the best clusters of art deco buildings in the nation, and the Dallas City Hall (1978), designed by I. M. Pei of New York, with its cantilevered, reverse tiers, has become a symbol for the driving ambition of the city.[2]

Dallas also inaugurated a 68-acre, nineteen-block downtown arts district with the Dallas Museum of Art (1984), Meyerson Symphony Center (1989), Nasher Sculpture Garden (2003), the AT&T Performing Arts Center (2008), and the Perot Museum of Nature and Science (2013).

Dallas had nurtured an audience for opera since the 1940s; growth

Dallas in 2013 as seen through the spans of the new Helen Hunt Hill Bridge, which crosses the Trinity River bottoms. Photograph by author.

was initially hindered by a poor venue at the old Music Hall in Fair Park. Seedy and cavernous, with twice the appropriate seating, singer Joan Sutherland said it "resembled a made-over aeroplane hangar."[3] It was embarrassing, and Mayor Bob Thornton growled to his choir of bankers in 1957 about the need for a better facility. "I don't give a damn about singing or dancing," he said, "but Dallas needs this, so you get behind it."[4]

The city remodeled the Music Hall, but it was still inadequate and located too far away. Opera fans nonetheless persisted, found patronage, and put together expensive, impressive seasons. Elsa Maxwell, an international socialite from New York, came regularly to hear the Dallas opera and commented in 1960, "It's really incredible—incredible—the greatest opera in the world in a little town like Dallas."[5]

Particularly gratifying, therefore, was the completion of the Winshear Opera House (2008), which was a part of four venues in the new AT&T center. Named for Bill and Margo Winshear, who donated $42 million, it was a twenty-first-century version of a nineteenth-century opera house, with horseshoe seating on four tiers facing the stage. Unique features were a ruby-red exterior, a huge, 318-rod retractable chandelier,

The Dallas City Hall, designed by I. M. Pei, 1978. Photograph by author.

The Winshear Opera House in Dallas, 2008. Photograph by author.

an encircling portico to shield the building from the sun, and splendid views of the city. Patron comments have praised the acoustics and grumbled about the parking, bathroom waiting lines, hard seats, lack of LEED certification (environmentally favorable engineering), lack of electronic libretto translations, and seats perilously close to the edge of the tiers. Also present was the old complaint about Dallas loneliness and darkness at night.

It remains to be seen whether or not the Winshear will attain a reputation like New York's venerable Carnegie Hall, but the effort of the city to form an arts district is interesting. It demonstrates an effort to improve high arts with up-to-date, dedicated venues. This is a historic trend that most maturing cities follow—as a city grows it becomes increasingly diverse and specialized. A large city, for instance, likely will possess not only a stadium for football but also specific stadiums for baseball, basketball, and soccer. So also, a city will build specialized individual venues for opera, theater, and symphony.

City Councilman Craig McDaniel justified it all in 1994: "These cultural institutions, this Arts District, this mosaic of cultural events are not worth further investment for arts' sake. They are worth further investment because they are critical to the success of Dallas and particularly to the success of downtown Dallas. A healthy central business district, which includes the Arts District will mean ... a better off city."[6] It was not art for the sake of art in Dallas; it was art for the sake of business. As long-time Dallas writer A. C. Greene commented, "Dallas salutes the person who can buy a piece of art, not the person who can create one."[7] Still, art was a beneficiary.

AUSTIN

The Texas capital was identified by Richard Florida as the leading creative city in the Lone Star State. It is the center of state political activity, symbolized by the nineteenth-century state capitol, and a link to the federal government, symbolized by the LBJ Presidential Library (1970). Both are buildings of excellence that carry special meaning.

When Johnson left office he transported 40 million pages of documents along with oral history transcripts to be managed by the National Archives in a monumental travertine library designed by modernist architect Gordon Bunshaft (1909–1990). Located on a ridge overlooking

The Lyndon B. Johnson Presidential Library at the University of Texas at Austin, dedicated in 1971. Photograph by author.

The Main Building, completed in 1937, at the University of Texas at Austin. Photograph by author.

the University of Texas, it is a fitting repository for the president who signed the Freedom of Information Act in 1966.

Within sight of the capitol is the University of Texas, an elite school that ranked forty-sixth on the *U.S. News and World Report* 2013 listing. The iconic twenty-seven-story Main Library tower in the center of the campus greets students and visitors who seek its wisdom with the biblical words, "Ye shall know the truth, and the truth shall make you free." *U.S. News and World Report* indicated that the university had an endowment that ranked among the top ten of the nation, with an administrative attitude that the money should be spent on libraries, intelligent students, buildings, and creative faculty.

The university currently ranks fifteenth among the top twenty-five research institutions in the country, and twenty-sixth best in the world. It possesses the fifth largest academic library, and produces the most doctorate degrees in the United States. In 2013 it had fifty-eight graduate programs in the top twenty-five in the nation; sixteen in the top five. Nine Nobel Laureates and at least one Pulitzer Prize winner were connected with the faculty. The university has been responsible for three hundred patents in the past decade and forty-six start-up companies in the past seven years.

With fifty thousand students in 2012, tripled since 1950, the university resolved the problem of diversity in its student body by automatically granting admission to the top 10 percent of graduating high school seniors in Texas. This strategy worked, but also took up all the student space. The legislature modified the rule by allowing the university to select 25 percent of the freshman class. The undergraduate mix of 50 percent white, 20 percent Hispanic, 18 percent Asian, 5 percent black, and 5 percent foreign is not too far from the state demographic distribution. The University of Texas at Austin is a powerhouse university.

In addition to the capitol and the university, Austin also has a vibrant high-tech industry. The city has long been noted for politics and education, but the Austin Chamber of Commerce began a growth effort in the 1950s to diversify the economy with electronics. The University of Texas made a start in 1942 with the Balcones Research Park, established to help the war effort. After the war civil engineering professor J. Neils Thompson developed a diverse engineering "think tank" that had thirty-seven government projects by 1951. A spin-off company, Tracor, was started in 1955 by mechanical engineer Frank McBee along with three university physicists; Tracor focused on acoustics research. By 1982 Tracor had $99 million in sales.

The first success for the Austin Chamber of Commerce was an IBM manufacturing plant to make computers in 1966. Gordon Moody, an IBM vice president, commented, "Austin sold itself. It offers a fine living and working environment, outstanding educational advantages, and impressive recreational and cultural features. The kind of people we need are here."[8] Texas Instruments followed in 1969, Motorola in 1974, and Advanced Micro Design in 1979. By the end of the century some three hundred technology-related companies had placed offices in the city.[9]

A watershed event came in 1983 when Admiral Bobby R. Inman brought his Microelectronic and Computer Technology Corporation (MCC) to Austin after nationwide competition and publicity. He wanted to improve national computer defense capability and to tap into the "atmosphere of genius" provided by the University of Texas.[10] Inman was an early investor in Michael Dell, an important actor in Austin's transformation to "silicon hills."

Dell grew up as a nerd in Houston, complete with horn-rimmed glasses and plastic shirt pocket protector, who liked to repair his friends'

Austin growth after World War II. The Capitol becomes obscured. Photograph by author.

computers. He continued this avocation in his freshman dorm room at the University of Texas and discovered that IBM computers, which sold for $3,000, contained only $700 in parts. At age nineteen he dropped out of school, set up a shop with $1,000 capital, and began to manufacture custom-made computers in 1984. By 1992 Dell, with an assembly plant north of the city, was the fifth largest computer maker in the world. By 2007 he was the second richest man in Texas and noted for his philanthropy.

To the good fortune of Austin in this rush for growth, which doubled its size between 1950 and 2000, a knotty problem of air transportation was resolved by the U.S. Air Force. Robert Mueller Municipal Airport had been patched continually since 1930 to facilitate war training in World War II, meet the demands of passengers, and accommodate the comings and goings of politicians during the Johnson administration in the 1960s. In 1990 the secretary of the air force began to decommission nearby Bergstrom Air Force Base (1942-1993) with its 4,000 acres and 12,250-foot runway. The city council accepted the free base and its property, and with voter approval borrowed $400 million to build a new airport. In 1999 Austin-Bergstrom International Airport opened and Mueller closed with a ceremony of arched streams of water over the final departure aircraft.[11]

KEEP AUSTIN WEIRD

Austin inhabitants, meanwhile, treasured their pleasant, open lifestyle. The city became a haven for the outlaw western music of Willie Nelson and an eclectic menu of music where Birkenstocks happily danced with Bostonians and Tony Lamas at the Armadillo World Headquarters (1970-1980). A local hippy store, Oat Willie's, sold bumper stickers with the motto "Onward: Thru the Fog," and later Red Wassenich, a librarian at Austin Community College, distributed a bumper sticker that read, "Keep Austin Weird." Imagination supplied various meanings to the widespread stickers, but they resonated with the populace.

The television program *Austin City Limits* combined the openness of the Armadillo with new television technology at the University of Texas to present concert performances of progressive country music on PBS starting in 1974. By the 2000s the program had expanded its focus and fan base to include rock, blues, folk, jazz, hip-hop, Latin, and world music. In March 1987, South by Southwest (SXSW), a music convocation, captured the city for the first time. Louis Black, editor of the *Austin Chronicle*, bi-weekly arts publication, Nick Barbaro, the publisher, and Louis Meyers, a booking agent, founded the company SXSW to showcase new musical talent. They expected 150 participants, but 700 showed up. "It was national almost immediately," said Black, a former film student from the University of Texas.[12]

They added film and media to the mix in 1994. Today SXSW hosts presentations, workshops, and a conference for music, film, and interactive media such as Facebook for some two thousand musical groups from around the world on eighty downtown stages and twenty thousand participants in the conference center. The 2011 festival brought $167 million to Austin. It was the largest single revenue event of the year, as visitors filled the hotels and motels of the metropolitan region.

For Austin residents, however, the attraction of the city was more than just a love of innovative music or high-tech industry. A large part of the population also cherished Austin as a place to live. They worked for the university or state government and did not share the business drive for profits and growth. This difference in attitude split the town in a surprising clash over Barton Springs, eventually transforming Austin into a unique, environmentally conscious city.

SAVE OUR SPRINGS

In 1918 Andrew Zilker, a politician and the first Coca-Cola bottler in town, gave 42 acres and later added 313 more acres to provide Zilker Park for his city. The land included Barton Springs, a rocky extension of Barton Creek that arose near Dripping Springs some 50 miles away. The creek dropped 1,000 feet in elevation as it moved toward the Colorado River and disappeared as it trickled water into the shallow limestone fissures of the Edwards Aquifer. In the aquifer the water mixed with other underground sources taken from a 365-square-mile watershed, and brought it all back to the surface at Barton Springs in Zilker Park—clean, clear, and cold as a mountain lake.

In the 1920s the city built a bathhouse and dam to form a swimming pool with a limestone bottom that eventually became 1,000 feet long, 150 feet wide, and 15 feet deep at the diving board. The spring water burbled forth at one end at a frigid 68 degrees and required no filtration or chlorination. With tree-lined and grassy banks Barton Springs became a

Barton Springs at Zilker Park shortly after World War I. Photograph courtesy of Austin History Center, Austin Public Library, PICA 01026.

recreational site for picnics, weddings, and sunbathing. Although it was illegal to skinny-dip, in the 1970s it became clear that no one objected to a woman who chose to leave her bathing suit top at home. University of Texas nature writer Roy Bedichek (1878–1959), who had a reserved space on "Bidi's Rock" under a cottonwood tree at the mouth of the spring, commented, "I go to Barton's every afternoon and have a delightful cooling off. What a poem this place is!"[13]

Barton Springs thus was a special place. It was also a canary in a coal mine, warning of danger. As Austin expanded in the 1980s, suburban land developers lusted to build on the springs recharge zone. The shallow aquifer had little filtration ability and pesticides, herbicides, fertilizer, dirt, and sewerage would appear at Barton Springs within twenty-four hours of a rainstorm. Water quality deteriorated and the pool had to be closed at times. In 1981, for example, the construction of a mall two miles away closed the pool for thirty-two days. This was a time of rising national environmental consciousness and local activists became aroused. The result was a confrontation to untrammeled business exploitation, and the use of political regulation to save a cherished community resource.

The city council, dominated by pro-growth businessmen, gave nodding acknowledgment of the problem at Barton Springs and passed tepid

The Barton Springs pool in April 1939. Photograph courtesy of Austin History Center, Austin Public Library, PICA 17301.

regulations, but they did not stop construction on the recharge zone even though the city drew its drinking water from the aquifer. The issue boiled over in 1990 when Jim Bob Moffett, a millionaire developer for Freeport McMoRan, sought city approval to build 2,500 houses, 1,900 apartments, 3.3 million square feet of shopping and offices, and four golf courses along Barton Creek. He said his plans would not affect the springs.

Some seven hundred environmentalists who knew better jammed an all-night session of the city council to jeer and offer contrary scientific testimony. The abashed council rejected the McMoRan proposal, declared a moratorium on building, and later offered a weak ordinance to allow construction with catchment and water diversion. It was not good enough, and a coalition of environmental groups called "Save Our Springs" (SOS) took to the streets.

This resulted in angry radio talk shows, a silent vigil at Barton Springs with a trumpeter playing "Taps," negative phone calls to city council members, and a thirty-five-thousand-signature petition to force a more restrictive ordinance. SOS director Brigid Shea stated, "The fundamental question before this community is whether or not the citizens of Austin have the right to control their own water quality or if it will be dictated by development interests."[14] It was a comment that hearkened to the age-old search for clean urban water.

The people voted 2:1 in favor of the SOS ordinance in 1992 to maintain the aquifer, and elected Shea to the council in 1994. Land developers, meanwhile, rushed to make claims ahead of the ordinance that would require later bond issues to buy them off. Barton Springs was saved and SOS remained as a watchdog organization to prevent water degradation of the Edwards Aquifer with a voice that echoed to the Rio Grande.

The city council was permanently sensitized to environmental issues, and developers no longer dominated the conversations. They had to learn to work with the environment, not just plow through it. Growth was not automatically good. Big box malls with extended pavement, for instance, required environmental scrutiny. Austin, thus, became a city with an abiding concern about quality of life, not just growth and wealth.[15] It had attained a special balance of excellence in urban governance that is rarely seen.

37

HOUSTON, A RENAISSANCE CITY

While Fort Worth, Dallas, and Austin provide examples of urban excellence, Houston has achieved excellence in many areas. In the early 1960s two events launched the confidence, image, and national reputation of Houston as a creative, renaissance city.[1]

MANNED SPACECRAFT CENTER

The first event was the space race of the 1960s. In the wake of the Soviet Union's successful flight of Sputnik, President John F. Kennedy (1917-1963) set a national goal to send men to the moon in a joint address to Congress on May 25, 1961. He repeated that goal in a speech at Rice University on September 12, 1962. On July 20, 1969, eight years later, astronaut Neil Armstrong (1930-2012) sent his message to earth from the surface of the moon: "Houston ... Tranquility Base here. The *Eagle* has landed!"[2]

During the interval between these messages Houston became the intellectual and technical leader of the space age. In 1961 the National Aeronautics and Space Administration (NASA) began to look for a site to place the Manned Spacecraft Center (MSC), the brains of the space effort. Through the cooperation of Congressman Albert Thomas (1898-1966),

Morgan J. Davis (president of Humble Oil Company), and George R. Brown (a principal in Brown and Root Construction and also chair of the board at Rice University), a timely swap was made. Humble Oil gave 1,000 acres of land to Rice in the middle of the 30,000-acre West Ranch they owned southeast of the city. Rice, in turn, offered it free to the federal government as the site. James E. Webb of NASA accepted. Brown and Root became the construction contractor, and Rice University received

City of Houston, 2008. Photograph by author.

Lovett Hall, cornerstone laid in 1911, Rice University. Photograph by author.

Johnson Space Center at Clear Lake in 1989. Courtesy of the National Aeronautics and Space Administration.

a research grant to set up a department of space science, the first in the nation.[3]

Today, Rice University ranks seventeenth in the nation in the *U.S. News and World Report* listing of the best national universities; its engineering program is just below that of the University of Texas. Rice is small, with two-fifths of the 5,200 students in the graduate schools. The faculty, including one Nobel Laureate and one Pulitzer winner, teach students drawn from the upper 5 percent of high school graduates in small classes. Recently the University of Houston, the traditional, shirtsleeve, commuter school of the metropolis, broke through the ranks of higher education and is considered one of four major research universities of the state.[4]

Humble Oil built a residential and industrial development on their land around the MSC, and the suburbs of Clear Lake City and Nassau Bay emerged. In five years the MSC attained its authorized personnel level of 4,900, with a payroll of $50 million. It was estimated that the MSC inspired sixty-five jobs for every hundred it created, and that 125 companies established offices to deal with the center.

Houston adopted the sobriquet of "Space City, U.S.A." and annexed most of the area in 1977. It was a place of intelligent, tech-minded, well-paid creative people that the Houston Chamber of Commerce continued to nurture. In regard to technological mastery, arguably the most important human characteristic, the Manned Spacecraft Center represented the greatest achievement of Western civilization. The newsworthy successes in space and the reflected glamour of the astronauts gave Houston the reputation of a "can-do" place where anything was possible.

ASTRODOME

The can-do image was underscored by the opening of the Astrodome in 1965. Engineering theory at the time said that it was possible to construct a building large enough to cover a baseball field, but no one had ever done it. The National League, which awarded a team to the Houston Sports Association (HSA) in 1960, required a new stadium to replace the home of the minor league Houston Buffalos. Led by the irrepressible Roy Hofheinz (1912–1982), politician and entrepreneur, the HSA conceived of a domed stadium large enough to cover a baseball field that could be air-conditioned and mosquito proof to counter Houston's oppressive summer environment.

Hofheinz was the driving force. The stadium was seven miles southwest of downtown on open land, thus helping to propel the decline of the central business district and spread the city. It was circular, with an elongated dome of translucent skylights higher than a pop-fly from home plate. The playing field was surrounded by a series of colored rings of cushioned seats. At the top were special, reserved skyboxes and an enormous 474-foot-long scoreboard. The stadium could seat forty-five thousand fans for baseball and fifty-two thousand for football when the seats were moved to form a rectangle.

Hofheinz changed the name of the baseball team to "Astros," called the stadium the "Astrodome," and built an apartment for himself behind the center-field wall. He solved the problem of glare from the skylights by painting them white, and the problem of dying grass by installing the first artificial AstroTurf. He paid for it—$45 million—with Harris County bonds approved by the people and with investment by the sports association.

The Astrodome was a sensation that drew attention to Houston as a place of daring technology. It was the first stadium to attract tourists

The Astrodome, opened in 1965. Four turret-like rampways on the perimeter marred the symmetry in 1989. Photograph by author.

since the ancient Roman Colosseum, about a half-million in the first year. Although it elicited snide comments from purists who wanted their sports served with the rains of summer and the snows of winter, its success dictated consideration of coverings wherever new stadiums were constructed.

The gentle arc of the white dome, moreover, provided feminine contrast to the jagged, phallic thrust of downtown skyscrapers. Urban skylines were never the same again. The Astrodome was the most culturally significant building ever constructed in Texas, and for a moment, it lived up to its nickname as the "Eighth Wonder of the World." Jerry Jones, who later built a billion-dollar stadium for the Dallas Cowboys in Arlington, Texas, reflected that when he first saw the Astrodome as a football player it sucked the wind out of him and left him breathless.[5]

ARCHITECTURE

Beginning in the 1960s, the downtown skyline became a showcase for the skills of famous contemporary architects that gave Houston a sharp, crisp, clean-lined modern appearance that affirmed the image of the city and the influence of architect Mies van der Rohe. Modernist architect Philip Johnson demonstrated his genius at the Menil House (1950), the University of St. Thomas (1958), Pennzoil Place (1976), Transco Tower (1983), and the University of Houston School of Architecture (1986). Johnson commented, "I like Houston, you know. It's the last great nineteenth-century city . . . what I mean is that Houston has a spirit about it that is truly American. An optimism, if you will. People there aren't afraid to try something new."[6]

FINE ARTS

Within the downtown, corporate canyons developed an arts district as Houston grew and became more specialized. Through the nudging of Ima Hogg, the symphony gradually improved, with a succession of conductors. Sir John Barbirolli took it on tour in 1964 to New York's Philharmonic Hall, where he was called for applause four times at intermission and six times at the conclusion of the performance, with people standing on their seats and gathering in front to shout "Bravo!"

His successor, André Previn, accompanied by his blithe companion

Mia Farrow in blue jeans and sandals, did not sit well with conventional Houston society, but Previn made a point that the orchestra needed more international experience. The city, meanwhile, supplied the handsome Jesse H. Jones Hall for the Performing Arts to replace the old, all-purpose City Auditorium.[7]

In 1962 John T. Jones, Jr., nephew of Jesse Jones and head of Houston Endowment, the philanthropic legacy of Jesse Jones, offered to replace the auditorium. Jesse Jones, who had amassed a fortune from real estate and finance, told his nephew not to forget that Houston needed a new opera house. The state-of-the-art structure, with cherry-red carpets and teak walls, was reminiscent of New York's Lincoln Center and provided an exclusive venue for the symphony. At its opening in 1966, music critic Carl Cunningham said, "Music burst forth like a sparkling bubble of champagne."[8] The science of acoustics is not precise, but Jones Hall fortunately obtained a passing grade.

During its construction in 1963, professional wrestling promoters protested the destruction of their venue at the old auditorium and wanted to share space with the symphony at the old Music Hall theater, where the symphony had fled in 1954. This was not allowed by the city council,

Jones Hall for the Performing Arts, completed in 1966. Photograph by author.

which served to emphasize the differentiation taking place between low and high culture.[9] The wrestlers were assigned to a peripheral venue. Houston was reaching for the stars.

Diagonally across the street from Jones Hall, the new Alley Theatre raised its curtains in 1968. It had begun in an alley in 1947 as an enthusiastic amateur theater group led by dynamic, blue-eyed Nina Vance (1914-1980). In time the group gathered Ford Foundation grants and evolved into an acclaimed, professional, repertory theater group. Houston Endowment donated property, Ford offered a matching grant, and the new building, with terraces and two inside theaters, became the site of avant-garde theater in Texas.

Competition for seats in Jones Hall from the Houston Grand Opera (1955-), the Houston Ballet (1955-), and the Society for Performing Arts (1975-), all of which booked traveling shows, resulted in the construction of the Wortham Center in 1987. It had a troubled birth due to the economic downturn, but emerged with two side-by-side theaters financed by donations and turned over to the city. Gus S. Wortham (1891-1976), who was a wealthy insurance man, had often made up the deficits of the symphony, and his foundation paid the bulk for the new center. It was noteworthy that both Wortham and Jones were members of the elite 8F Houston leadership group of the 1940s, which acted for the benefit of the city. Their influence was long reaching.

Simultaneously with Jones Hall in 1966, Jones Plaza, which was intended for free concerts and other events, became available across the street from Jones Hall on top of a landscaped, underground parking garage. In addition, in the downtown a reworked convention center with a movie complex, restaurants, and bars opened to the public in 1998; a labyrinth of air-conditioned tunnels between buildings replete with small shops and quick snacks evolved to provide respite from the heat; Minute Maid Park of the Astros, with a retractable roof, opened in 2000; and the Hobby Center for the Performing Arts replaced the depression-era Music Hall in 2002. The Theater District currently has thirteen thousand seats for live performances, second only to New York City, and attracts 1.5 million patrons per year. This is equal to the total annual attendance for all the professional sports of the city.[10]

It is not enough, however, just to have splendid venues; performances have to be creative and not merely present the pedestrian reproductions of the past. These organizations not only have pushed to present creative works of art, but also have played a role in training performers for the craft. The Houston Grand Opera, for example, provided scholarships for as many as twelve young people to work with the company for a season, and the Houston Ballet taught, trained, and maintained its own corps of dancers. Opera and symphony produce the world's most complicated music. It takes a great city to support and contribute to it.

Houston also assembled a loosely joined museum district. The Museum of Fine Arts, promoted by the Hogg family, came together in 1924-1927 between Rice Institute and downtown at the juncture of Montrose Boulevard and Main Street. Expansion became an issue after World War II, when the collection of four thousand objects began to increase. New wings were added in 1953 and 1958, and in 1974 the last design of Chicago architect Ludwig Mies van der Rohe gave the old building a modern entrance.

The Contemporary Arts Museum, across the street from the Museum of Fine Arts, added to the district in 1974. The Children's Museum in 1992 and the Museum of Health and Medical Science in 1995, six blocks away, established an eastern boundary. The Holocaust Museum, promoted by Houston's Jewish community, marked the northern border, five blocks distant, in 1996, and the Museum of Natural Science in Hermann Park in 1964, with the Cockrell Butterfly Center in 1995, established the southern line. All in all, it was not walkable in Houston heat and not a true "district." The conglomeration might be considered more of a neighborly association rather than a district.

Of greater national interest was the construction of the de Menil Collection in the Montrose residential area near the University of St. Thomas. John and Dominique de Menil of France had purchased modern art since 1931. They fled the German occupation of France in World War II, recovered their art, which they had left behind and hidden on a piece of high furniture, and ended up in Houston, where John was a principal of Schlumberger, an oil tools company.

In 1971 they built the Rothko Chapel on the campus of the University of St. Thomas. It was a small, plain brick structure that displayed fourteen huge black, abstract paintings by Mark Rothko. In a small reflection pool outside they placed Barnett Newman's sculpture dedicated to Martin Luther King, *The Broken Obelisk* (1970). It was a 26-feet high, truncated steel shaft, naturally rusted and balanced on a pyramidal point. It was considered to be one of the great pieces of sculpture of the twentieth century. "Only abstract art can bring us to the threshold of the divine," said Dominique.[11] A steady stream of pilgrims annually arrives from around the world to visit this place of quiet meditation.

After John died, Dominique continued to express her affection for their adopted city and arranged to display their art collection in a long gray-and-white gallery designed by Italian architect Renzo Piano. Other cities—Paris, Los Angeles, New York—tried to obtain the collection, but she preferred the informality of Houston. At the opening ceremony the residents of the neighborhood gathered outside in their shorts and raised their Lone Star beer cans in salute.

At the ceremony she said, "Artists are economically useless—yet they are indispensable. A political regime where artists are persecuted is stifling, unbearable. Man cannot live by bread alone. We need painters, poets, musicians, filmmakers, philosophers, dancers, and saints."[12] In 1995 she added an annex to house a collection of Cy Twombly's modern art. She said of the square, self-effacing gallery designed by Piano, "It is all on the inside. It is so modest on the outside and so rich on the inside."[13]

TEXAS MEDICAL CENTER

On South Main Street beyond the Arts District and Hermann Park, Houston's most important contribution to human life, the Texas Medical Center, emerged. Monroe D. Anderson, a wealthy cotton factor of the early twentieth century, left $20 million in 1936 in a trust to advance knowledge and alleviate human suffering. There was no specific project.

The state legislature, meanwhile, appropriated $500,000 and authorized a cancer research hospital under the vague direction of the University of Texas in 1941. At the time cancer was fearsome, perplexing, unmentionable, and deadly. Representative Arthur Cato, a druggist from Weatherford who had lost his father and wife's parents to the dreaded disease, introduced a bill to do something about it.[14]

Placing the hospital at Galveston with the University of Texas Medical Branch (UTMB), or perhaps even moving the entire Galveston school inland, was considered. UTMB was in serious departmental strife at the time, and the main campus in Austin was in turmoil over a clash between the regents and President Homer P. Rainey. The City of Galveston resisted. It did not want to lose its main source of income, and moreover, UTMB had been placed on the island by statewide vote.

The Anderson trustees sensed a purpose and an opportunity. At a meeting in Houston at Mayor Oscar Holcombe's office in 1942, it was arranged for the Anderson trustees to buy 134 acres of city land next to Hermann Hospital, with the approval of the electorate. The trustees then offered to the University of Texas a 21-acre portion and matched the amount given by the legislature. The university regents accepted, M. D. Anderson Cancer Center started, and the trustees found a pattern for future expenditure.

The University of Texas Dental Branch followed in 1943, and the Anderson trustees granted it $500,000 in support. Also in 1943 the Baylor University College of Medicine moved to Houston from Dallas. It was the only other medical school in Texas besides UTMB at the time. Unhappy in Dallas because of shaky funding, Baylor accepted an offer from the Anderson Foundation for a 21-acre site, $1 million for a new building, and $100,000 per annum support for ten years.

As was appropriate for a teaching college, the new Methodist Hospital was placed next door. The old hospital, located elsewhere in town, lacked air-conditioning, and the operating rooms depended upon the natural light of the windows. It was failing as a hospital. In the discussions of the hospital board, Ella Fondren (Mrs. Walter W. Fondren) a major supporter, said, "Now is the time to build, or to hide our faces as Methodists."[15]

The M. D. Anderson Cancer Center in 2012. Photograph by author.

The Anderson trustees offered land and a fund-raising matching grant of fifty cents for every dollar up to $500,000. Oilman Hugh Roy Cullen, who was noted for funding the University of Houston, easily met the goal with a $1 million gift. He actually gave $1 million to four hospitals within a few days in 1945. The land, a medical school, a hospital, a dental school, a cancer research facility, and ready philanthropy were the core essentials of the Texas Medical Center (TMC), which incorporated in 1945.

The new Methodist Hospital opened in 1951 and would expand four times. Neither the hospital nor Baylor University expressed a sectarian bias, and in 1968 the Baptist General Convention released the medical school from denominational ties. Medicaid and Medicare required integration in order to receive federal moneys, and consequently the hospitals and their staffs changed. Hermann Hospital went to court to break its exclusive white charter in 1962. Baylor admitted its first black to residency in 1953 and its first black student in 1969. M. D. Anderson Hospital changed immediately after a command in 1965 from the U.S. Department of Health, Education, and Welfare to desegregate or forego federal funding.[16]

MICHAEL E. DeBAKEY

Doctors hired at Methodist Hospital automatically became doctors at the school. The greatest success of this accommodation was the pioneering work of Dr. Michael E. DeBakey (1908-2008), who brought global renown to the Texas Medical Center. He was hired as chairman of the department of surgery at Baylor when he was thirty-nine years old, became president of Baylor for ten years, until 1979, and then was chancellor until 1996.

Meanwhile, DeBakey performed countless operations, and his inventions and innovations in heart surgery, such as utilizing Dacron grafts, made him world famous. He performed his first heart transplant in 1968. He worked to improve global health and received numerous awards, including the Medal of Freedom, the highest civilian honor, in 1969, the National Medal of Science in 1987, and the Congressional Gold Medal in 2008.[17] He worked tirelessly, with little sleep, and was said to be nourished by bananas and coffee. "Iron Mike" was prickly and perfectionistic, just the sort of person that people would want as their heart surgeon.

The Texas Medical Center (TMC) is now the largest medical center in the world, with fifty related medical institutions, fifteen hospitals, three

Dr. Michael DeBakey. Photograph courtesy of Baylor College of Medicine.

medical schools, and four nursing schools. All work is done on a nonprofit basis, with funds coming from donations, grants, fees, royalties, and patents. The facility occupies 1,000 acres, services 6 million patients per year in a concentrated environment, and employs 93,500 people, including 20,000 doctors.

TMC is the largest single employer in Houston, and it is all dedicated to the relief of human suffering. In September 2012, reminiscent of President John F. Kennedy's call to reach the moon, the M. D. Anderson Hospital announced a ten-year, $3 billion campaign with six teams to find a cure for eight specific types of cancer, including breast, ovarian, lung, prostate, melanoma, and leukemia. This is a noble quest and counts for greatness in a city.

38

THE INFRASTRUCTURE FOR EXCELLENCE

The urbanization examples in Texas suggest that certain basic elements seem necessary for modern urban greatness: democracy, law and order, a sustaining economy, philanthropy, and public education. These building blocks developed in the Lone Star State through time and are still evolving. They all have their own history and do not guarantee either the appearance or endurance of a great city. "For history shows," warned Peter Hall, "that golden urban ages are rare and special windows of light that briefly illuminate the world both within them and outside them, are then again shuttered."[1]

Yet, on occasion at a nexus in time, talented individuals or groups have used these blocks and resources to create something better—a computer, environmental sensitivity, a repertory theater, an opera house, a stadium, a control center for space exploration, a medical center—that pushes the envelope of civilization. This excellence is evidence of a creative urban people.

39

THE CITY AND THE STATE
A CONUNDRUM

The cities in Texas, as elsewhere in the United States, are often a political afterthought. Nonetheless, they are the key organizing units that attract creative people, and it would seem logical for a state to act for the benefit of its cities. Yet, in contemporary Texas, state deficiencies are blamed on the cities—illness, pollution, unemployment, racial problems, education problems, traffic congestion, and water shortages. The state, for instance, refuses to support Medicaid because it is an "intrusion into state sovereignty," with the result that the poor go to emergency wards of city hospitals supported by local taxes.[1]

Texas produces one-third of the greenhouse gases from industrial sources in the United States, and has not met Environmental Protection Agency goals for thirty years because the regulations are considered an overreach into state affairs.[2] Children who live within two miles of the Houston Ship Channel and its refineries, therefore, have a 56 percent greater chance of developing acute leukemia.[3] The state brags about having no income tax, using a regressive sales tax for funding. Such taxes strike the poor hardest, and in 2011 a record 14 percent of Texans depended upon federal food stamps in order to eat.[4] The state provision for higher education has been steadily cut: its contribution to the university budget dropped from 47 percent in 1984 to 14 percent in 2010.[5]

Texas' spending for grade school education has continually ranked with the lower portion of the other states, and in 2011 its high school seniors scored thirty points behind the national average for the National Scholastic Aptitude Test (SAT).[6]

Since educational accomplishment correlates with economic success, demographer Steve Murdock has predicted that by 2040 the state will be less educated and less able to pay its costs.[7] A new knowledge economy fueled by education is now in motion, and political scientist Cal Jillson of Southern Methodist University warns, "Texas hustle, grit, and bluff will not be enough. The days of the Texas wildcatter with a sixth-grade education who struck it rich are gone."[8]

Perhaps, the new natural gas bonanza, based upon fracking, will save the state. Perhaps, the increased state revenue will be invested wisely in health and education and water and roads. Perhaps, more money will ease the tension between city and state. Perhaps not, and mobile creative people will search for a better place to live. "Gone to Texas" may turn into a bitter jest, but that depends upon a future not quite here.

NOTES

INTRODUCTION: THEORIES, DEFINITIONS, HISTORIANS

1. See chapters 6 and 7 in David G. McComb, *Texas: A Modern History*, rev. ed. (Austin: University of Texas Press, 2010).
2. U.S. Patent and Trademark Office, "Patents by Country, State, and Year, 1963-2010." U.S. Patent and Trademark Office, "Statistical Reports Available for Viewing, Patents by State and Island Areas, 2009." The numbers by state of patents and copyrights, also a gauge of creativity, are elusive, but their increase parallels the growth of cities.
3. Bill Bishop with Robert G. Cushing, *The Big Sort: Why the Clustering of Like-Minded America Is Tearing Us Apart* (Boston: Houghton Mifflin, 2008), p. 134.
4. William Cronon, president of the American Historical Association in 2012, explains the symbiosis of synthesis and analysis in "Breaking Apart, Putting Together," *Perspectives on History* 50 (May 2012), pp. 5-6. For a general analysis of historical thinking see John Lewis Gaddis, *The Landscape of History: How Historians Map the Past* (New York: Oxford University Press, 2002).
5. Hope Tisdale, "The Process of Urbanization," *Social Forces* 20 (March 1942), pp. 311-312, 316. This is not far from a current Wikipedia definition of urbanization as "the physical growth of urban areas as a result of rural and urban migration."
6. Lewis Mumford, *The City in History: Its Origins, Its Transformations, and Its Prospects* (New York: Harcourt Brace and World, 1961), p. 576.
7. Peter Hall, *Cities in Civilization* (New York: Pantheon Books, 1998), p. 494.
8. A good summary of the field is provided by Raymond A. Mohl, "New Perspectives on American Urban History," in *The Making of Urban America*, 2nd ed. (Wilmington, DE: Scholarly Resources, 1997), pp. 335-374. Also, see the various issues of the *Journal of Urban History*, especially Mark H. Rose, ed., "Technology and Politics:

The Scholarship of Two Generations of Urban-Environmental Historians" in volume 30 (July 2004), pp. 769-785.
9. For a review of central place theory see Mario Polese, *The Wealth and Poverty of Regions: Why Cities Matter* (Chicago: University of Chicago Press, 2009), pp. 195-209.
10. Peter Hall, *Cities of Tomorrow: An Intellectual History of Urban Planning and Design in the Twentieth Century* (Oxford, UK: Basil Blackwell, 1988), pp. 326-335.

PART ONE: FIRST THINGS
1. THE LAY OF THE LAND

1. George B. Dealy, while manager of the *Dallas Morning News* in 1916, commented, "How much better if we devoted our time, energy, and thought to making Dallas the best town in Texas rather than the largest." Quoted by George Fuermann, *Reluctant Empire* (New York: Doubleday, 1957), p. 133. Ronald L. Davis, *Twentieth Century Cultural Life in Texas* (Boston: American Press, 1981), p. 49, quoted a Texas millionaire watching the University of Texas Band, "You know, to have the biggest of anything—that's something." Gail Collins of New York used the open space as a means to explain Texan feelings for independence and conservatism in her current critique of Texas in *As Texas Goes... How the Lone Star State Hijacked the American Agenda* (New York: Liveright, 2012), p. 27.

2. THE INFLUENCE OF THE NATIVE AMERICANS

1. William C. Foster, *Historic Native Peoples of Texas* (Austin: University of Texas Press, 2008), pp. xi, 244-245. The translation of "Tejas" is repeated by Fray Gaspar José de Solis in Mattie Austin Hatcher, ed., "Diary of a Visit of Inspection of the Texas Missions Made by Fray Gaspar Jose de Solis in the Years 1768-68," *Southwestern Historical Quarterly* 35 (July 1931), p. 60.
2. David La Vere, *The Texas Indians* (College Station: Texas A&M University Press, 2004), p. 54.
3. Andres Resendez, *A Land So Strange: The Epic Journey of Cabeza de Vaca* (New York: Basic Books, 2007), p. 185.
4. William C. Foster, *Spanish Expeditions in Texas, 1869-1768* (Austin: University of Texas Press, 1995), pp. 217-220. In *Old Texas Trails* (Burnet, TX: Eakin Press, 1979), p. 126, J. W. Williams insists that José Domingo Ramón, 1716, was the first road builder. Others left trails that did not become roads.

3. THE TOWNS OF THE SPANISH EMPIRE IN TEXAS

1. See for a general history Donald E. Chipman, *Spanish Texas, 1519-1821* (Austin: University of Texas Press, 1992).
2. John W. Reps, *Cities of the American West: A History of Frontier Urban Planning* (Princeton: Princeton University Press, 1979), pp. 37-42.
3. Marion A. Habig, *The Alamo Chain of Missions: A History of San Antonio's Five Old Missions* (Chicago: Franciscan Herald Press, 1968), p. 26. The dark brown robe of the Franciscans was universally adopted only in 1897.

4. Felix D. Almaraz, Jr., *The San Antonio Missions and Their System of Land Tenure* (Austin: University of Texas Press, 1989), pp. 6, 18, 20, 38, 40, 56.
5. Gilbert R. Cruz, *Let There Be Towns: Spanish Municipal Origins in the American Southwest, 1610-1810* (College Station: Texas A&M University Press, 1988), p. 46. In 1955 the City of El Paso annexed Yselta against the desires of its forty thousand inhabitants and submerged its history.
6. In 1768 Fray Solis observed numerous unbranded Spanish cattle and horses as a result of de León's release. Hatcher, "Diary of Fray Gaspar Jose de Solis," p. 56.
7. Noel M. Loomis and Abraham P. Nasatir, *Pedro Vial and the Roads to Santa Fe* (Norman: University of Oklahoma Press, 1968), p. 353.
8. James G. Partin et al., *Nacogdoches* (Lufkin, TX: Best of East Texas Publishers, 1995), pp. 34-38, 40.
9. Ibid., pp. 44-45. J. Villasana Haggard, "The House of Barr and Davenport," *Southwestern Historical Quarterly* 49 (July 1945), pp. 72-75, 77, 87.
10. Quoted in Cruz, *Let There Be Towns*, p. 57.
11. Reps, *Cities of the American West*, pp. 65-68; David G. McComb, *Spare Time in Texas: Recreation and History in the Lone Star State* (Austin: University of Texas Press, 2008), pp. 40-42.
12. Mattie Austin Hatcher, "The Municipal Government of San Fernando de Bexar, 1730-1800," *Southwestern Historical Quarterly* 8 (April 1905), pp. 293, 297, 305; Cruz, *Let There Be Towns*, pp. 76, 134-135.
13. Fray Juan Agustín Morfí, *History of Texas, 1673-1779*, trans. Carlos Eduardo Castañeda (Albuquerque: Quivira Society, 1935), p. 92.
14. Loomis and Nasatir, *Pedro Vial*, pp. 356-357.
15. Jack Johnson, *Los Mesteños: Spanish Ranching in Texas, 1721-1821* (College Station: Texas A&M University Press, 1986), pp. 131-132.
16. David J. Weber, *The Spanish Frontier in North America* (New Haven: Yale University Press, 1992), pp. 320-322.
17. Felix D. Almaraz, Jr., *The San Antonio Missions and Their System of Land Tenure* (Austin: University of Texas Press, 1989), p. 57; Jackson, *Los Mesteños, pp.* 252-253, 280-281, 294-295, 340, 412.
18. Cruz, *Let There Be Towns, pp.* 94 95, 103.
19. Alicia V. Tjarks, "Comparative Demographic Analysis of Texas, 1777-1793," *Southwestern Historical Quarterly* 77 (January 1974), pp. 296-299, 301-313.
20. Ibid., pp. 323-326.
21. Jesús F. de la Teja, "Why Urbano and Maria Trinidad Can't Get Married: Social Relations in Late Colonial San Antonio," *Southwestern Historical Quarterly* 112 (October 2008), p. 146. See also Mark M. Carroll, *Homesteads Ungovernable: Families, Sex, Race, and the Law in Frontier Texas, 1823-1860* (Austin: University of Texas Press, 2001), pp. 1-3.
22. Cruz, *Let There Be Towns*, pp. 140-143.

4. THE COMING OF THE AMERICANS

1. W. Eugene Hollon, *The Lost Pathfinder: Zubulon Montgomery Pike* (Norman: University of Oklahoma Press, 1949), p. 156.
2. Elliot Coes, ed., *The Expeditions of Zebulon Montgomery Pike...* (New York: F. P.

Harper, 1895), vol. 2, pp. 783 (first quote), 784 (second quote), 786 (third quote), 784 (fourth quote).
3. Ibid., p. 287.
4. Michael C. Meyer and William L. Sherman, *The Course of Mexican History* (New York: Oxford University Press, 1979), p. 288. "Gachupine" is a pejorative word for a European-born Spaniard. The use of the word at the time also was a general expletive for the Spanish upper class.
5. Jack Johnson, *Los Mesteños: Spanish Ranching in Texas, 1721-1821* (College Station: Texas A&M University Press, 1986), p. 546.
6. See for the Magee-Gutiérrez expedition Harry McCorry Henderson, "The Magee-Gutierrez Expedition," *Southwestern Historical Quarterly* 55 (July 1951), pp. 45-60; Henry P. Walker, ed., "William McLane's Narrative of the Magee-Gutierrez Expedition, 1812-1813," *Southwestern Historical Quarterly* 66 (January, April 1963), pp. 236, 247-249, 458, 460-466, 474-478; Felix D. Almaraz, Jr., *Tragic Cavalier: Governor Manuel Salcedo of Texas, 1808-1813* (Austin: University of Texas Press, 1971), pp. 159, 164-172, 175-181; Julia Kathryn Garrett, *Green Flag over Texas* (Austin: Pemberton Press, 1939), pp. 225-228.
7. Meyer and Sherman, *The Course of Mexican History*, pp. 335-336.
8. Eugene C. Barker, "The Government of Austin's Colony, 1821-1831," *Southwestern Historical Quarterly* 21 (January 1918), pp. 243 n. 76, 245.
9. Noah Smithwick, *The Evolution of a State; or, Recollections of Old Texas Days* (Austin: University of Texas Press, 1983), p. 50.
10. Ibid., pp. 49, 53, 55 (second quote), 56 (first quote); Gregg Cantrell, *Stephen F. Austin, Empresario of Texas* (New Haven: Yale University Press, 1999), p. 197. According to Margaret Swett Henson in *Samuel May Williams: Early Texas Entrepreneur* (College Station: Texas A&M University Press, 1976), pp. 16-17, and J. H. Kuykendall, "Recollections: Reminiscences of Early Texans," *Quarterly of the Texas State Historical Association* 7 (July 1903-April 1904), pp. 49-50, Dr. Lewis B. T. Dayton, who opposed Stephen F. Austin, wrote this parody of a barroom ballad and distributed the words in 1827. Austin's friends arrested Dayton, held a trial in a saloon, dumped tar and feathers on Dayton's head, and escorted him out of town. Dayton was not seen again. See also J. Frank Dobie, "More Ballads and Songs of the Frontier Folk," in *Follow de Drinkin' Gou'd* (Dallas: Southern Methodist University Press, 1928), pp. 155-158.
11. Smithwick, *The Evolution of a State*, pp. 46-47 (quote); Cantrell, *Stephen F. Austin*, pp. 237-238.
12. Hatcher, "Diary of Fray Gaspar José de Solis," pp. 42 (first quote), 43 (second quote), 44 (third quote).
13. Ibid., p. 73.
14. Ibid., p. 76.
15. Nettie Lee Benson, "Bishop Martin de Porras and Texas," *Southwestern Historical Quarterly* 51 (July 1947), pp. 18, 21, 29 (quote).
16. Andres Tijerina, *Tejanos and Texas under the Mexican Flag, 1821-1836* (College Station: Texas A&M University Press, 1994), pp. 4, 11, 17, 38, 46, 87, 98-99.
17. Benjamin Heber Johnson and Jeffrey Gusky, *Bordertown: The Odyssey of an American Place* (New Haven: Yale University Press, 2008), pp. 46-48.
18. José Mariá Sánchez y Tapia, "A Trip to Texas in 1828," Carlos Castañeda, trans., *Southwestern Historical Quarterly* 29 (April 1926), pp. 250, 251 (quote), 251; Jean Louis

Berlandier, C. H. Muller, and Katherine K. Muller, eds., *Journey to Mexico during the Years 1826 to 1834* (Austin: Texas State Historical Association, 1980), vol. 2, pp. 262, 271, 272, 274, 275, 276, 276, 282, 284.
19. Jesús F. de la Teja and John Wheat, "Bexar: Profile of a Tejano Community, 1820-1832," *Southwestern Historical Quarterly* 89 (July 1985), pp. 9-10.
20. Sánchez, "A Trip to Texas in 1828," pp. 258-259, 258 (quote).
21. Joseph Chambers Clopper, "J. C. Clopper's Journal and Book of Memoranda for 1828," *Southwestern Historical Quarterly* 13 (July 1909), pp. 68-74, 73 (first quote), 76 (second quote).
22. Jack Jackson, ed., *Texas by Terán: The Diary Kept by General Manuel de Mier y Terán on His 1828 Inspection of Texas*, trans. John Wheat (Austin: University of Texas Press, 2000), p. 45.
23. Sánchez, "A Trip to Texas in 1828," p. 271 (quotes); Jackson, *Texas by Terán*, p. 56.
24. Sánchez, "A Trip to Texas in 1828," p. 274.
25. Ibid., p. 282; Jackson, *Texas by Terán*, pp. 80-81 (quote).
26. William Seale, "San Augustine in the Republic of Texas," *Southwestern Historical Quarterly* 72 (January 1969), pp. 348, 349; Margaret Swett Henson and Deolece Parmelee, *The Cartwrights of San Augustine* (Austin: Texas State Historical Association, 1993), pp. 59-61.
27. Carlos Castañeda, trans., "Statistical Report on Texas by Juan N. Almonte," *Southwestern Historical Quarterly* 28 (January 1925), pp. 183-184, 193, 196, 197, 205, 209 (quote), 215-216; Helen Willits Harris, "Almonte's Inspection of Texas in 1834," *Southwestern Historical Quarterly* 41 (January 1939), pp. 209, 210.

5. THE TOWNS OF THE TEXAS REVOLUTION

1. Alwyn Barr, *Texans in Revolt: The Battle for San Antonio, 1835* (Austin: University of Texas Press, 1990), pp. 46-50.
2. Ibid., p. 57.
3. Stephen L. Hardin, *Texian Iliad: A Military History of the Texas Revolution, 1835-1836* (Austin: University of Texas Press, 1994), pp. 79-91.
4. See ibid.; Lon Tinkle, *The Alamo* (New York: Signet Book, 1960; Walter Lord, *A Time to Stand* (New York: Pocket Books, 1963); James W. Pohl and Stephen L. Hardin, "The Military History of the Texas Revolution: An Overview," *Southwestern Historical Quarterly* 89 (January 1986), pp. 269-308; James E. Crisp, *Sleuthing the Alamo: Davy Crockett's Last Stand and Other Mysteries of the Texas Revolution* (New York: Oxford University Press, 2005); and Randy Roberts and James S. Olson, *A Line in the Sand: The Alamo in Blood and Memory* (New York: Free Press, 2001).
5. Reference to San Antonio quoted in Gregg J. Dimmick, *Sea of Mud* (Austin: Texas State Historical Association, 2004), p. 264; William Bollaert quoted in *William Bollaert's Texas*, ed. W. Eugene Hollon and Ruth Lapham Butler (Norman: University of Oklahoma Press, 1956), p. 181, reported in 1843 that San Felipe was a deserted village with weeds and bushes grown up in the streets.
6. José Enrique de la Peña, *With Santa Anna in Texas: A Personal Narrative of the Revolution*, trans. Carmen Perry (College Station: Texas A&M University Press, 1975), pp. 165-166.
7. Dimmick, *Sea of Mud*, p. 277.

PART TWO: THE DIRT ROAD FRONTIER, 1836-1900

6. MAJOR EVENTS

1. Ralph A. Wooster, "Wealthy Texans, 1870," *Southwestern Historical Quarterly* 74 (July 1970), pp. 24-25, 26, 28-29, 32; Thad Sitton and Dan K. Utley, *From Can See to Can't: Texas Cotton Farmers on the Southern Prairies* (Austin: University of Texas Press, 1997), p. 27.
2. This is based on a survey of governors listed in the *Handbook of Texas Online*.

7. THE DIRT ROAD

1. Frederick Law Olmsted, *A Journey through Texas; or, a Saddle-Trip on the Southwestern Frontier* (Austin: University of Texas Press, 1978), p. 55.
2. A. Joachim McGraw, John W. Clark, Fr., and Elizabeth A. Robbins, eds., *A Texas Legacy, The Old San Antonio Road and Caminos Reales: A Tricentennial History, 1691-1991* (Austin: Texas Department of Transportation, January 1998), p. 43. The old highway is practically impossible to trace. See Stephen Harrigan, "Highway 1," *Texas Monthly* 19 (January 1991), pp. 96-118.
3. McGraw et al., pp. 4, 12, 27. 33, 230, 234.
4. Arnoldo De León, *They Called Them Greasers: Anglo Attitudes toward Mexicans in Texas, 1821-1900* (Austin: University of Texas Press, 1983), p. 26.
5. G. Arthur Bell, "Breeds of Draft Horses," *USDA Farmer's Bulletin* 619, November 16, 1914.
6. J. W. Williams, "The National Road of the Republic of Texas," *Southwestern Historical Quarterly* 47 (January 1944), pp. 208, 216, 221; "National Road," *The New Handbook of Texas*, vol. 4, ed. Ron Tyler (Austin: Texas State Historical Association, 1996), p. 945; W. L. Newsom, "The Postal System of the Republic of Texas," *Southwestern Historical Quarterly* 20 (October 1916), pp. 106, 119.

8. MIGRATION: GONE TO TEXAS

1. Archie P. McDonald, *Hurrah for Texas: The Diary of Adolphus Stern, 1838-1851* (Waco, TX: Texian Press, 1969), p. 14 (first quote), p. 80 (second quote).
2. Terry G. Jordan with John L. Bean, Jr., and William M. Holmes, *Texas: A Geography* (Boulder: Westview Press, 1984), pp. 48, 71-73.
3. Ibid., p. 73, 77-81.
4. J. D. B. Debow, *The Seventh Census of the United States: 1850* (Washington, DC: Robert Armstrong, Public Printer, 1853), p. 504; Department of Interior, Census Office, *Twelfth Census of the United States, Taken in the Year 1900. Population, Part I* (Washington, DC: United States Census Office, 1901), p. 613.
5. Mark M. Carroll, *Homesteads Ungovernable: Families, Sex, Race, and the Law in Frontier Texas, 1823-1860* (Austin: University of Texas Press, 2001), pp. 98-99.
6. John William Rogers, *The Lusty Texans of Dallas* (New York: E. P. Dutton, 1951), p. 70.
7. Elizabeth Jameson, "Women as Workers, Women as Civilizers: True Womanhood in the American West," in Susan Armitage and Elizabeth Jameson, eds., *The Women's West* (Norman: University of Oklahoma Press, 1987), p. 150.

8. Elizabeth York Enstam, *Women and the Creation of Urban Life: Dallas, Texas, 1843-1920* (College Station: Texas A&M University Press, 1998), pp. 75-78.
9. Ann Patton Malone, *Women on the Texas Frontier: a Cross-Cultural Perspective* (El Paso: Texas Western Press, 1983), pp. 14 (second quote), 56 (first quote); Mary Austin Holey, in *Texas* (Austin: Texas State Historical Association, 1990), pp. 135-136, tells of a frontier woman living alone, raising her children, teaching herself and her children to read, and providing meat by hunting. After shooting a deer, and not being strong enough to put it on the horse, she cut it into quarters with a tomahawk, linked the pieces together, and carried them home with the quarters balanced on each side of the horse.
10. John Salmon Ford, *Rip Ford's Texas*, ed. Stephen B. Oates (Austin: University of Texas Press, 1963), p. 442 (both quotes).

9. THE EVOLUTION OF SAN ANTONIO

1. Mary A. Maverick, *Memoirs of Mary A. Maverick*, ed. Rena Maverick Green (Lincoln: University of Nebraska Press, 1989), p. 27.
2. Ibid., pp. 32-33.
3. W. Eugene Hollon and Ruth Lapham Butler, eds., *William Bollaert's Texas* (Norman: University of Oklahoma Press, 1956), p. 219.
4. Noah Smithwick, *Evolution of a State; or, Recollections of Old Texas Days* (Austin: University of Texas Press, 1983), p. 151.
5. David Montejano, *Anglos and Mexicans in the Making of Texas, 1836-1986* (Austin: University of Texas Press, 1987), p. 28.
6. Ibid., p. 26. For the rise of prejudice see also James R. Crisp, *Sleuthing the Alamo: Davy Crockett's Last Stand and Other Mysteries of the Texas Revolution* (New York: Oxford University Press, 2005), pp. 27-60.
7. Jesús F. de la Teja, ed., *A Revolution Remembered: The Memoirs and Selected Correspondence of Juan N. Seguín* (Austin: State House Press, 1991), p. x.
8. Arnoldo De León, *The Tejano Community, 1836-1900* (Albuquerque: University of New Mexico Press, 1982), p. 29.
9. Jo Ella Powell Exley, *Texas Tears and Texas Sunshine: Voices of Frontier Women* (College Station: Texas A&M University Press, 1985), p. 119. Mary Maverick records cholera in San Antonio in 1849 that killed their child, Augusta. Maverick, *Memoirs*, p. 97. Five hundred people died that year.
10. Frederick Law Olmsted, *A Journey through Texas; or, a Saddle-Trip on the Southwestern Frontier* (Austin: University of Texas Press, 1978), p. 160.
11. Arnoldo De León, *Mexican Americans in Texas: A Brief History* (Wheeling, IL: Harlan Davidson, 1999), pp. 49-50.
12. Montejano, *Anglos and Mexicans*, p. 40.
13. Larry Knight, "The Cart War: Defining American in San Antonio in the 1850s," *Southwestern Historical Quarterly* 109 (January 2006), p. 322.
14. Olmsted, *A Journey through Texas*, p. 157.
15. Ibid., p. 151.
16. Ferdinand Roemer, *Texas*, trans. Oswald Mueller (San Antonio: Standard Printing, 1935), pp. 124-125.

17. Abbe Domenech, *Missionary Adventures in Texas and Mexico* (London: Longman, Brown, Green, Longmans, and Roberts, 1858), p. 39.
18. Maverick, *Memoirs*, pp. 50-51.
19. David R. Johnson, "Frugal and Sparing: Interest Groups, Politics, and City Building in San Antonio, 1870-85," in Char Miller and Heywood T. Sanders, eds., *Urban Texas, Politics and Development* (College Station: Texas A&M University Press, 1990), pp. 35-36. It is difficult to account for the Mexican population because the U.S. Census did not count Mexican Americans as an ethnic group until 1970. Therefore, surnames are used as an indication of ethnicity. Consider also the entanglement of defining the words "Mexican," "Mexicano," "Tejano," "Texas Mexican," "Mexican American," "Anglo," "white," "Anglo Texan," and "Anglo immigrant." See the preface of Kenneth L. Stewart and Arnoldo De León, *Not Room Enough: Mexicans, Anglos, and Socio-economic Change in Texas, 1850-1900* (Albuquerque: University of New Mexico Press, 1993).
20. Quoted in Donald E. Everett, "San Antonio Welcomes the 'Sunset'—1877," *Southwestern Historical Quarterly* 65 (July 1961), p. 47.
21. Raymond Boryczka, "'The Busiest Man in Town': John Hermann Kampmann and the Urbanization of San Antonio, Texas, 1848-1885," *Southwestern Historical Quarterly* 115 (April 2012), pp. 356, 358.
22. Montejano, *Anglos and Mexicans*, pp. 92-95.
23. Ibid., p. 42.
24. Lewis F. Fisher, "Preservation of San Antonio's Built Environment," in Char Miller, ed., *On the Border: An Environmental History of San Antonio* (San Antonio: Trinity University Press, 2005), pp. 206-207.

10. THE GERMAN TOWNS OF TEXAS

1. Seymour V. Connor, *The Peters Colony of Texas: A History and Biographical Sketches of the Early Settlers* (Austin: Texas State Historical Association, 1959), pp. 104, 107, 110.
2. Frederick Law Olmsted, *A Journey through Texas; or, a Saddle-Trip on the Southwestern Frontier* (Austin: University of Texas Press, 1978), p. 81.
3. Glen E. Lich, *The German Texans* (San Antonio: Institute of Texan Cultures, 1996), pp. 155-156; David G. McComb, *Spare Time in Texas: Recreation and History in the Lone Star State* (Austin: University of Texas Press, 2008), pp. 23-25.

11. THE COASTAL PORTS

1. Richard V. Francaviglia, *From Sail to Steam: Four Centuries of Texas Maritime History, 1500-1900* (Austin: University of Texas Press, 1998), pp. 128-135, 161-162, 229-230, 260, 262. Francaviglia noted that schooners would take a week to sail from New Orleans to Galveston. Steamships would make the run in under two days (p. 132).
2. Ellen Beasley, *The Alleys and Back Buildings of Galveston: An Architectural and Social History* (Houston: Rice University Press, 1996), p. 14. It is remarkable that there are few comments about garbage and human excrement disposal in historical references. This book is an exception. See also Martin V. Melosi, *Garbage in the Cities: Refuse, Reform, and the Environment* (Pittsburgh: University of Pittsburgh Press, 2005).
3. Much of the information about Galveston comes from David G. McComb, *Galveston:*

A History (Austin: University of Texas Press, 1986). The quotation from Cuney is cited in Maud Cuney Hare, *Norris Wright Cuney: A Tribune of the Black People* (Austin: Steck-Vaughn, 1968), p. 31.
4. Ralph A. Wooster, "Wealthy Texans, 1870," *Southwestern Historical Quarterly* 74 (July 1970), p. 34.
5. Jesse A. Ziegler, *Wave of the Gulf* (San Antonio: Naylor, 1938), p. 202.
6. Bronson Malsch, *Indianola: The Mother of Western Texas* (Austin: Shoal Creek, 1977), p. 121.
7. Bill Walraven, *Corpus Christi: The History of a Texas Seaport* (Woodland Hills, CA: Windsor, 1982), p. 39. For a discussion of Corpus Christi and Texas myth see Alan Lessoff, "A Texas City and the Texas Myth: Urban Historical Identity in Corpus Christi," *Southwestern Historical Quarterly* 100 (January 1997), pp. 305-329.
8. W. S. Henry, *Campaign Sketches of the War with Mexico* (New York: Harper and Brothers, 1847), pp. 18 (quote), 45.
9. Robert H. Thonhoff, "Taylor's Trail in Texas," *Southwestern Historical Quarterly* 70 (July 1966), pp. 8-9, 14.
10. Mary Jo O'Rear, *Storm over the Bay: The People of Corpus Christi and Their Port* (College Station: Texas A&M University Press, 2009), p. 19.
11. Coleman McCampbell, *Texas Seaport: The Story of the Growth of Corpus Christi and the Coastal Bend Country* (New York: Exposition Press, 1952), pp. 65-67; Walraven, *Texas Seaport*, p. 75; Dan E. Kilgore, "Corpus Christi: A Quarter Century of Development," *Southwestern Historical Quarterly* 75 (April 1972), p. 434.
12. Erin M. Hill, Brien A. Nicolau, and Paul V. Zimba, "History of Water and Habitat Improvement in the Nueces Estuary, Texas, USA," *Texas Water Journal* 2 (December 2011), p. 98; Atlee M. Cunningham, *Corpus Christi Water Supply: Documented History, 1852-1997* (Corpus Christi: Texas A&M University-Corpus Christi, 1998), pp. 6, 8, 19.

12. THE RIVER PORTS

1. Francis R. Lubbock, *Six Decades in Texas*, ed. C. W. Rains (Austin: Ben C. Jones, 1900), p. 46; David G. McComb, *Houston, a History* (Austin: University of Texas Press, 1981), pp. 9-15. Much of the material about Houston is taken from this book.
2. Wooster, "Wealthy Texans, 1870," p. 34.
3. George C. Werner, "Railroads," in Ron Tyler, ed., *The New Handbook of Texas*, vol. 5 (Austin: Texas State Historical Association, 1986), p. 411.
4. *Tri-Weekly Telegraph*, September 24, 1858.
5. Jesse A. Ziegler, *Wave of the Gulf* (San Antonio: Naylor Company, 1938), pp. 31-33.
6. McComb, *Houston*, p. 70.
7. Ibid., pp. 89-90.
8. Fred Tarpley, *Jefferson: Riverport to the Southwest* (Austin: Eakin Press, 1983), pp. 53, 57, 70, 91, 100, 125, 125-134, 172.
9. James W. Daddysman, *The Matamoros Trade: Confederate Commerce, Diplomacy, and Intrigue* (Newark: University of Delaware Press, 1984), pp. 118-119.
10. Pat Kelly, *River of Lost Dreams: Navigation on the Rio Grande* (Lincoln: University of Nebraska Press, 1986), pp. 34-35, 54, 57, 63, 70.

13. THE POLITICAL TOWNS

1. Semour V. Conner, "The Evolution of County Government in the Republic of Texas," *Southwestern Historical Quarterly* 55 (October 1951), pp. 170-171, 177, 199; Luke Gournay, *Texas Boundaries: Evolution of the State's Counties* (College Station: Texas A&M University Press, 1995), pp. 30-33.
2. Gournay, *Texas Boundaries*, pp. 28, 79, 244.
3. James L. Haley, *Sam Houston* (Norman: University of Oklahoma Press, 2002), p. 214; Stanley Siegel, *The Poet President of Texas: The Life of Mirabeau B. Lamar, President of the Republic of Texas* (Austin: Jenkins, 1977), pp. 97-102; Alexander W. Terrell, "The City of Austin from 1839 to 1865," *Southwestern Historical Quarterly* 14 (October 1910), pp. 114, 123.
4. Madge Thornall Roberts, ed., *The Personal Correspondence of Sam Houston, Volume I: 1839-1845* (Denton: University of North Texas Press, 1996), p. 125.
5. Llerena Friend, *Sam Houston: The Great Designer* (Austin: University of Texas Press, 1954), p. 79.
6. David C. Humphrey, *Austin: A History of the Capital City* (Austin: Texas State Historical Association, 1997), p. 4. Historian Keith Bryant claimed that midwestern farmers who grumbled about primitive roads chanted: "Hardly jackassable; the roads are impassable; I think those that travel 'em; should turn out and gravel 'em." Keith L. Bryant, Jr., "The Development of North American Railroads," in William D. Middleton, George M. Smerk, and Roberta L. Diehl, eds., *Encyclopedia of North American Railroads* (Bloomington: Indiana University Press, 2007), p. 2.
7. W. Eugene Hollon and Ruth Lapham Butler, eds., *William Bollaert's Texas* (Norman: University of Oklahoma Press, 1956), p. 198.
8. David C. Humphrey, "A 'Very Muddy and Conflicting' View: The Civil War as Seen from Austin, Texas," *Southwestern Historical Quarterly* 94 (January 1991), p. 414.
9. Kenneth Hafertepe, "Austin Buildings," in Hank Todd Smith, ed., *Austin: Its Archiects and Architecture (1836-1986)* (Austin: American Institute of Architects, 1986), p. 36.
10. Marjory Harper, "Emigrant Strikebreakers: Scottish Granite Cutters and the Texas Capitol Boycott," *Southwestern Historical Quarterly* 95 (April 1992), p. 483, 484.
11. Emily Fourmy Cutrer, "'The Hardy, Stalwart Son of Texas': Art and Mythology at the Capitol," in *The Texas State Capitol: Selected Essays from the Southwestern Historical Quarterly* (Austin: Texas State Historical Association, 1995), pp. 90-91, 94-95, 104, 110.
12. David G. McComb, *Spare Time in Texas: Recreation and History in the Lone Star State* (Austin: University of Texas Press, 2008), pp. 28-29.
13. Humphrey, *Austin*, pp. 29-33.

14. THE MILITARY TOWNS

1. W. Turrentine Jackson, *Wagon Roads West: A Study of Federal Road Surveys and Construction in the Trans-Mississippi West, 1846-1869* (Berkeley: University of California Press, 1952), pp. 36-37, 42-43, 44-45; Robert Wooster, *Soldiers, Sutlers, and Settlers: Garrison Life on the Texas Frontier* (College Station: Texas A&M University Press, 1987), p. 205.
2. David G. McComb, *Spare Time in Texas: Recreation and History in the Lone Star State* (Austin: University of Texas Press, 2008), p. 21.

3. Walter Nugent, "The People of the West since 1890," in Gerald D. Nash and Richard W. Etulain, eds., *The Twentieth-Century West: Historical Interpretations* (Albuquerque: University of New Mexico Press, 1989), pp. 42, 68 n. 4.
4. Wooster, *Soldiers*, p. 82.
5. Ty Cashion, *A Texas Frontier: The Clear Fork Country and Fort Griffin, 1849-1887* (Norman: University of Oklahoma Press, 1996), p. 137.
6. Quoted in Benjamin Heber Johnson and Jeffrey Gusky, *Bordertown: The Odyssey of an American Place* (New Haven: Yale University Press, 2008), p. 64.
7. Quotation in Henry N. Ferguson, *The Port of Brownsville* (Brownsville: Springman-King Press, 1976), p. 191. See also John Woodhouse Audubon, *Audubon's Western Journal: 1849-1850* (Glorieta, NM: Rio Grande Press, 1969), p. 53.
8. Caleb Coker, ed., *The News from Brownsville: Helen Chapman's Letters from the Military Frontier, 1848-1852* (Austin: Texas State Historical Association, 1992), p. 136.
9. James A. Irby, "Line of the Rio Grande: War and Trade on the Confederate Frontier," PhD diss., University of Georgia, 1969, p. 4.
10. Wooster, *Soldiers*, pp. 22-23.
11. Joe A. Gibson, *Old Angelo* (San Angelo: Educator Books, 1971), pp. 15-16.

15. THE RAILROAD TOWNS

1. Charles P. Zlatkovich, *Texas Railroads: A Record of Construction and Abandonment* (Austin: Bureau of Business Research, 1981), pp. 3, 11.
2. John S. Spratt, *The Road to Spindletop: Economic Change in Texas, 1875-1901* (Austin: University of Texas Press, 1970), p. 33.
3. James Marshall, *Santa Fe: The Railroad That Built an Empire* (New York: Random House, 1945), pp. 220-221; Keith L. Bryant, Jr., *History of the Atchison, Topeka and Santa Fe Railway* (Lincoln: University of Nebraska Press, 1974), pp. 132-133.
4. George C. Werner, "Railroads," in Ron Tyler, ed., *New Handbook of Texas*, vol. 5 (Austin: Texas Historical Association, 1996), p. 411. St. Clair Griffin Reed, *A History of Texas Railroads* (Houston: St. Clair, 1941), pp. 131, 134, counts 39 million acres and $2,361,000 in bonds from cities and counties. Michael Ariens, *Lone Star Law: A Legal History of Texas* (Lubbock: Texas Tech University Press, 2011), pp. 83-84; S. G. Reed, "Land Grants and Other Aids to Texas Railroads," *Southwestern Historical Quarterly* 49 (April 1946), pp. 520-521, 523. Severe criticism of railroad development and management has come from historians Richard White in *Railroaded: The Transcontinentals and the Making of Modern America* (New York: Norton, 2011) and Robert Fogel in *Railroads and American Economic Growth* (Baltimore: Johns Hopkins University Press, 1964).
5. John S. Spratt, Sr., *Thurber, Texas: The Life and Death of a Company Coal Town*, ed. Harwood P. Hinton (Austin: University of Texas Press, 1986), p. 25.
6. Frank MacD. Spindler, "The History of Hempstead and the Formation of Waller County, Texas," *Southwestern Historical Quarterly* 63 (January 1960), p. 407.
7. Writers' Program, *The WPA Dallas Guide and History*, ed. Gerald D. Saxon and Maxine Holmes (Denton: University of North Texas Press, 1992), p. 138.
8. *Montgomery Ward and Company Catalogue*, (1895; reprint,, New York: Dover, 1969), p. 198; *Sears Roebuck and Company Catalogue* (reprint; Northfield, IL, Digest Books, 1971), p. 261.

9. Thomas C. Jepsen, *Ma Kiley: The Life of a Railroad Telegrapher* (El Paso: Texas Western Press, 1997), pp. 11-12.
10. Theresa A. Case, *The Great Southwest Railroad Strike and Free Labor* (College Station: Texas A&M University Press, 2010), p. 21.
11. Jack Maguire, *Katy's Baby: The Story of Denison, Texas* (Austin: Nortex Press, 1991), p. 15.
12. Graham Landrum, *Grayson County: An Illustrated History of Grayson County, Texas* (Fort Worth: University Supply, 1960), pp. 29. 36. 38; Maguire, *Katy's Baby*, pp. 2, 9, 11, 13, 19-33.
13. Sam Acheson, *Dallas Yesterday* (Dallas: Southern Methodist University Press, 1977), p. 3.
14. Philip Lindsley, *A History of Greater Dallas and Vicinity* (Chicago: Lewis, 1909), vol. 1. p. 36, 40; Michael V. Hazel, *Dallas: A History of "Big D"* (Austin: Texas State Historical Association, 1997), pp. 7-9.
15. John William Rogers, *The Lusty Texans of Dallas* (New York: E. P. Dutton, 1951), pp. 81, 84.
16. Hazel, *Dallas*, pp. 16-17.
17. Spratt, *Road to Spindletop*, pp. 62-63, 82-83.
18. Robert A. Calvert, "Nineteenth Century Farmers, Cotton, and Prosperity," *Southwestern Historical Quarterly* 73 (April 1970), pp. 510-511, 519-520 (quotes).
19. Historians have been inattentive to the study of Dallas development in the last part of the nineteenth century. During the Great Depression, however, unemployed historians were set to work recording the past of several major Texas cities. Many of the facts about Dallas growth were taken from this source. See Writers' Program, *WPA Dallas Guide and History*, ed. Gerald D. Saxon and Maxine Holmes (Denton: University of North Texas Press, 1992), pp. 130-132, 238, 309-312.
20. See David G. McComb, *Spare Time in Texas: Recreation and History in the Lone Star State* (Austin: University of Texas Press, 2008), pp. 130-134.
21. Nancy Wiley, *The Great State Fair of Texas* (Dallas: Taylor, 1985), pp. 12-13, 52.
22. Richard F. Selcer, *Fort Worth: A Texas Original!* (Austin: Texas State Historical Association, 2004), pp. 7, 9.
23. Leonard Sanders, *How Fort Worth Became the Texasmost City* (Fort Worth: Amon Carter Museum, 1973), p. 31.
24. Richard F. Selcer, "Fort Worth and the Fraternity of Strange Women," *Southwestern Historical Quarterly* 96 (July 1992), p. 71.
25. Oliver Knight with Cissy Stewart Lale, *Fort Worth: Outpost on the Trinity* (Fort Worth: Texas Christian University Press, 1990), p. 73.
26. Thomas H. Thompson, *The Ware Boys* (Canyon, TX: Staked Plaines Press, 1978), p. 133.
27. McComb, *Spare Time in Texas*, pp. 30-31.
28. Selcer, *Fort Worth*, pp. 30-38.
29. Quoted in Marion Travis, ed., *Waco's Champion: Selections from the Papers of Roger Norman Conger* (Waco: Historic Waco Foundation, 1990), pp. 99-100.
30. Patricia Ward Wallace, *Waco: Texas Crossroads* (Woodland Hills, CA: Windsor, 1983), pp. 33, 35-36, 43; Travis, *Waco's Champion*, pp. 83-90, 122; Harry E. Ellis, *Dr Pepper: King of Beverages* (Dallas: Gaylor, 1979), 23-24, 37-38; Phillip J. Shank, "A History of the Early Variety Theatres and Legitimate Theatres in Waco, Texas from the Beginnings to 1928," MA thesis, Baylor University, 1977, pp. 4-6, 15-17, 24-31, 76; Lavonia

Jenkins Barnes, *The Texas Cotton Palace Heritage Society of Waco* (Waco: Texian Press, 1964), pp. 2-5.
31. Charles Carver, *Brann and the Iconoclast* (Austin: University of Texas Press, 1957), p. 123.
32. Jamers McEnteer, *Fighting Words: Independent Journalists in Texas* (Austin: University of Texas Press, 1992), pp. 28-32, (quote on p. 32).
33. Katharyn Duff, *Abilene on Catclaw Creek* (Abilene: Reporter, 1969), pp. 56, 97-100.
34. Ibid., pp. 63, 73 (quote).
35. Hugh E. Cosby, ed., *History of Abilene* (Abilene: Cosby, 1955), p. 134.
36. Mary H. Turner, *These High Places* (Amarillo: Russell, 1941), pp. 51-52; Mary H. Turner, *Into the West* (Amarillo: Russell, 1938), pp. 14 (quote), 23.
37. W. H. Timmons, *El Paso: A Borderlands History* (El Paso: Texas Western Press, 1990), pp. 141-143, 144, 146, 157.
38. Ibid., pp. 161, 175; Owen White, *Out of the Desert: The Historical Romance of El Paso* (El Paso: McMath, 1923), p. 185.
39. Leon C. Metz, *Turning Points in El Paso, Texas* (El Paso: Mangan Books, 1985), p. 51.
40. C. L. Sonnichsen, *Pass of the North: Four Centuries on the Rio Grande* (El Paso: Texas Western Press, 1968), vol. 1, pp. 220-224 (quote on p. 220), 242-246.
41. Ibid., pp. 231-246, 251-254.
42. Ibid., pp. 262-268; Conrey Bryson, *Down Went McGinty: El Paso in the Wonderful Nineties* (El Paso: Texas Western Press, 1977), pp. 17, 20, 31.
43. White, *Out of the Desert*, pp. 206-207.
44. Nancy Ellen Farrar, "The History of the Chinese in El Paso, Texas: A Case Study of an Urban Immigrant Group in the American West," master's thesis, University of Texas at El Paso, 1970, pp. 56-57.
45. Timmons, *El Paso*, pp. 185, 187-190.

16. THE LUMBER TOWNS

1. Thad Sitton and James H. Conrad, *Nameless Towns: Texas Sawmill Communities, 1880-1942* (Austin: University of Texas Press, 1998), pp. 9, 10, 14, 19-20, 71, 132, 141, 156.

17. THE END OF THE DIRT ROAD FRONTIER

1. John Tyler Bonner, *Why Size Matters: From Bacteria to Blue Whales* (Princeton: Princeton University Press, 2006), p. 101.
2. "AHR Conversation: Historical Perspectives on the Circulation of Information," *American Historical Review* 116 (December 2011), pp. 1396-1403.

PART THREE: THE AMENITIES OF CITY LIFE, 1900-1950

18. THE RURAL TO URBAN SHIFT

1. Christopher S. Davies, "Life at the Edge: Urban and Industrial Evolution of Texas, Frontier Wilderness—Frontier Space, 1836-1986," *Southwestern Historical Quarterly* 89 (April 1986), p. 521.
2. Winfred G. Steglich, "Population Trends," in Lawrence L. Graves, ed., *A History*

of *Lubbock: Part Three, The Cultural Emergence of Lubbock* (Lubbock: West Texas Museum Association, 1961), pp. 422-425, 430, 433.
3. Ellis Amburn, *Buddy Holly: a Biography* (New York: St. Martin's Press, 1995), p. 13.
4. Beth Anne Shelton et al., *Houston: Growth and Decline in a Sunbelt Boomtown* (Philadelphia: Temple University Press, 1989), p. 94.

19. THE GREAT GALVESTON STORM

1. Isaac M. Cline, *Storms, Floods and Sunshine* (New Orleans: Pelican, 1945), pp. 92-93. In a fictionalized account Erik Larson blames the weather service and Cline for lack of proper warning (*Isaac's Storm* [New York: Crown, 1999]).
2. Patricia Bellis Bixel and Elizabeth Hayes Turner, *Galveston and the 1900 Storm* (Austin: University of Texas Press, 2000), p. 84.
3. The account of the storm is taken from David G. McComb, "The Great Storm and the Technological Response" in *Galveston: A History* (Austin: University of Texas Press, 1986), pp. 121-149. See Bixel and Turner, *Galveston*, for excellent photographs.

20. SPINDLETOP AND BEAUMONT

1. Allen W. Hamill, "Spindletop: The Lucus Gusher," Oral History of the Oil Industry, University of Texas Archives, Austin, typescript, pp. 18-19.
2. Judith Walker Linsley, Ellen Walker Rienstra, and Jo Ann Stiles, *Giant under the Hill* (Austin: Texas State Historical Association, 2002), p. 3.
3. Ibid., pp. 140-143; Diana Davids Olien and Roger M. Olien, *Oil in Texas: The Gusher Age, 1895-1945* (Austin: University of Texas Press, 2002), pp. 49-50.
4. Linsley et al., *Giant under the Hill*, p. 153.

21. THE OIL TOWNS

1. This background information on the oil bonanza comes from David G. McComb, *Texas: A Modern History*, rev. ed. (Austin: University of Texas Press, 2010), pp. 118-121.
2. Quoted in Diana Davids Olien and Roger M. Olien, *Oil in Texas: The Gusher Age, 1895-1945* (Austin: University of Texas Press, 2002), p. 75.
3. George Parker (George Parker Stroker), *Oil Field Medico* (Dallas: Banks Upshaw, 1948), pp. 136-137.
4. Diana Davids Olien, "Domesticity and the Texas Oil Fields: Dimensions of Women's Experience, 1920-1950," in Fane Downs and Nancy Baker Jones, eds., *Women and Texas History: Selected Essays* (Austin: Texas State Historical Association, 1993), p. 126.
5. Everette DeGolyer, "Anthony F. Lucas and Spindletop," *Southwest Review* 30 (Fall 1945), p. 86. Evidence suggests that oil production from the current fracking bonanza will start to decline in 2020. See *USA Today*, November 4, 2013.
6. Robert L. Martin, *The City Moves West: Economic and Industrial Growth in Central West Texas* (Austin: University of Texas Press, 1969), p. 157.
7. Roger M. Olien and Dianna Davids Olien, *Oil Booms: Social Change in Five Texas Towns* (Lincoln: University of Nebraska Press, 1982), pp. 64, 78-82.
8. Bobby D. Weaver, *Oilfield Trash: Life and Labor in the Oil Patch* (College Station: Texas A&M University Press, 2010), pp. 128-129 (quote on p. 128).

9. H. Gordon Frost and John H. Jenkins, *I'm Frank Hamer: The Life of a Texas Peace Officer* (Austin: Jenkins, 1968), pp. 143-144.
10. Ibid., pp. 79 (quote), 150, 232-233.
11. Lucille Glasscock, *A Texas Wildcatter* (San Antonio: Naylor, 1952), p. 64.
12. Roger Biles, "The New Deal in Dallas," in Raymond A. Mohl, ed., *The Making of Urban America*, 2nd ed. (Wilmington, DE: Scholarly Resources, 1997), p. 253.
13. Joseph A. Pratt, *The Growth of a Refining Region* (Greenwich, CT: JAI Press, 1980), pp. 54-55.
14. John O. King, *Joseph Stephen Cullinan: A Study of Leadership in the Texas Petroleum Industry, 1897-1937* (Nashville: Vanderbilt University Press, 1970), pp. 151, 182, 213.

22. THE ELITE RULE OF THE CITIES

1. See C. Wright Mills, *The Power Elite* (New York: Oxford University Press, 2000), new edition. Mills wrote about the national power influence in the mid-twentieth century of leaders in business, military, and politics.
2. Quoted in Bradley Robert Rice, *Progressive Cities: The Commission Government Movement in America, 1901-1920* (Austin: University of Texas Press, 1977), p. 107. Under disaster conditions the elite often feel out of control, they panic, and a power struggle takes place. See Rebecca Solnit, *A Paradise Built in Hell: The Extraordinary Communities That Arise in Disaster* (New York: Penguin, 2010), pp. 21, 127-131.
3. For a general history of these events see David G. McComb, *Galveston: A History* (Austin: University of Texas Press, 1986), pp. 134-137. An example of the myth can be found in Harold M. Hyman's commissioned family history *Oleander Odyssey: the Kempners of Galveston, Texas, 1854-1980s* (College Station: Texas A&M University Press, 1990), pp. 138-162.
4. Rice, *Progressive Cities*, p. 109.
5. McComb, *Galveston*, pp. 186-189 (quote on p. 189).
6. Joe R. Feagin, *Free Enterprise City: Houston in Political-Economic Perspective* (New Brunswick, NJ: Rutgers University Press, 1988), pp. 120-127, 129, 133, 138; Joseph A. Pratt and Christopher J. Castaneda, *Builders: Herman and George R. Brown* (College Station: Texas A&M University Press, 1999), pp. 158-161. Not all Houston elites were members of this group. Notable exceptions were oilman Hugh Roy Cullen, Judge Roy Hofheinz, and wildcat oilman Glenn McCarthy.
7. Quoted in Fran Dressman, *Gus Wortham: Portrait of a Leader* (College Station: Texas A&M University Press, 1994), p. 92.
8. Jan de Hartog, *The Hospital* (New York: Atheneum, 1964), p. 119.
9. David G. McComb, *Houston, a History* (Austin: University of Texas Press, 1981), pp. 178-182.
10. Feagin, *Free Enterprise City*, pp. 142, 147.
11. Quote in Darwin Payne, *Big D: Triumphs and Troubles of an American Supercity in the Twentieth Century* (Dallas: Three Forks Press, 2000), p. 199; Patricia Evridge Hill, *Dallas: The Making of a Modern City* (Austin: University of Texas Press, 1996), pp. 109-110, 116-117.
12. Payne, *Big D*, pp. 199-200, 214, 316-321, 340, 414-441.
13. Oliver Knight, *Fort Worth: Outpost on the Trinity* (Fort Worth: Texas Christian University Press, 1990), p. 220 (quotes).

14. David G. McComb, *Texas: A Modern History*, rev. ed. (Austin: University of Texas Press, 2010), p. 174.
15. Victoria Buenger and Walter L. Buenger, *Texas Merchant: Marvin Leonard and Fort Worth* (College Station: Texas A&M University Press, 1998), p. 143.
16. Mary Jo O'Rear, *Storm over the Bay: The People of Corpus Christi and Their Port* (College Station: Texas A&M University Press, 2009), pp. 120-121, 128 (quote).
17. Stacy R. Lester, "Bryan Callaghan versus the Reformers: 1905-1912," master's thesis, Trinity University, San Antonio, 1976, p. 42 (quote).
18. David R. Johnson, Derral Cheatwood, and Benjamin Bradshaw, "The Landscape of Death" in Char Miller, ed., *On the Border: An Environmental History of San Antonio* (San Antonio: Trinity University Press, 2005), p. 102.
19. Char Miller, *Deep in the Heart of San Antonio* (San Antonio: Trinity University Press, 2004), pp. 33-34.
20. Pat Ireland Nixon, *A Century of Medicine in San Antonio: The Story of Medicine in Bexar County, Texas* (San Antonio: P. A. Nixon, 1936), pp. 307-310.
21. Donald L. Zelman, "Alazan-Apache Courts: A New Deal Response to Mexican American Housing Conditions in San Antonio," *Southwestern Historical Quarterly* 87 (October 1983), p. 135 (quote).
22. Ibid, pp. 120-121.
23. Ibid., pp. 89-91; Heywood Sanders, "Empty Taps, Missing Pipes," in Char Miller, ed., *On the Border: An Environmental History of San Antonio* (San Antonio: Trinity University Press, 2005), p. 151.
24. C. L. Sonnichsen, *Pass of the North: Four Centuries on the Rio Grande* (El Paso: Texas Western Press, 1968), vol. 1, pp. 364-367, 370-376.
25. W. H. Timmons, *El Paso: A Borderlands History* (El Paso: Texas Western Press, 1990), p. 186.

23. THE WORLD WAR I ERA

1. Ralph W. Wooster, *Texas and Texans in the Great War* (Buffalo Gap, Texas: State House Press, 2009), p. 53.
2. Robert V. Haynes, *A Night of Violence: The Houston Riot of 1917* (Baton Rouge: Louisiana State University Press, 1976), pp. 318, 322.
3. Rogers M. Smith, "The Waco Lynching of 1916: Perspective and Analysis," master's thesis, Baylor University, 1971, pp. 60-90 (quote p. 90).
4. Walter L. Buenger, *The Path to a Modern South: Northeast Texas between Reconstruction and the Great Depression* (Austin: University of Texas Press, 2001), p. 168.
5. Charles C. Alexander, *Crusade for Conformity: The Ku Klux Klan in Texas, 1920-1930* (Houston: Texas Gulf Coast Historical Association, 1962), pp. 7, 11, 41, 62-64, 71.
6. Elizabeth York Enstam, *Women and the Creation of Urban Life: Dallas, Texas 1843-1920* (College Station: Texas A&M University Press, 1998), pp. 58, 112, 156.
7. Judith N. McArthur and Harold L. Smith, *Texas through Women's Eyes: The Twentieth-Century Experience* (Austin: University of Texas Press, 2010), pp. 25, 27, 30-31, 137-141; Randolph B. Campbell, *Gone to Texas: A History of the Lone Star State* (New York: Oxford University Press, 2003), p. 439.

24. THE ENTICEMENTS OF THE CITY

1. Much of the information about recreation in Texas comes from David G. McComb, *Spare Time in Texas* (Austin: University of Texas Press, 2008), pp. 12-34.
2. Shine Philips, *Big Spring: The Casual Biography of a Prairie Town* (New York: Prentice-Hall, 1943), p. 53.
3. Nelson Manfred Blake, *Water for the Cities: A History of the Urban Water Supply Problem in the United States* (Syracuse, NY: Syracuse University Press, 1956), pp. 263-264.
4. Simon W. Freese and Deborah Lightfoot Sizemore, *A Century in the Works: Freese and Nichols Consulting Engineers, 1894-1994* (College Station: Texas A&M University Press, 1994), pp. 11-35, 39 (quote on p. 20).
5. Joel A. Tarr, *The Search for the Ultimate Sink: Urban Pollution in Historical Perspective* (Akron, OH: University of Akron Press, 1996), p. 116; Martin V. Melosi, *Garbage in the Cities: Refuse, Reform, and the Environment* (Pittsburgh: University of Pittsburgh Press, 2005), p. 151.
6. Freese and Sizemore, *Century*, p. 55. It was a long-standing joke. When Houston began to use Trinity River water sixty years later people in Dallas quipped, "Flush twice. Houston needs the water."
7. David G. McComb, *Houston, a History* (Austin: University of Texas Press, 1981), pp. 146-147.
8. David R. Johnson, Derral Cheatwood, and Benjamin Bradshaw, "The Landscape of Death," in Char Miller, ed., *On the Border: An Environmental History of San Antonio* (San Antonio: Trinity University Press, 2005), pp. 102-105.
9. Quoted in McComb, *Houston*, p. 152.
10. See Richard Schroeder, *Lone Star Picture Shows* (College Station: Texas A&M University Press, 2001), pp. 11-27, 40-72.
11. William H. Crain, "Karl St. John Hoblitzelle," in Ron Tyler, ed., *The New Handbook of Texas*, vol. 3 (Austin: Texas State Historical Association, 1996), p. 642.
12. Ronald Garay, *Gordon McCendon: The Maverick of Radio* (New York: Greenwood Press, 1992), pp. 1-18, 19 (quote).
13. Margo Jones, *Theatre-in-the-Round* (New York: McGraw-Hill, 1965), p. 93.
14. Helen Sheehy, *Margo: The Life and Theatre of Margo Jones* (Dallas: Southern Methodist University Press, 1989), p. 41.
15. *Houston Post*, April 13, 1953.
16. *Dallas Morning News*, December 31, 1989.
17. Rosenberg's quotation is chiseled on the cornerstone of the library.
18. Dan Rather with Peter Wyden, *I Remember: Growing up in Texas* (Boston: Little, Brown, 1991), p. 193 (first quote), p. 194 (second quote).
19. Patrick Cox, *The First Texas News Barons* (Austin: University of Texas Press, 2005), pp. 9, 27.
20. For general information see H. Roger Grant, "'Interurbans Are the Wave of the Future': Electric Railway Promotion in Texas," *Southwestern Historical Quarterly* 84 (July 1980), pp. 29-48.
21. Clay McShane, *Down the Asphalt Path: The Automobile and the American City* (New York: Columbia University Press, 1994), pp. 103-105, 107-109.
22. Ibid., pp. 59, 79.

23. Howard J. Erlichman, *Camino del Norte: How a Series of Watering Holes, Fords, and Dirt Trails Evolved into Interstate 35 in Texas* (College Station: Texas A&M University Press, 2006), pp. 157-160.
24. Note the fate of *Motorius* in note 6, about Victor Gruen, in chapter 34.
25. Darwin Payne, *Big D: Triumphs and Troubles of an American Supercity in the Twentieth Century* (Dallas: Three Forks Press, 2000), p. 39.
26. Paul H. Carlson, *Amarillo: The Story of a Western Town* (Lubbock: Texas Tech University Press, 2006), p. 68.
27. McShane, *Asphalt Path*, pp. 193 (quote), 201; McComb, *Houston*, p. 72.
28. Cheryl Caldwell Ferguson, "River Oaks: 1920s Suburban Planning and Development in Houston," *Southwestern Historical Quarterly* 104 (October 2000), p. 204.
29. McComb, *Houston*, pp. 74, 123, 127.
30. Roger Bilstein and Jay Miller, *Aviation in Texas* (Austin: Texas Monthly Press, 1985), pp. 46-47.
31. Kenneth B. Ragsdale, "Barnstormers, Businessmen, and High Hopes for the Future: Austin, Texas, Enters the Modern Air Age," *Southwestern Historical Quarterly* 107 (April 2004), p. 255.
32. Kate Seyen Kirkland, *The Hogg Family and Houston: Philanthropy and the Civic Ideal* (Austin: University of Texas Press, 2009), pp. 55 (quote), 69-74; McComb, *Houston*, p. 97.
33. Kirkland, *Hogg Family*, pp. 206-214.
34. Ibid., pp. 182-187.
35. Alison Isenberg, *Downtown America: A History of the Place and the People Who Made It* (Chicago: University of Chicago Press, 2004), pp. 20, 24, 83, 91-92, 162.
36. Jackie McElhaney, "Going Downtown to Shop: Sanger's, Titche's, Volk's, and More," *Legacies* 21 (Spring 2009), p. 16.
37. Stanley Marcus, *Quest for the Best* (New York: Viking Press, 1979), pp. 151-152.
38. *Houston Chronicle*, August 4, 2008.

25. THE GREAT DEPRESSION

1. John C. Dawson, Sr., *High Plains Yesterdays* (Austin: Eakin Press, 1985), pp. 182-183, 183 (quote).
2. Merton L. Dillon, "Religion in Lubbock," in Lawrence L. Graves, ed., *A History of Lubbock: Part Three, The Cultural Emergence of Lubbock* (Lubbock: West Texas Museum Association, 1961), p. 483.
3. Quoted in David G. McComb, *Texas: A Modern History*, rev. ed. (Austin: University of Texas Press, 2010), p. 142.
4. Howard J. Erlichman, *Camino del Norte: How a Series of Watering Holes, Fords, and Dirt Trails Evolved into Interstate 35 in Texas* (College Station: Texas A&M University Press, 2006), p. 181.
5. *Houston Post*, November 26, 1933.
6. Roger Biles, "The New Deal in Dallas," in Raymond A. Mohl, ed., *The Making of Urban America*, 2nd ed. (Wilmington, DE: Scholarly Resources, 1997), pp. 254, 256-257, 258, 259.
7. Kenneth B. Ragsdale, *The Year America Discovered Texas–Centennial '36* (College Station: Texas A&M University Press, 1987).

26. WORLD WAR II

1. J'Nell L. Pate, *Arsenal of Defense: Fort Worth's Military Legacy* (Denton: Texas State Historical Association, 2011), pp. 73, 77, 79.
2. Ibid., pp. 117-121.
3. Ann Markusen et al., *The Rise of the Gunbelt: The Military Remapping of Industrial America* (New York: Oxford University Press, 1991), pp. 8-9, 13.
4. Writers' Program, American Guide Series, *San Antonio: A History and Guide* (San Antonio: Clegg, 1941), p. 5.
5. David R. Johnson, "The Failed Experiment: Military Aviation and Urban Development in San Antonio, 1910-40," in Roger W. Lotchin, ed., *The Martial Metropolis: U.S. Cities in War and Peace* (New York: Praeger, 1984), p. 104.
6. Darwin Payne, *Big D: Triumphs and Troubles of an American Supercity in the Twentieth Century* (Dallas: Three Forks Press, 2000), pp. 249-250.
7. "Plastics: Will They Boost the Boom," *Houston* 28 (April 1957), p. 17.

PART FOUR: GREAT TEXAS CITIES, 1950-2012
28. POPULATION AND URBAN EXPANSION

1. Peter Hall, *Cities in Civilization* (New York: Pantheon, 1998), pp. 283-286.
2. Charles Murray, *Human Accomplishment: The Pursuit of Excellence in the Arts and Sciences, 800 B.C. to 1950* (New York: Harper Collins, 2003), pp. 355-361.
3. Richard Florida, *The Rise of the Creative Class: And How It's Transforming Work, Leisure, Community, and Everyday Life* (New York: Basic Books, 2004), pp. 68, 218, 223, 237-239, 246-247, 249, 292. See also John Howkins, *The Creative Economy: How People Make Money from Ideas* (New York: Penguin Books, 2001), and Margaret Pugh O'Mara, *Cities of Knowledge: Cold War Science and the Search for the Next Silicon Valley* (Princeton: Princeton University Press, 2005).

    Of interest, *Smithsonian*, in "The Twenty Best Small Towns in America" (vol. 44, April 2013, pp. 46-47), noted exceptional concentrations of museums, art galleries, orchestras, theaters, historic sites, and institutions of higher learning.
4. On this point I follow the lead of Murray, *Human Accomplishment*, pp. 59-86. Excellence in science refers to truth that can be verified; in technology and medicine excellence involves the use of truth to obtain desired results; in arts it reflects high aesthetic value as judged by experts. Murray disavows that he is concerned about the rise and fall of civilizations (p. xvii), although much of his material involves Western civilization.
5. See Elizabeth Cruce Alvarez, ed., *Texas Almanac, 2012-2013* (Denton: Texas State Historical Association, 2012), pp. 421-447.
6. Peter Hall, *Cities in Civilization* (New York: Pantheon, 1998), pp. 282-283.
7. Darwin Payne, *Big D: Triumphs and Troubles of an American Supercity in the Twentieth Century* (Dallas: Three Forks Press, 2000), pp. 249-250.
8. David G. McComb, *Houston, a History* (Austin: University of Texas Press, 1981), p. 141.
9. *Houston Post*, May 4, 1962.
10. David R. Johnson, John A. Booth, and Richard J. Harris, eds., *The Politics of San Antonio: Community, Progress, and Power* (Lincoln: University of Nebraska Press, 1983), pp. 165-173.

11. John M. Donahue and Jon Q. Sanders, "Mediation and Resolution of Water Conflicts," in Char Miller, ed., *On the Border: An Environmental History of San Antonio* (San Antonio: Trinity University Press, 2005), pp. 185, 193-195; *San Antonio Express-News*, March 5, 2014.
12. Peter Hall, in his study of major world cities in their "golden ages," notes concentrations of workers in specific crafts. Present corporations also concentrate workers, which would allow Texas cities to both sprawl and experience the spark of creative minds. Peter Hall, *Cities in Civilization* (New York: Pantheon, 1998), pp. 283-286, 494.

29. SUBURBS AND SUBDIVISIONS

1. For a comparison of Houston, San Antonio, and Dallas see Robert B. Fairbanks, "Public Housing for the City as a Whole: The Texas Experience, 1934-1955," *Southwestern Historical Quarterly* 103 (April 2000), pp. 403-424.
2. Beth Ann Shelton et al., *Houston: Growth and Decline in a Sunbelt Boomtown* (Philadelphia: Temple University Press, 1989), pp. 73 (quote), 75. For a view of Houston segregation at mid-century see the articles in *Houston History* 8(1) (Fall 2010), including the editorial comments by Joseph Pratt. "Ward" is a divisional anachronism left from the aldermanic government before 1905 and still used for general designations in Houston.
3. David G. McComb, *Houston, a History* (Austin: University of Texas Press, 1981), p. 162.
4. Robert B. Fairbanks, "From Consensus to Controversy," *Legacies* 1 (Fall 1989), pp. 38-41.
5. Roger Biles, *The Fate of Cities: Urban America and the Federal Government, 1945-2000* (Lawrence: University of Kansas Press, 2011), p. xi.
6. McComb, *Houston*, pp. 124, 233 n. 136. In 1971-1972 Sharp was caught in a scandal that involved bribing legislators to pass favorable laws for his bank and given three years probation. The event involved top Democratic leaders and offset the Nixon scandal in Texas.
7. Jan Jarboe, "Gone to Texas," *Texas Monthly* 21 (February 1993), pp. 172-174 (quote), 175.
8. *Houston Chronicle*, March 6, 2012.
9. George T. Morgan, Jr., and John O. King, *The Woodlands: New Community Development, 1964-1983* (College Station: Texas A&M University Press, 1987), pp. 8, 9, 36-37, 46, 94, 147.
10. Bill Bishop with Robert G. Cushing, *The Big Sort: Why the Clustering of Like-Minded America Is Tearing Us Apart* (Boston: Houghton Mifflin, 2008), pp. 5, 53, 97, 131.

30. SEGREGATION AND INTEGRATION

1. Brian D. Behnken, "The 'Dallas Way': Protest, Response, and the Civil Rights Experience in Big D and Beyond," *Southwestern Historical Quarterly* 111 (July 2007), p. 29.
2. Merline Pitre, "Black Houstonions and the 'Separate but Equal Doctrine': Carter W. Wesley versus Lulu B. White," *Houston Review* 12 (January 1990), p. 34.
3. Gary M. Lavergne, *Before Brown: Heman Marion Sweatt, Thurgood Marshall, and the Long Road to Justice* (Austin: University of Texas Press, 2010), pp. 280-281.

4. Judith N. McArthur and Harold L. Smith, *Texas through Women's Eyes: The Twentieth-Century Experience* (Austin: University of Texas Press, 2010), p. 159.
5. Michael Phillips, *White Metropolis: Race, Ethnicity, and Religion in Dallas, 1841-2001* (Austin: University of Texas Press, 2006), p. 157.
6. Gerald S. McCorkle, "Busing Comes to Dallas Schools," *Southwestern Historical Quarterly* 111 (January 2008), p. 332.
7. *USA Today*, September 8, 2008.
8. Alexander Wolff, "Ground Breakers," *Sports Illustrated* 103 (November 7, 2005), pp. 62 (quote), 64.
9. Robert J. Robertson, *Fair Ways: How Six Black Golfers Won Civil Rights in Beaumont, Texas* (College Station: Texas A&M University Press, 2005), pp. xi-xii.
10. David G. McComb, *Galveston: A History* (Austin: University of Texas Press, 1986), p. 213.
11. David G. McComb, *Spare Time in Texas: Recreation and History in the Lone Star State* (Austin: University of Texas Press, 2008), p. 46.
12. David G. McComb, *Houston, a History* (Austin: University of Texas Press, 1981), pp. 169-171.
13. Dwight D. Watson, *Race and the Houston Police Department, 1930-1990: A Change Did Come* (College Station: Texas A&M University Press, 2005), pp. 12 (quote), 77, 112-116, 127.
14. Robert B. Fairbanks, *For the City as a Whole: Planning, Politics, and the Public Interest in Dallas, Texas, 1900-1965* (Columbus: Ohio State University Press, 1998), p. 191. The FHA "redlining" to restrict black ownership continued into the 1960s.
15. Darwin Payne, *Big D: Triumphs and Troubles of an American Supercity in the Twentieth Century* (Dallas: Three Forks Press, 2000), pp. 294-302.
16. Ibid., pp. 340-343.
17. Stanley Marcus, *Minding the Store* (Boston: Little, Brown, 1974), pp. 368, 371.
18. Victoria Buenger and Walter L. Buenger, *Texas Merchant: Marvin Leonard and Fort Worth* (College Station: Texas A&M University Press, 1998), p. 145.
19. Oliver Knight, *Fort Worth: Outpost on the Trinity* (Fort Worth: Texas Christian University Press, 1990), pp. 247-248.
20. Robin C. Bean, "The Role of the Commercial-Civic Elite in the Desegregation of Public Facilities in Waco, Texas," master's thesis, Baylor University, 1990, pp. 75-75, 84.

31. THE HISPANIC IDENTITY

1. Thomas H. Kreneck, *Del Pueblo: A History of Houston's Hispanic Community* (College Station: Texas A&M University Press, 2012), pp. 59, 63, 74, 80.
2. Armando Navarro, *Mexican American Youth Organization: Avant Garde of the Chicano Movement in Texas* (Austin: University of Texas Press, 1995), pp. 80, 81, 89.
3. Ibid., p. 94.
4. W. H. Timmons, *El Paso: A Borderlands History* (El Paso: Texas Western Press, 1990), pp. 251, 253 (quotes).
5. David R. Johnson, John G. Booth, and Richard Harris, eds., *The Politics of San Antonio: Community Progress and Power* (Lincoln: University of Nebraska Press, 1983), pp. 76-105.

6. Judith N. McArthur and Harold L. Smith, *Texas through Women's Eyes: The Twentieth-Century Experience* (Austin: University of Texas Press, 2010), p. 235.

32. JOHN F. KENNEDY AND DALLAS

1. See Earl Warren, *Report of the President's Commission on the Assassination of President Kennedy* (Washington, DC: U.S. Government Printing Office, 1964); and William Manchester, *The Death of a President, November 20–November 25, 1963* (New York: Harper and Row, 1967).
2. Judith Garrett Segura, *Belo: from Newspapers to New Media* (Austin: University of Texas Press, 2008), pp. 110-117.
3. Warren Leslie, *Dallas: Public and Private* (New York: Grossman, 1964), p. 11.
4. Lawrence Wright, "Why Do They Hate Us So Much," *Texas Monthly*, 11 (November 1983), p. 250.

33. THE VOTING RIGHTS ACT AND THE CITIES

1. Wendell M. Bedichek and Neal Tannahill, *Public Policy in Texas*, 2nd ed. (Glenview, IL: Scott, Foresman, 1986), pp. 75-81, 295-297.
2. Ruth P. Morgan, *Governance by Decree: The Impact of the Voting Rights Act in Dallas* (Lawrence: University Press of Kansas, 2004), pp. 268-278, argues that single-member districts were no panacea for good government, but offers no better resolution for the problem of equal representation.
3. David G. McComb, *Houston, a History* (Austin: University of Texas Press, 1981), p. 173.
4. Bedichek and Tannahill, *Public Policy in Texas*, p. 296.
5. Darwin Payne, *Big D: Triumphs and Troubles of an American Supercity in the Twentieth Century* (Dallas: Three Forks Press, 2000), p. 446.
6. Molly Ivins, *Molly Ivins Can't Say That, Can She?* (New York: Vintage, 1992), p. 198. The diverse roles of women in Texas history can be found in the various historical plaques of the official Texas historical markers. See Dan K. Utley and Cynthia J. Beeman, *History along the Way: Stories beyond the Texas Roadside Markers* (College Station: Texas A&M University Press, 2013), pp. 266-270.
7. Joe B. Frantz, *The Driskill Hotel* (Austin: Encino Press, 1973), p. 52.

34. LAND TRANSPORTATION

1. *Houston Chronicle*, December 7, 1985.
2. Howard J. Erlichman, *Camino del Norte: How a Series of Watering Holes, Fords, and Dirt Trails Evolved into Interstate 35 in Texas* (College Station: Texas A&M University Press, 2006), pp. 222-226.
3. Linda Scarbrough, *Road, River and Ol' Boy Politics: A Texas County's Path from Farm to Supersuburb* (Austin: Texas State Historical Association, 2005), pp. 293-296.
4. Jane Jacobs, *The Death and Life of Great American Cities* (New York: Vintage, 1961), pp. 151-152.
5. Edward Glaeser, *Triumph of the City: How Our Greatest Invention Makes Us Richer, Smarter, Greener, Healthier, and Happier* (New York: Penguin Press, 2011), p. 248.
6. M. Jeffrey Hardwick, *Mall Maker: Victor Gruen, Architect of an American Dream*

(Philadelphia: University of Pennsylvania Press, 2004), pp. 166-189. Gruen frequently told the story of a mythical planet called *Motorius* where car drivers spent their lives on an eighty-six-lane expressway. They slept and bred in their machines and viewed the outside world from their windshields. Buildings had been demolished for more freeways and the planet was 92 percent covered in asphalt. Driving was perfectly synchronized, but one day a driver had a blowout that resulted in massive gridlock. The motorists then all died of starvation in their cars. "Spread causes further spread, congestion causes further congestion," warned Gruen. "Freeways bear new freeways, and anti-city begets more of its own malformed type" (pp. 182-183).

35. AIRLINES AND AIRPORTS

1. Roger Bilstein and Jay Miller, *Aviation in Texas* (Austin: Texas Monthly Press, 1985), p. 231. Data reported in *The Week*, October 26, 2012, p. 18, taken from WashingtonPost.com.
2. Stanley H. Scott and Levi H. Davis, *A Giant in Texas: A History of the Dallas-Fort Worth Regional Airport Controversy, 1911-1974* (Quanah, TX: Nortex Press, 1974) p. 49.
3. Kinky Friedman, *How to Get to Heaven or Hell without Going through Dallas-Fort Worth* (New York: Cliff Street, 2001), p. 36.
4. Darwin Payne, *Big D: Triumphs and Troubles of an American Supercity in the Twentieth Century* (Dallas: Three Forks Press, 2000), p. 423 n.
5. Ben F. Love, *Ben Love: My Life in Texas Commerce* (College Station: Texas A&M University Press, 2005), p. 310.

36. URBAN EXCELLENCE IN TEXAS

1. U.S. News and World Report, *Best Colleges*, 2013 edition (Washington, DC: U.S. News and World Report, 2012), p. 72. Rankings are always contentious, but the U.S. News specializes in this effort for the benefit of prospective students. It gives a weighted measurement to peer opinion, graduation and retention rates, class sizes, faculty pay and degrees, student selectivity, alumni giving, and college spending on students. The data comes from the colleges, and every year they nervously await the outcome. Any ranking is arguable, but rankings do give a general idea of merit.
2. Art historian Richard B. Brettell praised Dallas architecture, but ranked it behind Houston in "Architecture in Dallas," *Legacies: A History Journal for Dallas and North Texas* 9 (Fall 1997), pp. 56-59.
3. Joan Sutherland, *A Prima Donna's Progress* (Washington, DC: Regnery, 1997), p. 94.
4. Ronald L. Davis, *La Scala West: The Dallas Opera under Kelly and Rescigno* (Dallas: Southern Methodist University Press, 2000), p. 14.
5. Ibid., p. 2.
6. *Dallas Morning News*, June 19, 1994.
7. A. C. Greene, *Dallas USA* (Austin: Texas Monthly Press, 1984), p. 239.
8. *Austin American Statesman*, December 10, 1966.
9. Joshua Long, *Weird City: Sense of Place and Creative Resistance in Austin, Texas* (Austin: University of Texas Press, 2010), p. 39; Margaret P. O'mara, *Cities of Knowledge: Cold War Science and the Search for the Next Silicon Valley* (Princeton,: Princeton University Press, 2005), pp. 1-2, 10, 12-13, 221.

10. *Houston Chronicle*, January 14, 1985 (quote).
11. Kenneth B. Ragsdale, *Austin, Cleared for Takeoff* (Austin: University of Texas Press, 2004), pp. 180–181, 192–193, 206.
12. *Daily Texan*, March 18, 2010.
13. Quoted in David C. Humphrey, *Austin: A History of the Capital City* (Austin: Texas State Historical Association, 1997), p. 52.
14. *Austin American-Statesman*, November 19, 1994.
15. William Scott Swearingen, Jr., *Environmental City: People, Place, Politics, and the Meaning of Modern Austin* (Austin: University of Texas Press, 2010), pp. 2–3, 169, 221.

37. HOUSTON, A RENAISSANCE CITY

1. The word "renaissance" usually refers to the humanistic upsurge of art, literature, and architecture in medieval Italy and Europe. It can also be used to refer to broad intellectual accomplishments in arts and sciences, as in the phrase, "Renaissance man [or woman]." That is the sense here. It does not mean that Houston has solved all of its problems. Its seesaw struggle with its environment—clean air, clean water, solid waste, subsidence, heat, humidity, floods, hurricanes, air-conditioning—for instance, are only partially resolved. See Charles P. Kaplan, "Houston and the Twentieth-Century Environmental Ideal," in *Houston: A Twentieth Century Urban Frontier* (Port Washington, NY: Associated Faculty Press, 1983), pp. 160–181; and Martin V. Melosi and Joseph Pratt, *Energy Metropolis: An Environmental History of Houston and the Gulf Coast* (Pittsburgh: University of Pittsburgh Press, 2007).
2. *Houston Post*, July 21, 1969.
3. Stephen B. Oates, "NASA's Manned Spacecraft Center at Houston, Texas," *Southwestern Historical Quarterly* 67 (January 1964), pp. 354–355.
4. The University of Houston, with forty thousand students, was the city commuter university, with three hundred degree programs. It ranked 184th in the *U.S. News and World Report* in 2013 and was considered a top 50 research university. Its student body—34 percent white, 22 percent Hispanic, 20 percent Asian, and 13 percent black—reflects the demographic mix of the city. In 2011 the University of Houston was placed in the Carnegie Foundation's top tier of research universities (based on dollar grants) along with Rice, Texas A&M, and the University of Texas.
5. See *Chicago Tribune Sports*, September 19, 2010. Jones has often said that the Astrodome has been his inspiration for stadium building since he was a twenty-two-year old player for the University of Arkansas. The Astrodome has been displaced by the barn-like Reliant Stadium (2002) and the clamshell (capable of enclosure) Minute Maid Stadium (2002). Lest stadiums be seen as an urban panacea, San Antonio hopefully built the $186 million Alamodome in 1993 to attract a professional football team that never came.
6. Phil Patton, "Philip Johnson: The Man Who Changed Houston's Skyline," *Houston City Magazine* 4 (January 1980), p. 46. Architectural historian Richard R. Brettell states, "Put simply, Dallas is a national and regional architectural center, while Houston is an international one" ("Architecture in Dallas: Where Are We," *Legacies: A History Journal for Dallas and North Central Texas* 9 [Fall 1997], p. 56).
7. David G. McComb, *Houston, a History* (Austin: University of Texas Press, 1981), p. 183. Helpful for general information about musical development is Laurie E. Jasinski, ed.,

The Handbook of Texas Music, 2nd ed. (Denton: Texas State Historical Association, 2012).
8. *Houston Post*, October 4, 1966.
9. Kyle Shelton, "Culture War in Downtown Houston: Jones Hall and the Postwar Battle over Exclusive Space," *Southwestern Historical Quarterly* 116 (July 2012), p. 8.
10. Drexel Turner provides an architect's view of the Theater District in "Neighborhood of Make-Believe: The Houston Theater District," in Barrie Scardino, William F. Stern, and Bruce C. Webb, eds., *Ephemeral City: Cite Looks at Houston* (Austin: University of Texas Press, 2003), pp. 161-172. Historian Hyland B. Packard provides a contrast between Chicago and Houston arts districts in "Houston's High Culture: Patterns of Institutionalization and Changing Definitions of Function and Community," in Francisco A. Rosales and Barry J. Kaplan, eds., *Houston: A Twentieth Century Urban Frontier* (Port Washington, NY: Associated Faculty Press, 1983), pp. 100-114.

    The six miles of tunnels proved a liability during tropical storm Allison in 2001, when they flushed floodwaters into Jones Hall, Alley Theater, and Wortham Center. Elsewhere, the water damaged basement record keeping and power sources at the Texas Medical Center.
11. Dominique Browning, "What I Admire I Must Possess," *Texas Monthly* 11 (April 1983), p. 208.
12. Greg Smith, "Art for Houston's Sake," *Images*, July 17, 1987, p. 4.
13. Patricia Johnson, "Why Twombly?" *Zest, Houston Chronicle*, February 5, 1995, p. 9.
14. Frederick C. Elliott, *The Birth of the Texas Medical Center* (College Station: Texas A&M University Press, 2004), pp. 14-15.
15. Marilyn McAdams Sibley, *The Methodist Hospital of Houston: Serving the World* (Austin: Texas State Historical Association, 1989), p. 92.
16. Ibid., p. 112.
17. Sibley, *Methodist Hospital*, pp. 112-114, 208.

38. THE INFRASTRUCTURE FOR EXCELLENCE

1. Peter Hall, *Cities in Civilization* (New York: Pantheon, 1998), pp. 3-4.

39. THE CITY AND THE STATE: A CONUNDRUM

1. *Houston Chronicle*, December 8, 2010.
2. Cal Jillson, *Lone Star Tarnished: A Critical Look at Texas Politics and Public Policy* (New York: Routledge, 2012), p. 222; *Houston Chronicle* (editorial), December 31, 2010; January 10, 2011.
3. *Dallas Morning News*, July 29, 2007.
4. *Houston Chronicle*, November 14, 2011.
5. Paul Burka, "Storming the Ivory Tower," *Texas Monthly* 40 (October 2012), pp. 290, 394, 300.
6. Jillson, *Lone Star Tarnished*, pp. 125-126 (table 5.4).
7. Steve Murcock, "Lecture," *Texas Tribune*, February 28, 2011.
8. Jillson, *Lone Star Tarnished*, p. 102.

SUGGESTIONS FOR FURTHER READING

Global aspects of cities are addressed in Lewis Mumford, *The City in History: Its Origins, Its Transformations, and Its Prospects* (New York: Harcourt, Brace and World, 1961), and Peter Hall, *Cities in Civilization* (New York: Pantheon, 1998). Central place theory is summarized by Mario Polese in *The Wealth and Poverty of Regions: Why Cities Matter* (Chicago: University of Chicago Press, 2009).

Comments about urbanization and various Texas cities can be found in bits and snatches in the following general histories of Texas: Randolph B. Campbell, *Gone to Texas: A History of the Lone Star State* (New York: Oxford, 2003) and David G. McComb, *Texas: A Modern History* (Austin: University of Texas Press, 2010). The same is true for period histories, such as Donald E. Chipman, *Spanish Texas, 1519-1821* (Austin: University of Texas Press, 1992); David J. Weber, *The Spanish Frontier in North America* (New Haven: Yale University Press, 1992); Gilbert R. Cruz, *Let There Be Towns: Spanish Municipal Origins in the American Southwest, 1610-1810* (College Station: Texas A&M University Press, 1988); David Montejano, *Anglos and Mexicans in the Making of Texas, 1836-1986* (Austin: University of Texas Press, 1987; Diana Davids Olien and Roger M. Olien, *Oil in Texas: The Gusher Age, 1895-1945* (Austin: University of Texas Press, 2002); and Walter L. Buenger, *The Path to the Modern South: Northeast Texas between Reconstruction and the Great Depression* (Austin: University of Texas Press, 2001).

For individual cities, the best source for concise, authoritative summaries is Ron Tyler, ed., *The New Handbook of Texas* (Austin: Texas State Historical Association, 1996), 6 vols., and *The Handbook of Texas Online*, which keeps the information updated. The *Handbook* contains an article on urbanization and brief bibliographies at the end of entries. The Texas State Historical Association has also published a series of popular city histories and guides for Galveston, Austin, Dallas, and Fort Worth.

The best comprehensive urban biographies are C. L. Sonnichsen, *Pass of the North: Four Centuries on the Rio Grande* (El Paso: Texas Western Press, 1968, 1980); David G. McComb, *Houston, a History* (Austin: University of Texas Press, 1981) and *Galveston: A History* (Austin: University of Texas Press, 1986); Oliver Knight with Cissy Stewart Lale, *Fort Worth: Outpost on the Trinity* (Fort Worth: Texas Christian University Press, 1990); W. H. Timmons, *El Paso: A Borderlands History* (El Paso: Texas Western Press, 1990); Darwin Payne, *Big D: Triumphs and Troubles of an American Supercity in the Twentieth Century* (Dallas: Three Forks Press, 2000); and Mary Jo O'Rear, *Storm over the Bay: The People of Corpus Christi and Their Port* (College Station: Texas A&M University Press, 2009). Unusual but pertinent are T. Lindsay Baker's *Ghost Towns of Texas* (Norman: University of Oklahoma Press, 1986) and *More Ghost Towns of Texas* (Norman: University of Oklahoma Press, 2005).

INDEX

Page numbers in italics refer to figures.

Abercrombie, James, 176
Abilene, Texas, 133
Adams, Nathan, 168
air transport, 214-215; DFW airport, *274*, *275*; Fort Worth versus Dallas, 273-274
Alley Theatre, 299
Amarillo, Texas, 134, *135*
Ames, Jesse Daniel, 189
Armstrong, John S., 125
Asians: and diversity of population, 241; in El Paso, 1900, 139
Aubrey, William P., 83
Austin, Texas, 99; and Bergstrom Air Force Base, 228, 287; and building of modern capitol, *103*, 104; confirmed as capital, 101; and dam failure, 106; 1839 city plan of, 100; growth of black settlement in, 101; and high-tech industry, 286; and moonlight towers, *105*, 106; and music culture, 287; and rowdy social life, 104; and Save Our Springs, 288-291, *289*, *290*; and Sweet Home Missionary Baptist Church, *102*; and the University of Texas, 101, 283, *283*, *284*
automobiles, 209, 212-214; and interstate system, 264-269, *265*, *266*

Baker, T. Lindsay, 9
Ball, Thomas H., 170
Barton, Clara, 153
Beaumont, Texas, 140; and boomtown growth, 158; and race riot, 159; and Spindletop, 157
Bellinger, Charlie, 182
Belo, Alfred H., 80
Berry, James T., 134
Bexar. *See* San Antonio
blacks: in Austin, 101; and Beaumont race riot, 151; and diversity in population, 236, 241, 243; and El Paso, 139; in Houston, 91; and Houston race riot, 188; and integration, 244-252; and Ku Klux Klan, 189-190; and lynching, 188-189; and migration, 148; and slavery, 50, 61, 78; and voting 259-260

Bomar, W. P., 180
boomtowns: lumber, 140, 142; military, 109; oil, 162-163
Borger, Texas, 165
Brackenridge, George W., 71
Brann, William C., 132
Bremond, Paul, 90, 142
Brown, George, and Suite 8F group, 176, 177, 178
Brown, Herman, 177, 178
Brownsville, Texas, 110, 111
Bryan, John Neely, 121
Buck, Frank "Bring 'Em Back Alive," 205
Buffalo Bayou, Brazos and Colorado Railway (BBB&C), 89
Buffalo Gap, Texas, 133
Bussel, Dick, 108
Byrd, James, 263

Callaghan, Bryan, 182
Carlson, Paul H., 9
Carter, Amon, 179; and Seventh Street Gang, 180
Castroville, Texas, 73
Chambers, C. M., 182
Christaller, Walter, 9
Cisneros, Henry, 238, 255
Clarendon, Texas (Old Clarendon), 134
Cline, Isaac, 152-153
Cockrell, Alexander, 121
Cockrell, Lila, 262
Conrad, James H., 9
Corpus Christi, Texas, 83, 84-85
Corsicana, Texas, 160
Courtwright, "Longhair Jim," 128-129
Craft, Juanita, 244
Cruz, Gilbert R., 9
Cullinan, Joseph S., 161, 171
Cuney, Norris Wright, 78
Cutrer, Lewis W., 237

Dallas, Texas: the arts in, 279-282; banking in, 124, 168; black population in, 122; and Bush recession, 2008, 275-276; and Citizen's Council, 178-179; and Cotton Bowl, 204; and East Texas oil boom, 168; 1872 map of, *123*; founding of, 121; and George W. Bush Presidential Library, 277; Great Depression in, 221; growth of, 121-122, 125; and Kennedy assassination, 257-258, *258*; and La Reunion, 121; and Las Colinas, 269; and the Metroplex, 275; and railroads, 122, 123, 124; recreation in, 125; and Sanger Brothers, 122-123; sports in, 275; and State Fair of Texas, 125; and Voting Rights Act, 260; and WRR radio station, 201
DeBakey, Michael E., 303, *304*
De Hartog, Jan, 177
De Leon, Alonzo, 19
Dell, Michael, 286
De Menil, Dominique, 300-301
Denison, Texas, 120
Dowd, C. F., 117

Eberly, Angelina, 99
Elkins, James A., Sr., 176
El Paso, Texas: Anson Mills constructs map and name of, 135; Butterfield Stage stop in, 136; Dallas Stoudenmire as marshal of, 138; and early missions, 18-20; and Fort Bliss, 138; growth and population mix of, 139; and McGinty Club, 139; and Mexican revolutions, 185, *185*; and railroads, 1881, 137, *137*; as a "sin city," 138, 184; and University of Texas at El Paso, 186; and water supply, 185
Enstam, Elizabeth York, 63

Farenthold, Francis, 262
F. de la Teja, Jesus, 9, 30; and Caminos Reales, 56
Feagin, Joe R., 176
Florence, Fred F., 178

Florida, Richard, and creative cities, 234
Fondren, Ella (Mrs. Walter W.), 302
Fort Worth, Texas: art in, 278; and Carswell Air Force Base, 227; cattle in, 127; and Consolidated Aircraft Corporation, 227; growth of, and urban amenities in, 129-130; and "Hell's Half Acre," 127; and Liberator Village, 227; and railroads, 128; settlement of, 126; and Victor Gruen, 270-271; and WBAP radio, 202; zoo in, 279
Foster, William C., 14
Foyt, A. J., 265
Fuqua, H. B., 180

Galleria (Houston), 267-269, *268*
Galveston, Texas: and commission form of city government, 173; and Deep Water Committee, 80, 172; 1860 population of, 51; and Fort Crockett, 174; founding of, 77; and the "Free State of Galveston," 174-176, *175*; and the great storm of 1900, 152-156, *154*, *155*; harbor in, 80; Juneteenth Day in, 78; as largest and richest Texas city in 1870 and 1880, 80; and problems of yellow fever, fresh water, sewerage, and fire control, 79; ruling families of, 174-176; state medical school established in, 81
Gaston, William H., 125
Gentry, Abram Morris, 90
Glaeser, Edward, 270
Glidden, Joseph F., 135
González, Henry B., 238
Great Depression in Texas cities: 220, 221
Gresham, Walter, 180
Gulf, Colorado, and Santa Fe Railway, 113

Hall, Peter, 7, 234, 305
Hamill, Allen W., 157
Hawley, John B., 195
Hefertepe, Kenneth, 101
Henley, J. J., 51

Hines, Gerald, 269
Hispanics: in El Paso, 139; and Hispanic identity, 253-254; as largest minority, 149-150; and Mexican invasions, 65; and Mexican revolutions, 32-35, 185; and population decline, 71; in San Antonio, 182-183; and Spanish Empire, 16-30, 31-43; and Texas Revolution, 44-48; and voting, 259-260
Hobby, Oveta Culp, 176
Hobby, William, 176, 181
Hoblitzelle, Karl St. John, 179, 200-201
Hofheinz, Roy, 295-296, *296*
Hogg, Ima, 216, 297
Hogg, Mike, 213
Hogg, William, C., 213, 215
House, Thomas W., 88
Houston, Texas: arts in, 300; and Astrodome, 295, *296*; and Buffalo Bayou, 92; and de Menil Collection, 300; founding of, by Augustus C. and John K. Allen, 87, *87*; and fresh water, 92-93; and Manned Spacecraft Center, 292, 295, *295*; and Mexican American school boycott, 254; Minute Maid Park, 299; pavement of streets in, 91, 92; and petrochemicals for World War II, 229; and railroads, 89, 90; and Rice University, 293, *295*; and River Oaks, 213; and Rothko Chapel, 300-301; shipbuilding for World War II in, 229; and ship channel, 92-93, 169, 170, *170*, 229, *230*; and slaves, 90-91; suburban growth in, 230; and Suite 8F group, 176; and Texas Medical Center, 301-303, *301*; and trade, 88, 89; and Voting Rights Act, 260
Houston and Great Northern Railroad, 90
Houston and Texas Central Railroad (H&TC), 90
Hugman, H. H. Robert, 222
Humphrey, David C., 101
Hutcheson, Joseph C., 169
Indianola, Texas, 81, 82

Inman, Bobby R., 286
integration. *See* racial integration
Ivins, Molly, 262

Jacksboro, Texas, 109
Jacobs, Jane, 270
Jaworski, Leon, 176, 177
Jefferson, Texas, 93; and Red River raft, 93–94
Jillson, Cal, 307
Johnson, David R., 70
Johnson, Philip, 258, 269, 297
Joiner, Columbus Marvin "Dad," 161
Jones, Jesse H.: and Great Depression, 220, *221*, 298; and Houston Ship Channel, 170; and Suite 8F group, 176
Jones, John T., 298
Jones, Margo, 202–203
Jones, Walter C., 153
Jordan, Barbara, 260, *261*

Kampmann, John H., 71
Kempner, Isaac H., 173
Kempner, Ruth Levy, 176
Kenedy, Mifflin, 94
Kennedy, John F., 257
Kessler, George E., 215
Kilby, Jack St. Clair, 275
Kilgore, Texas, 166, *167*; and Rangerettes, 166
King, Richard, 51, 94
Kinney, Henry L., 83
Kirby, John Henry, 143
Ku Klux Klan, 189–190; and state election of 1924, 190

La Bahia, Texas, 28, 38
Laredo, Texas: founding of, 28–29; railroads in, 94; visited by Manuel de Mier y Teran expedition in 1828, 39
Leonard, Marvin, 180
libraries, 205–207, *206*
Lich, Glen E., 75

Longview, Texas, 168
Lott, Uriah, 84
Lubbock, Texas, 149, 219
Lucas, Anthony F., 157, 163
Lutcher, Henry Jacob, 141

Malone, Ann Patton, 63
Marcus, Stanley, 217–218
Marquis de Rubi, Cayetano Maria Pignatelli, 20
Marsalis, Thomas, 125
Marshall, Texas, 119
Maverick, Mary A., 64, 69
Maverick, Maury, Sr., 184
Maverick, Samuel Augustus, 66
McClellan, Carole Keeton, 262
McClendon, Gordon, 202
McDaniel, Myra, 262
McKinney, Thomas F., 77
Melosi, Martin V., 9
Menard, Michael B., 77
Menger, William A., 70
Mexican Americans. *See* Hispanics
Midland, Texas, 163
Miller, Char, 9
Miller, Henry Pomeroy "Roy," 180, 181
Missouri, Kansas and Texas Railroad (the Katy), 120
Mitchell, George, and Woodlands, Texas, 242
Moody, William L., 80
Moore, G. Bedell, 141
Morgan, Charles, 76, 82
Mumford, Lewis, 7
Murdock, Stephen, 307
Murray, Charles, 234

Nacogdoches, Texas: early missions in, and Antonio Gil Ibarvo, 20–21; and observations by Teran expedition of 1828, 42–43; and trade, 21–22
National Association for the Advancement of Colored People (NAACP), 244

Neiman-Marcus (department store), 217
New Braunfels, Texas, 74
newspapers, 208
Nixon, Lawrence A., 255

Odessa, Texas, 164
Olien, Diana Davids, 9
Olien, Roger M., 9
Olmsted, Frederick Law: and old Camino Real, 56; in San Antonio in 1850s, 68
Orange, Texas, 141, 142
O'Rear, Mary Jo, 9

Parker, Annise, 262
Parker, George, 162
Payne, Darwin, 9
Pike, Zebulon M., 31-32
population, 51; and diversity, 236; and frontier and urban spine, 51-52; and Mexican Americans as the largest minority group, 149, 150; and results of size, 144; and the shift to the cities, 148; and Texas urban growth, 1950-2010, 235
Port Arthur, Texas, 142
Port Lavaca, Texas, 82
Potter, Alexander, 93, 169
Pratt, Joseph, 9
public health: and garbage, 199; and sewerage, 197-199; and water, 194-197

racial conflict: and lynching, 189; and World War I, 188; and World War II, 232
racial integration: in business and society, 249-252; in education, 245-247, 254; and Mexican Americans, 253-256; in military, 256; in sports, 247-248, *248*
Ragsdale, Kenneth B., 225
railroads: and culture, 116, 117, *145*, 146; decline of, 273; financing of, 115; and lumber, 142; and technology, 115, 119; and telegraphs, 119; and trackage, *114*; and urban success, 51, 89, 90, 94, 115, 116, 119

Rice, H. Baldwin, 170
Rice, William Marsh, 88
Richards, Ann, 262
Richardson, Sid, 180
Ropes, Elihu Harrison, 85
Rosenberg, Henry, 205
Ross, Shapley P., 63
Ruby, George T., 78

Sakowitz, Bernard, 267
San Angelo, Texas, and Fort Concho, livestock trade in, 112
San Antonio, Texas (known as Bexar until Texas Revolution): and the Alamo, taken by Santa Anna, 48; and the Alamo as a tourist site, 72; and arrival of Galveston, Harrisburg and San Antonio Railroad, 70; and Battle of Mission Concepción, 45; and capture of Mexican General Martin Perfecto de Cos, 46-47; and cholera, 67; and Council House Fight, 1840, 64; and Fort Sam Houston, 70, *71*; founding of, 22-25; and free public schools, 67; and machine politics, 182; Mexican, German, and Anglo population in, after Civil War, 70, 71; and Mexican American Youth Organization (MAYO), 254; observation about, by José María Sánchez y Tapía (1828), 40; observation about, by Joseph Chambers Clopper (1828), 41-42; observations about, by William Bollaert (1843), 65; and observations of Frederick Law Olmsted (1850s), 68-69; occupation of, during Gutiérrez rebellion, 33-35; and pecan shellers, 182; and Pike at Bexar in 1807, 31-32; poverty and *corrales* in, 183, *183*; and river bathing, 69; and River Walk, 222, *223*; and San Pedro Springs, 23, 71; tourism in, 72; and Voting Rights Act, 260; and water, 184, 238-239; World War II training bases in, 228

San Augustine, Texas, 43
Sanborn, Henry B., 135
San Felipe, Texas, 36-38
Sealy, John, 51
Seguin, Juan Nepomuceno, 66
Sherman, Sidney, 89
Sherman, Texas, 120
Sherman, Walter Justin, 113
Short, Luke, 129
Sitton, Thad, 9
Smith, R. E. "Bob," 176
Smithwick, Noah, 37, 66
Sonnichsen, C. L., 9
Southwest Conference (sports), 204
Spanish Empire: accomplishments of, 30; and "Caminos Reales," 56-58, 57; and Indians, 14-17; and King's Census 1777-1793, 29; and roads, 14-15, 38, 40, 41, 42; and role of the Roman Catholic Church, 16-18; and urban orientation and Laws of the Indies, 17; Zebulon M. Pike comments about, 31-32
Staub, John E., 213
Stillman, Charles, 94; and Brownsville, Texas, 110
Stilwell, Arthur, 142
Strauss, Annette, 262
street pavement, 210; and expressways, 211
Stripling, W. K., 180
suburbs: black Fifth and Third wards (Houston), 240; and Bruce Alger, 241; and Las Colinas, 269; and low-cost housing, 241; middle-class Bellaire, West University (Houston), Oak Cliff (Dallas), Terrill Hills (San Antonio), 240; and racial integration, 242, 243; and satellite cities, 269-270; and Sharpstown, 241-242; wealthy River Oaks (Houston), Highland Park (Dallas), Alamo Heights (San Antonio), 240; and Woodlands, 242
Sweatt, Heman Marion, 245

Tatum, Clarence. A., Jr., 178
Tenayuca, Emma, 183
Texas and New Orleans Railroad (T&NO), 90
Texas and Pacific Railroad (T&P), 113
Texas Centennial: and River Walk, 222; and San Jacinto Monument, 223, 223; and State Fair, 224-225, 224
Texas League baseball, 203
Texas Medical Center: and growth, 301-303; and Harris County Medical Society, 177; and Michael E. DeBakey, 303
Texas Railroad Commission, 113, 117
Thomas, J. B., 180, 270
Thompson, Ben, 104
Thompson, J. Neils, 285
Thornton, Robert L. "Bob," and Citizen's Council, 178
Timmons, W. H., 9
Tisdale, Hope, 6, 9
Tobin, John R., 182
Tobolowsky, Hermine, 262
tourism: and Astrodome, 295; and automobiles, 212-213; and Cotton Bowl, 204; in Fort Worth, 127; in Houston, 300; and Save Our Springs, 288-291; and State Fair of Texas, 125
Tranchese, Carmelo, 183
trolleys, 208, 213
Trost, Henry C., 166
Turner, Frederick Jackson, 8, 52

urbanization: and boundary wars over city limits, 237-239; creativity of, 3; definition of, 6-7; growth of, 4, 52; and migration, 61; and physiography, 13; and population shift from rural to urban areas, 1-3, 4, 6, 52; and the urban spine along the Balcones Escarpment to the Rio Grande, 51 52; and World War I, 187; and World War II, 226, 231-232. *See also the maps of major Texas*

INDEX   341

roads and cities (5), rainfall (12), and city populations (53-55)

vices: alcohol, 192-193; prostitution, 193-194
Voting Rights Act, 1965, 259

Waco, Texas: and "Dr Pepper," 132; establishment of, as cattle town, 130; higher education in, 132; and the *Iconoclast*, 132; railroads in, 131; and Waco Bridge Company, 130-131, *131*
Wade, Richard C., 8
Waggoner, William T., 161
wagon and horse technology, 58-59; impact of, on cities, 59-60; and road systems, 59
Walker, Doak, 204

Waller, Edwin, 99; map of Austin, Texas, 100
Washington-on-the Brazos, Texas, 46
Webb, Walter P., 9
White, Lulu, 244
Whitmire, Kathy, 262
Williams, Samuel May, 77
women, 62; and Equal Rights Amendment, 262; suffrage of, 189, 190-191; and Voting Rights Act, 260, 262
Wooldridge, Alexander P., 106
Wooster, Robert, 109
Wortham, Gus S., 176, 177, 299

Youngblood, Theodore, 263

zoos, 205